Exotic England

Also by Yasmin Alibhai-Brown

The Settler's Cookbook: A Memoir of Love, Migration and Food

Mixed Feelings: The Complex Lives of Mixed-Race Britons

Who Do We Think We Are?: Imagining the New Britain

Exotic England

The Making of a Curious Nation

Yasmin Alibhai-Brown

Research assistant
Dawn Solman

Portobello
BOOKS

Published by Portobello Books 2015

Portobello Books
12 Addison Avenue
London
W11 4QR

Copyright © Yasmin Alibhai-Brown 2015

Yasmin Alibhai-Brown has asserted her moral
right under the Copyright, Designs and Patents Act, 1988,
to be identified as the author of this work.

A CIP catalogue record for this book
is available from the British Library

2   4   6   8   9   7   5   3   1

ISBN 978 1 84627 419 0
eISBN 978 1 84627 497 8

Text designed and typeset in Bodoni by Patty Rennie

Printed and bound by CPI Group (UK) Ltd,
Croydon CR0 4YY

www.portobellobooks.com

MIX
Paper from
responsible sources
FSC® C020471

For Leila, Rafe and Lara.

Three beautiful, exotic Englanders

and for all those who have made them.

Contents

Acknowledgements

THIS BOOK TOOK MUCH too long to write. I got carried away by the endlessly fascinating subject. I thank my agent Natasha Fairweather for her patience and firm guidance. Philip Gwyn Jones and Tasja Dorkofikis commissioned the book. Their encouragement and advice was invaluable. Laura Barber got me to be more disciplined with my material and had faith we would get there. Her warm support is much appreciated. Daphne Tagg, my editor, was sensitive, exact and a delight to work with.

I am very grateful to the Churchill Fellowship for awarding me a travel grant that enabled me to go to India and the Middle East. I was in Egypt and Jordan just after the first uprisings. Spring was in the air but it felt temporary even then. Springs always are. Some opinion research was carried out at the University of Lincoln and also Middlesex University, where I am a part-time professor. A number of my students gathered views of young people about England and the East, and conversations with academic staff helped to clarify my thoughts and ideas. I would like to express my gratitude to the students and lecturers from both institutions.

Several politicians, academics, journalists, artists, authors, thinkers and public intellectuals gave me their precious time, shared many insights and taught me much about the English nation. In no particular order, I am indebted to Neil

MacGregor, Jeremy Paxman, Andrew Marr, Tristram Hunt, Jon Cruddas, Norman Davies, Kwasi Kwarteng, Jesse Norman, Lord Malloch-Brown, Rory Stewart, Mark Perryman, Billy Bragg, Michael Boyd, Brian Sewell, Greg Doran, Charles Cotton, Graham Johnson, Simon Schama, William Dalrymple, Meera Syal, Mihir Bose, Jemima Khan, Prince Hassan bin Talal, Princess Sarvath Ikramullah, Fadia Faqir, Ranjeet Singh, Suchdev Singh, Mr Mehta, Saadi al-Timimi, Kate Hickman, Brigid Keenan Wadham, Omari Benn, Hugh Bochel, Edgar Gerrard Hughes, Geordie Greig, Richard Bean, Gitanjali Prasad, Shastri Ramachandaran, Gamal el-Ghitani, Mahmoud el Wardany, Professor Mohammad Al Masalha, Dr Kamel Abu Jaber, Dr Majeda Omar, Professor Khamesh, Suad al-Attar and Jameel, Wisaam al Zawahie, Hisham el-Leithy, Hussein Chalayan, Shaimaa Khalil, Dr Rim Turkmani, Saleem Arif Quadri, Salwa Jarrah, Tim Supple, Rahul da Cunha, Shernaz Patel, Rajit Kapur, George Hawatmeh, Tessa Portobello, Lyn Heppner, Sam Harvey, Khalil Fahmi, the British Council in Egypt, Jordan and India, Mustapha and Faten Karkouti, Ali Rafaei, Bassam Andari, Carl Miller, Elyse Dodgson, Chris Campbell, Carl Miller, Ala'a Karkouti, Sabah Mohmoud.

To those strangers who were happy to talk to me in England, Jordan, Egypt and India, and to all those who let me stay with them and who fed and looked after me, I cannot thank you enough.

I met my English husband at Bristol railway station in 1989. Since that chance meeting, he has loved me unconditionally (not easy) and encouraged me to explore and know his homeland. Colin, I owe you and love you. My precious son Ari and second daughter Liz are part of that story of England.

x

Introduction

'The english have an opportunity to discard myths and face a reality which
could be so much better. Otherwise the vaunted 'reawakening of England'
will be only a prolongation of dreams or the stirring of nightmares.'

Felipe Fernandez-Armesto[1]

England is where I live, work, play, cry, laugh, suffer and
flourish. Fate brought me to these shores and now I would not, could not, live
anywhere else. Almost gone are those deep yearnings for Uganda, my birthplace,
from whence I was exiled in 1972. This England – merry, stormy, warm, cold,
unchanging, always changing – is my homeland. I speak to it and sometimes for it,
not out of audacity but affection, grown over many decades.

It has been tough at times. Hostility to migrants, settlers and minorities
pollutes the atmosphere, saps hope. But the nation's open spirit, its liberalism
and cultural litheness offset the negative ions. Most migrants to Britain can't dis-
entangle their convoluted emotions about a land that is duplicitous and yet
remarkable, truly great. Many who want to belong cannot do so, because their
overtures are regarded with suspicion or rejected. Or because it feels like a
betrayal of their previously subjugated countries. Or is it fear that such attachments and affirmations would be unseemly? Yet every day, Englanders and

outsiders reach out to each other, touch, trust, share, transfer ideas and knowledge, build resilient relationships, form ties that bind. This is their story, and mine too.

An Englishman I met at Bristol railway station has cherished me and my son too, whose father was, like me, a Ugandan Asian. Our daughter Leila is brown-skinned with brown eyes, but so, so like Colin, her blue-eyed English father. He is descended from old Sussex folk who've been roaming across the South Downs forever, swimming in the wild sea, watching boats, and pulling in outsiders from the cold, offering them warmth and piping hot tea.

I was in Brookwood cemetery, Woking, when the first thoughts of this book started forming. My parents are interred there. Blood in the soil has made the grounds lush and fecund. The vast burial ground is a place of abiding loveliness, with big redwood trees like sequoias and still, dappled glades that shelter, in spring, propitious snowdrops and bluebells. It is the England of poets and landscape painters. Nature garlands Albion while birds sing in praise.

Today, for most people, Albion is England, but the whole mainland, until the Romans renamed it Britannia, was known as Albion. It is a pre-Celtic word, some say, derived from Latin, meaning 'white', as in the cliffs of Dover, but two hours away from Woking. That chalky appellation has been muddied by providence and events, and by incautious citizens themselves. Here in bucolic Surrey, where true-born English men, women and children are laid to rest, various unfamiliar incomers have joined them, in their own demarcated plots, making a palimpsest, a multicoloured mosaic of the departed. There are sections for Zoroastrians, people of mixed faith, Latvians, members of the Turkish Air Force, Ahmadi Muslims.

I am in the enclosure reserved for us Shia Ismaili Muslims. Ismailism is a minority Muslim sect.[2] Our men and women pray together, modernism nudges tradition, evolution prevents stagnancy and conservatism. For literalist Muslims, Ismailism is an abomination. They shun us and keep our dead out of their grave-yards. In contrast, Christian England lets in our dear departed. Bodies of Ismailis, in plain white sheets and simple coffins, are gently lowered into graves dug in Brookwood. Their last resting place is in Middle England and will be mine too. What a tale of the unexpected this is. There are rumours of ghosts in this necrop-olis – shapes are seen in the green mist and a strange babble is heard. Maybe restless phantoms – indigenous and immigrant – are speaking in a new, composite tongue, a patois, as they moan and yearn for peace.

On my mum Jena's grave, I placed her favourite English roses. I cannot locate the spot where my father, Kassam, was buried back in the 1970s. Our relationship had broken down irrecoverably many years before he died, after I played Juliet in a school play to a black Romeo. I was a teenager and he, then in his fifties, an unconventional, insubordinate, irresponsible, autodidactic and intriguing man. He'd read every one of Shakespeare's plays and made me read bits aloud to him, so I too could love the language and drama. I did, and still do, passionately, on the page and on the stage. In Uganda, the races did not mix, touch or kiss, even in a school play, but when I played Juliet, I was her, an ardent, pulsating young woman, not careful, unable to hold back from forbidden love. Sadly for me, transgressive female sexuality, in drama and real life, terrified dear Papa. He never spoke to me again, carried his deadly, unforgiving silence to the other side, perhaps regretting he had led me to the Bard. Sometimes I feel he watches me now, still worried I will slip into wantonness. Shakespeare, England's greatest son, pulled us closer together and ripped us apart.

Born in Karachi, in undivided India in around 1905, Papa Kassam behaved like an Edwardian Englishman and wore what he called 'Graham Greene suits'. He must be happy here, I thought as I ambled around Brookwood, my mother even more so. After moving from Uganda to London, Jena became irrepressibly patriotic. In spite of wounding experiences of racism, she felt freer, happier and more secure in London than anywhere else. How grateful she was for her small supplementary state pension and cramped council flat. She had faith: England had looked after her well in life and would in death. I can imagine the natives in their graves shuffling up to make a little more room, as they do on busses and in waiting rooms. On that cold, sunny afternoon in April, I knew my next book would be about England. It was as if my parents had sent a message to my mind's inbox.

When I first introduced Jena to Colin (who unwisely wore a hoop earring and a cerise pink shirt), she had stern words with me in Kutchi, our language: 'Look at him. Long hair, dressing like a girl. First husband, one of us, betrayed you. You think this man will be better? The English are very nice people, best in world, but don't understand family at all. Only at Christmas maybe. Give presents. No real care.'

Five years before her death, Jena wrote out a list of who should get her precious bits of jewellery. My English husband was to get a small diamond stud – she had lost the other. And in her last days in hospital, she instructed me to make sure Colin was one of her pall-bearers: 'He is more than my own son. He showed me so many places I never saw before in this beautiful country. His mother Vera – look after her. Kind, both so kind. He must hold the *kaffan* (coffin).' This was her asking for the impossible: our funerals are intensely private and restricted to believers. (Some injunctions are changing as more of us marry out, but non-Ismailis can only sit in an ante-room, not see the body nor go to the graveside.) I had to persuade the elders to let Colin be part of all the prayers and rituals, to help carry the coffin. After secret meetings they agreed. So the Englishman she so mistrusted helped lay her down in Brookwood. And wept.

Englanders of all classes are attracted to and enlivened by enigmatic strangers and exotic cultures. (I really don't understand why the beautiful word 'exotic' has become tarnished and is intolerable to post-colonial thinkers.[3]) I have worn saris in villages in England and been greeted with rapturous, excessive praise. In rural France the same flowing silk garment produced contemptuous looks. While researching this book, I came upon a host of colourful characters, including Jack Philby, father of Kim, a polyglot Arabist and ardent convert to Wahabi Islam; Samson Rowlie, aka Hassan Aga, a powerful eunuch in the Ottoman court; the artist William Hodges, who painted Indian landscapes infused with wonder, divine light and religious ecstasy; the high-born Jane Digby, who happily became a Bedouin wife. They are exemplars not of English eccentricity but of England's openness to the 'Other' – an incorrigible aspect of the Anglo-Saxon identity.

Princess Diana had two Muslim lovers, the heart surgeon Hasnat Khan and Dodi Fayed. Undeterred by disapprovers, she let her heart go east, following other daring romantics of her tribe. Prince Charles is also pulled to the East, but more with his head: he heaps praise on Islamic art, design and faith, leading some Americans and Britons to suspect he is a secret Muslim convert, at once dotty and treacherous.[4] Diana and Charles were more alike than they realized. Their sensitive and searching psyches were shaped by the diverse streams and rivers of England's history.

Over time, that part of the national story was curbed, bypassed and so faded from the collective consciousness. And Englanders were stereotyped as snobs, unreconstructed imperialists, dull, devious, rule-bound, cold, tight-lipped, repressed, tight folk. The mordant list was ratified by preeminent insiders.

P. G. Wodehouse, for example, asked contemptuously: 'There will always be an England, but who wants an England full of morons reading the *Express*?'[5] For George Orwell, the country was like a stuffy Victorian family,[6] and D. H. Lawrence utterly despaired of his 'cursed, rotten, bored, pappy-hearted countrymen'.[7] Such sleights and quips are careless and unfair, for these nationals have also been hearty and lusty, physically and culturally – much more so than the 'hot-blooded' Mediterranean nations – and bold.

The Empire Came Home

In 1889, a small terraced property in Liverpool was turned into a place for daily Islamic prayer by one William Quilliam (1856–1932), a charismatic English Muslim who converted hundreds of fellow middle-class English men and women to the faith.[8] Though these worshippers were resented and attacked by some natives of Liverpool, there were many who admired the man and his mission.[9] By that time there were already a good number of Africans, Indians, Chinese and various children of the Empire in English towns and cities. In 1886, Dr Gottlieb Leitner, a European migrant and multilingual academic, was appointed principal of a higher education college in Punjab, India, and became interested in Islam. He moved to Woking, bought some land and set up a centre for oriental languages, culture and history. It attracted many Muslims students and scholars who, Dr Leitner believed, were entitled to a place of worship nearby. Begum Shah Jehan, Queen of Bhopal, agreed to pay for the mosque, and the project took off. English converts backed the idea wholeheartedly.

An English architect, W. L. Chambers, was chosen; his drawings show an abode of quiet solace, with a dome, minarets, an ablution pool and contemplative worshippers in turbans and loose clothes – a visual invocation. He proudly wrote about his vision and its progress in the *Building News and Engineering Journal*.[10] No objections were raised by local people or planners, and in 1889, the same year that Quilliam opened his modest house of worship, the mosque in Woking was completed, one of the first to be built in Western Europe.

The white, blue-green and gold mosque, still attended by many, seems to lay a whispering claim to the verdant habitat around it. Queen Victoria's Muslim servants prayed there and she took a keen interest in their faith. England then seemed to be profoundly moved by the essence and aesthetics of Islam. Incredible really. Other worshippers included upper-class converts such as Rowland George Allanson-Winn, the fifth Baron Headley; Marmaduke Pickthall, a novelist and widely respected translator of the Koran,[11] whose ancestors were knighted by William the Conqueror; and the third Baron Stanley of Alderley, who was the first Muslim member of the House of Lords.[12] The first two are buried in Brookwood. By 1910, there were an estimated 10,000 Muslims in England and a tenth of them were converts.

Brookwood's Muslim burial ground goes back to 1917, when consecrated land was laid aside in Horsewell Common for Indian-Muslim soldiers who had died in the First World War. Beautified with Islamic arches and domes, the site was designed by T. H. Winney, the builder was Ashby Horner Ltd, and Messrs Neal of Wandsworth landscaped the gardens – again all Englishmen.[13] Sikh and Hindu victims were respectfully cremated in other designated spots. Injured Indian soldiers were taken to the makeshift wartime hospital in the Brighton Pavilion. Great care was taken to meet their dietary and other religious requirements. The signs naming the separate kitchens are still there, carved in stone.

In 2011, research by Swansea University found that some 100,000 Britons had turned to Islam in the first decade of the new millennium, a period of Islamicist terrorism, Western 'wars on terror', and growing mistrust between the monotheistic faiths. (The figure obviously did not include those who have never come out as Muslims.) A large proportion of these converts were English and female. Admittedly such conversions are rising throughout the modern Western world, but elsewhere the trend is recent and tied to contemporary dilemmas and geopolitical dramas; in England these leaps of faith and culture have been taken over several centuries, as this book will attest. They are embedded in society and the national psyche.

England is, in spite of itself, more open and accommodating than other European nations, a truth acknowledged by innumerable third-world migrants, including ferocious anti-colonialists, such as myself. The Afro-French footballer Benoit Assou-Ekotto, who plays in the English Premier League, reflects that '[In France] you would be fiercely proud of being African. But here it is different. People might say that their parents are from the Ivory Coast or Nigeria or whatever, but they are fiercely proud of being here and the society accepts that.' Fellow footballer Sébastien Bassong, also Afro-French, agrees: 'It's just a fact … people know they will get a chance no matter how they dress or where they're from. In England minds are more open and that's why French players who play in England don't want to go back to France.'[14] I wonder how Anglo-Saxon patriots react to these accolades. Are they flattered or alarmed? Both, I expect.

Why did the English develop this openness? Experts and thinkers explained it was a combination of geography, religion, ambition and national temperament. Neil MacGregor, Director of the British Museum, offered some of his own, considered views: 'These island people were vulnerable to attacks, needed to be extraordinarily alert and energetic, make alliances, deal skilfully with outsiders.'[15]

England's physical position determined and drove its story of war, global trade and migration. Once Francis Drake had circumnavigated the world in the sixteenth century, the nation was unbounded, its imagination illimitable. Shakespeare named his new theatre 'The Globe', a sign, surely, that even as England named itself, it included the world in its imagined entity.

The historian Norman Davies made further observations: 'England is a small nation and though it had a relatively big navy, its people knew they couldn't conquer the world with battleships . . . They really didn't have the same degree of triumphalism of many other nations, not in the earlier centuries anyway. Right from the start the English were conscious of their limitations and felt they had to know other people, cooperate with locals. French and Spanish imperialists did not do that, they behaved very differently.'[16] Kwasi Kwarteng, the British-Ghanaian Tory MP,[17] agreed those smooth skills were used to cunning effect to co-opt subjects: 'Empire wouldn't have worked without local agents or a large degree of compliance and acquiescence and respect.'[18]

Even those who were uncompromising liberationists, such as Mahatma Gandhi and Jawaharlal Nehru, both educated in England,[19] could not but admire English institutions and culture. They fought to end the British Empire, yet some of their closest ties were with English men and women. Gandhi and Charles Freer Andrews, an Anglican priest, were lifelong friends and allies, and when final negotiations over Indian independence were going on, Nehru and Edwina, wife of Lord Mountbatten, apparently embarked on a passionate affair. Photographs show the couple, arms around each other, eyes for no one else (while Mountbatten looks away, as a gentleman must).[20]

With the sea beckoning, Englanders could not stay put or content within a small, proscribed landmass. This restlessness is typically English, according to

Lord Malloch-Brown, a former UN diplomat: 'The small island thing gives us an internationalist feel from a very early age. I was born in Sussex, brought up on tales about what lay beyond. I wanted to go there'.[21] In 1947 an English tea planter in Ceylon expressed the same sentiment: 'It was not the lure of money that took me to the East . . . I was led there, as so many others are, by the spirit of adventure. There is something in our blood that will not let us rest.'[22] After Kwarteng's *Ghosts of Empire* was published, readers in provincial England wrote to him about the times when they were abroad, living the dream: 'We look at these people and places as settled, boring and monocultural, but they have memories and extensive experiences in far-flung places like Burma and the Gold Coast. Their Empire made them arrogant and also receptive.' They knew what it was be to be truly alive once.

MacGregor convinced me that the split with the Catholic Church in the sixteenth century was at the root of England's eclecticism: 'Religion was the litmus test for so much. They deliberately constructed a church where, though the centre was strong, the edges were vague and so could allow and accommodate many different views within it. They had to.' So the English Reformation's carefully nurtured pragmatism and permeability led to a nation that was exceptionally versatile and inclusive: 'The English understood very early . . . that truth that we all have many identities and that being English doesn't stop you being other things. It was one of the great insights of the Elizabethan age and of the Anglican Church. The whole polity is based on that idea, it is deeply embedded in the political tradition. That is why an authoritarian insistence now on cultural uniformity and conformity is unlikely ever to succeed in England.' According to Macgregor, Scotland's trajectory was different: 'It has always been an emigrant nation, so there are contacts, but there isn't as much coming and going of foreigners in Scotland . . .

The Scottish Reformation was popular and profound but didn't admit the 'Other'. The French Reformation also led to conformity. In 1685, the Edict of Nantes, granting civil rights to Protestants, was revoked and large numbers of Huguenots fled to England. There was no room for difference in France and there isn't really today.'

It seems incontrovertible that the English are comfortable with diversity, indeed excited by civilizations of excess, sumptuousness and high emotion, they are also instinctively conservative, need the conformity and security of their homes and hearths. These internal and external tussles, I believe, are uniquely Anglo-Saxon.

Other nationals in Europe and the UK can be open too, but not to the same extent. And yet the English are routinely described as particularly jingoistic and colonialist, which, in truth, many are. Exclusive England and exotic England are conjoined twins, symbiotically linked. Most migrants to the UK choose to live in England, which could not purge them without destroying its own body and soul.

So putative 'little England' appears pinched and hostile, erects ramparts, but its native sons and daughters breach the walls, welcome outlanders, sneak out to find foreigners, steal out to weird and wondrous places, bringing back goodness knows what. Though stringent laws are passed and attitudes towards incomers harden, migrants, itinerants and dissenters will not be kept out. And, in time, they will join England's cultural waterways and genetic bloodstreams, lay claim to the land and its fabulous story. These peculiarities, paradoxes and incongruities are explored in the book.

'New' England

In the twenty-first century, diversity has become the most contested aspect of modern Englishness, despite the fact that England has been ethnically mixed since before the Norman conquests.[23] Since 2000, high migration from Europe and other parts of the world has enabled Britain to remain competitive in the global market. It has also increased pressures on public services. Attitudes have hardened for this reason and because inflows are described almost wholly in negative terms by sections of the media and some political factions. The recession which hit the UK after 2008 inevitably made things worse. However, as the economy begins to recover, 'outsiders' feel even more unwanted. Abuse and attacks against asylum seekers, Muslims and people of colour have gone up but crime in general has gone down.[24]

When I first came to Britain in 1972, millions of white citizens were just as hostile, and politicians such as Enoch Powell who railed against 'coloured' migrants were hugely popular. Racism slapped you in the face in public spaces. (In my case, literally, on two occasions, in London. One was a woman with sharp red fingernails who caught an earring, pulled and cut my ear.) But at that time and earlier, during the 1960s, most mainstream politicians did not capitulate to this swell of opinion and racism. There was a cross-party liberal consensus – internationalist, reasonable and against discrimination. Included in this alliance were Roy Jenkins, Edward Heath, Michael Foot, William Whitelaw, Barbara Castle and others. Broadcasters, especially the BBC, shared those values. That accord has gone. The internet and other modern developments have, in my view, made society coarser and meaner, while politicians and the media now follow hostile public attitudes, meekly, ingratiatingly. It is a particularly vicious circle. But, as ever, this is not the whole story. Happily, virtuous circles give hope by offering an optimistic counter-narrative.

The 2012 London Olympics brought assorted Britons together in a hot, sweaty, happy embrace. For a few weeks the voices of rancorous neo-Powellites could not be heard above the unifying applause, joy and partying. As the excitement abated, myths of homogeneity were reasserted with increased volume. England is re-discovering itself. Like daybreak, there is an awakening, but no one can predict what will follow. The outward-looking nation could, may, withdraw into a hermetic enclave and constrictive nationalism. The historian Linda Colley warns that: 'For any people to pin down their identity as though it is a captive butterfly is simply wrong. People are able to have more than one identity.'[25] The post-Reformation English knew that; less so their modern descendants.

What will new England, the coming Jerusalem, be? Reactionary English nationalists cannot win the argument because that would mean editing out their colourful and dashing past. England 'has always been a hybrid nation which thrived on assimilating generations of immigrants'.[26] But no one can predict with confidence what will come to pass. John Sentamu, the Ugandan-born Archbishop of York, asks delicately: 'Can it be an identity we can all share? Will it be flexible enough to recognize new aspects of Englishness while remaining authentic enough to proudly name and recognize its own history?'[27]

That is my hope. That the England of maypoles, Morris dancers, Yorkshire pudding, re-enactments of Lady Godiva and Boudicca, imperial wistfulness and celebrations of St George and Shakespeare, will rejoice in Diwali fireworks, Hanukkah and Eid feasts, black actors playing English monarchs, people of colour getting medals and seats in Parliament, cross-racial love, and eat lots of kebabs and curry.

Speaking Personally

Why do I take on a subject that isn't naturally mine? Because insider/outsider insights are fresh and may even be necessary, as the Indian-born American professor Krishan Kumar argues: 'traditional approaches to English national identity . . . have tended to consider the character of "Englishness" from within, from inside the national culture . . . of such kind are the famous works of cultural analysis, such as Priestley's *English Journey* and Orwell's *The English People*. Invaluable as they are, they . . . cannot be the starting point. They take for granted the very thing that needs investigation: the wider world within which England and Englishness find their meaning. English national identity cannot be found from within the consciousness of the English themselves. We need to work from outside in.'[28]

More than sixty years ago, another Indian, Ranjee Shahani, asked audaciously in his book *The Amazing English*: 'Can I, a roaming Asiatic, hope to succeed where people of the same race, subjected to more or less the same historical forces, have failed ? The very idea is ludicrous . . . Fortunately, I am not trying to reveal the inwardness of England.'[29] Me neither. As another roaming Asiatic, I am attempting to explore her outwardness, follow that mystery, but in our times.

That means looking afresh at prevailing orthodoxies even if the reappraisal tests the political instincts of this author. For example, Edward Said's *Orientalism* has been an almost sacred text for post-colonial writers such as polymath Ziauddin Sardar: '[Orientalism] is a lie about the nature of the West and about the nature of the great cultures and civilizations to the east of the West, a lie about "Us and Them" . . . by no means limited to Islam and Muslims . . . it was applied equally forcefully to all other orients, Chinese, Indian, south-east Asian and others.'[30] To me, though, it seems the Orientalist paradigm can itself be myopic and inflexible. I did once try, without success, to discuss those misgivings with Said.

Be wary of unequivocal constructs, however brilliant and persuasive. Norman Davies reckons that the sum of the past '. . . can only be likened to a forest of those giant tropical lianas which coil upwards out of earth and twist their way through the jungle cover towards the light'.[31] He is absolutely right.

A key aim of this book is to initiate a more nuanced, unbiased conversation about England and the 'Other'. It challenges Muslim firebrands who have persuaded themselves that since the crusades Christian Westerners have only ever felt hatred for their people and faith. And jingoists who use a bleached history as propaganda.

Part I focuses on England's responses to the 'Other' at home and abroad. Beyond the chauvinism and expansionism lie hinterlands of subterfuge, cravings, respect and forbidden love. In Part II, I have chosen particular topics to illustrate in more detail how the Orient affected and influenced England and vice versa. I hope by the end readers will appreciate that Exotic England's story is a riposte to the pernicious divide of Them and Us.

I myself have been on a marvellous journey of discovery, have learnt much from the experts and thinkers who talked to me and from the published sources I used. In order to finish what I started in this lifetime, a vast amount of material had to be left out. I have drawn on primary and secondary sources, published surveys and commentaries, the research of willing academics and enthusiastic students who helped me, and taped interviews I conducted in England, Egypt, Jordan and India.

I spoke to over a hundred new and old migrants in English conurbations. Some are from rich nations – the US, Australia, Qatar, Japan, Singapore – others from rising economies like India and Brazil, and the rest from Eastern Europe and African nations. At least half of them felt intolerance was spreading. Yet hardly any want to go back to their own homelands or elsewhere in the West. Why? Because of the openness and sense of opportunity the French footballers noted, and for these reasons articulated by Imran Quereshi, an old poet and factory worker from Kashmir: 'Here they eat our food, smile and will not be rude even if they don't like us. That is self-control. That is humanity. I can forgive them for many bad things because they are so humane. I thought before, one day I will go back. What to go back to after a life of quiet and freedom? My Urdu poems are about love between us Easterners and England.' We were having tea in his lovely little garden full of sweet-smelling English roses and lavender.

In contrast, in a pretty Berkshire village one Asian shopkeeper I spoke to brusquely refused to answer any of my questions: 'Please go now. I am a very busy man. Nothing to do with us. Their business.' He is wrong. England is our business because history threw us together. Its destiny is our destiny.

PART I

1 *England Stirs*

'England . . . can change only in certain directions . . . that is not to say the
future is fixed, merely that certain alternatives are possible, others are not.'

George Orwell[1]

ALL'S NOT WELL WITH the sceptred isle. Since the 1990s, the
bones of England have got brittle, the body seems liverish and blood pressure
precariously high. Confidence has buckled, doubts enervate certainties.
Geopolitical influence and economic might are slipping away and elected leaders
are lost as they confront challenges facing England in the new millennium: the
pressures on the United Kingdom in the aftermath of the Scottish independence
referendum; hostility to the expanding European Union; and the rise of aggressive, increasingly xenophobic nationalism as a response to continuing immigration.

Britain was a colonial power from 1583 to 1945. Then the imperial sun went
down, was much missed, and is saved in the national memory bank. After the
Second World War, powerful figures, including Winston Churchill, began to
envision a 'United States of Europe' to prevent future outbreaks of war on the
continent – and, in my view, to pick up after decolonization, shake off regret,
regroup and create a new power base.[2] In 1973 Ted Heath took Britain into the
European Community. This English prime minister was a zealous European. His

successor Margaret Thatcher was defiantly not. She was a patriotic small islander, who evoked Empire, Protestantism and manifest destiny in her rousing speeches. Europe was elsewhere and full of aliens. But in her time as PM she sold off many of Britain's assets to 'bloody foreigners' and, being strategic, stuck with the EU project. For Professor Bernard Crick, 'Thatcherism, with its contradictory combination of an intense free-market ideology and an intense chauvinism, was an attempt to find a new sense of English identity.'[3]

As the European Union got bolder and bigger Britain turned rebellious, questioning and disrupting its aims and policies. Thatcher was a masterful irritant and power broker within the EU. I am not sure she would have wanted to quit the club. A good number of her devotees seem to want that now. To them the pan-national project is moribund and burdensome. The anti-EU UK Independence Party (Ukip), led by Nigel Farage, has gained millions of English supporters. This discontent is surely a sign of deeper troubles.

Long gone is the triumphalism of the 1980s when Margaret Thatcher and Ronald Reagan seemed unassailable and omnipotent. Their ideological passions and laissez-faire, small-state economic model spread across the globe. After the Cold War ended, the dominance of Western capitalism was secured and Britain, as the best mate of the US, was at the top table. Albion's pride found a place to go and be special again.

Nobody predicted then that, as soon as they could, Eastern Europeans would move west or that Russian oligarchs would head for Europe's capitals – London in particular – and buy influence, power and palatial properties. A landowning duke[4] confessed to me his feelings of rage that England, his England, was now occupied by 'Commies and charlatans who, unlike our Empire folk, know us not, never can know us. That's not to say I think we should have allowed every ex-colonial Tom, Dick, Harry, Khan and Singh into the country. But at least there was a historical connection. And they did work hard. Our old gardener was from the Punjab, knew Father in the Indian army. Damn good chap. Made excellent chai too.'

The duke, in his posh way, articulated the biggest national anxiety of this epoch. Post-war migrants were unwanted, but natives learnt to put up with them. Those who came to stay had to endure racism and make good. Some did not survive. (This is Britain's archetypal immigrant story from the sixteenth century onwards.) The supply of cheap labour from the old colonies helped drive economic growth and delivered ever higher living standards for the majority. Integration happened organically and laws ensured some fairness. However, in the new millennium, animosity engulfs the nation. Continuing inflows from poor countries and the EU (which allows free movement of nationals within the union) is inflaming citizens from right to left and even earlier immigrants and their thoroughly British families. Work-hungry migrants, those seeking refuge, and undocumented itinerants are increasingly seen as invasive and an affront to national integrity.

Globalization and the unstoppable rise of India and China are also upsetting the comfortable old order. Other nations, previously subjugated by European powers, are catching up fast. The Empire finally strikes back. England feels the blows most deeply. This was not how it was meant to be.

Meanwhile the Scots and Welsh are more assertive and self-assured than ever before in history. Though historic grievances will never be forgotten, they are focussed on the future. Like other minorities, they are more full of verve and purpose than are Englanders, less apprehensive too about globalization and the expanding EU. The Republic of Ireland and Britain are developing closer ties, setting aside the injustices and furies of past centuries. Catholics and Protestants in Northern Ireland, still largely unreconciled, are having to deal with this out-break of goodwill.

In the 2010 election, Labour lost power and an awkward coalition government was formed between the anti-devolutionist Conservative party and the Liberal Democrats, enthusiastic decentralists. A year later the SNP won the Scottish Parliamentary elections and pledged a plebiscite on independence from the UK. England was rattled and provoked by the promise. In September 2014, the Scots voted to stay in the UK, but everyone knows the old union is no more.

And the other union – between European nations – is as problematic. After centuries of mutual suspicion, deadly wars, trade rivalries and religious hostili-ties, this unwieldy and imperfect enterprise has achieved peace, economic accord and cooperation. But the drums of jingoism beat, oblivious to these considerable achievements. The political historian David Marquand is concerned that in England virulent anti-European scepticism has 'morphed into phobia'.[5]

These extreme reactions are not found elsewhere in the UK. One Plaid Cymru member of the Welsh Assembly, who did not want to be identified, said to me: 'We are for the EU, so is the SNP. And we see globalization as an opportunity. The English are scared of change, of losing power. You have to pity the English.' Has it come to this? No. You don't have to pity the English, but to understand their desires and demands. They yearn to be a distinct, recognizable, respected tribe.

Devolution

In 1977, Tam Dalyell, then MP for West Lothian, put this question to Parliament: 'For how long will English constituencies and English honourable members tolerate . . . honourable members from Scotland, Wales and Northern Ireland exercising an important, and probably often decisive, effect on English politics while they themselves have no say in the same matters in Scotland, Wales and Northern Ireland?'[6] He articulated the internal competitiveness between the four UK partners and sensed that the centre would not hold for long.

Partial decentralization was pushed through by New Labour in 1998, some twenty years after Dalyell's speech. The Scottish Parliament, Northern Irish and Welsh Assemblies were set up with new, albeit limited, powers. England was cursorily offered regional autonomy, of sorts. Its piqued nationalists spurned the deal and went into a long sulk, quite justifiably, in my view.

An *Economist* journalist noted at the time, most Middle Englanders believed that Britain was 'an organic nation with a definite identity, lashed together by hundreds of years of shared customs, privations, wars and culture',[7] while Jeremy Paxman declared: 'England scarcely exists as a country: nationalism was and remains a British thing . . . It is a mark of self-confidence: the English have not spent a great deal of time defining themselves because they haven't needed to. Is it necessary to do so now? I can only answer that it seems something the English can no longer avoid . . .'[8]

The politicians who championed devolution should have recognized that the new settlement was much more than a constitutional realignment and an overdue concession to the other three British nations. Devolution splintered the mirror the English looked into, shattered their self-image. Their nation seemed to be losing its vim. The aftershock began to transfigure everything.

The new millennium dawned. Even as the bells tolled and the Thames glittered and shimmied as if it was a river of gold, mighty England must have felt denuded and diminished. It had to fight back, make its own history.

Scotland and Wales have changed in ways that will be either a lesson for or warning to England. Strongly revivalist, too many Scots and Welsh citizens and myth-makers zealously promote ancestral stories and emotive histories in which the usual villains are the English. Outsiders rarely get to join in as equals to shape the nation.

Though modern Scotland is enthusiastically European and genuinely committed to diversity, I feel its soul looks back to *Braveheart* and Burns. The conservative MP Rory Stewart disagreed with this view, and robustly reminded me that a disproportionate number of Scots went forth to the East and happily adopted local cultural habits.[9] The journalist Andrew Marr was keen to stress that the modern SNP 'is the most pro-immigrant of all the parties. These Scots have worked hard to change their image and promote civic nationalism.'[10] Still, at best, it is a work in progress.

I have been taken aback by my fellow Britons' strong antipathy to tentative English patriotism. In Wales and Scotland none of my interviewees welcomed the development; though several were lyrical about their own nationalisms. Some were fearful of it, others dismissive. Mr Ahmed, a Pakistani shopkeeper in Glasgow, told me: 'One thing with the Scottish – they are nice people. Another type altogether are the English. They have done so many bad things and if they get their own parliament will do it again. They are like that.'

Then, when the tape was off he went off message, disclosed that abusive anti-Muslim graffiti had been daubed on his shop windows and that racism has got worse in Scotland since the foiled attempt by an Iraqi doctor and his accomplice to bomb Glasgow airport in 2007: 'London and Birmingham are different – we people feel at home there. Here we have to say all the time Scotland is so great. In England they don't expect that so much'.

Wales, meanwhile, which has third-generation mixed-race citizens, cannot consolidate its romanticized past, persistent parochialism and global ambitions into a convincing narrative. Northern Ireland is still attempting to forge a common cause between Protestants and Catholics and so, for now, cannot attend adequately to the wider mix of its fast-altering society. Non-white immigration into both Northern and Southern Ireland is testing the people and politicians. The Irish have sent their sons and daughters to every part of the world for many centuries, but that hasn't made them culturally receptive.

In 2009, I met a smart young Kenyan migrant in Belfast. His bags were packed, he said, for the onward journey: 'In some ways it is easier here, because we are still a novelty, you know, black people who are competent, not with begging bowls. But I am always explaining myself, always answering stupid questions. They are casually racist, don't get me, my desires, plans. England will be hard, but the people there stopped asking these questions many years ago.' His faith will either have been affirmed or broken by the time I write this. All I know is that he did move to London and then to Bristol.

SPLITTING ENGLAND FROM BRITAIN

There have always been a minority of Englanders who have never, ever felt British. The novelist John Fowles, for example, recoiled from the red, white and blue of the Union Jack; for him it represented 'the Britain of the Hanoverian dynasty and the Victorian and Edwardian ages; of the Empire; of the Wooden Walls and the Thin Red Line; of "Rule Britannia" and Elgar's marches; of John Bull; of Poona and the Somme; of the old flog-and-fag public school system; of Newbolt, Kipling and

Rupert Brookes, of clubs, codes and conformity; of an unchangeable status quo; of jingoism at home and arrogance abroad; of the paterfamilias; of caste, cant and hypocrisy.'[11] To Fowles, England was different, its colour green, fresh and fecund, a poetic sanctuary. In reality, however, many of the items he contemptuously listed as 'British' are essentially English.

The interchangeable use of 'English' and 'British' once seemed normal and incontestable. The historian A. J. P. Taylor was certain, like the rest of his compatriots, that 'It really does not matter. Everyone knows what we mean, whether we call our subject English history or British history. It is a fuss over names, not over things.'[12] In the 1970s, the punk rockers Angelic Upstarts, famous for their patriotic song *England*, tossed 'Britain' into the lyrics as if they were one and the same.[13]

I believe this English mindset has a lot to do with numbers. The vast majority of Britons are of Anglo-Saxon ancestry and in a democracy that counts, or should, and seems not to now. They were born great, achieved greatness and were more than happy to have further greatness (including great expectations) thrust upon them.

England and Britain are still used synonymously and unthinkingly by many English people. It could just be an old habit that is hard to shake off, or a mark of implicit superiority. After all, the national, now global, language has their name on it. Outsiders have followed suit, submerging the whole nation into its biggest part. This conflation, I believe, will drop away as English self-awareness continues to grow.

A survey in 1999[14] found 43 per cent of the English described themselves as 'English' and 41 per cent as 'British', a switch of allegiance that would, once, have been unthinkable. By 2004, 58 per cent of those polled said they were English.[15]

The Economic and Social Research Council confirmed the drift to Englishness.[16] In 2007, 72 per cent of the English wanted a holiday on St George's Day and when asked to say what they thought England was, for 55 per cent of the respondents the place was 'historical' and for 48 per cent, interestingly, it was 'multicultural'.[17] Research reports published in 2012 concluded that voters in England had become more assertive and placed more emphasis on their English rather than their British identity.[18] This was confirmed by a short internet survey commissioned for this book. For 40 per cent of respondents, the reasons were tied to devolution, while 18 per cent said it was because being English meant a sense of fairness and tolerance of a multicultural society. History was very important to more than half the respondents; 73 per cent believed you had to be born English and yet only 17 per cent said ethnicity best described Englishness. In fact nearly 39 per cent emphasised 'mixed blood' or diversity as a central definer. The countryside was considered a key identifier by 56 per cent, and 30 per cent still think it is the Empire.[19]

ALL FOR ST GEORGE

In the past there was no need for noisy nationalism. History had made the English top dog. There was 'inhibition in the matter of national self assertiveness' observed Professor Kumar, not from inborn modesty but from hauteur.[20] They felt they 'owned' the kingdom, its tongue, traditions and aggrandizing chronicles. In Andrew Marr's words: '[They] felt themselves better than the hot-blooded, untrustworthy and unstable peoples around them. The Anglo-Normans were the unifiers, the builders of the world-beating institutions, the grown-up race.'[21]

The novelist E. M. Forster found his compatriots hideously narrow-minded, yet also free-ranging, quixotic and dreamy: 'the nation that produced Elizabethan drama and the Lake Poets cannot be a cold and un-poetical nation. We can't get fire out of ice . . . there must be in the English nature hidden springs of fire to produce the fire we see – the warm sympathy, the romance, the imagination must exist in the nation as a whole.'[22] Kumar today hails the England which 'can produce spine-chilling effects. It has served . . . to focus ideas and ideals. It has been the subject of innumerable eulogies and apostrophes [*sic*] by poets and play-wrights. From Shakespeare to Rupert Brooke, it has been lauded as the font of freedom and standard of civilization, a place of virtue as well as beauty.'[23]

Past glories and poetic praise will always make them exultant, but the English now want to be recognized as a great, modern nation with a distinct identity. The Campaign for an English Parliament asserts: 'There has been a decisive resurgence in English self definition and awareness. The tide will not be turned back.'[24] England's sap rises in the month of April, around St George's Day and Shakespeare's birthday. Each year more bright red crosses than ever before appear on proud bosoms, chests and heads, call out from windscreens and windows. St George, who is thought to have been born in Turkey to a Palestinian mother,[25] is leading his troops in an unmapped political topography.

For some thinkers and policy makers the surge is a mood not a movement.[26] But moods are temporary and change and this national consciousness is spreading and deepening.

It started with a kick. During Euro '96 many fans wore the red cross on their flushed faces. It felt then like whimsy, an amusing craze. It was, in fact deadly serious.

Harbouring coiled grudges, a growing tribe of Anglo-Saxons threw gloomy portents and auguries, filled up with angst. Foreigners, migrants, the EU,

Scotland, multiculturalism were regularly blamed for the disquiet. Islamicists added real terror to the mix. At the time of writing, the extremist English Defence League (EDL) was soothing fears and fanning them at the same time. Ukip's popularity among Anglo-Saxons signalled more isolationism and less expansiveness.[27]

Perhaps reacting to the fortress mentality, an alternative English patriotism also began to emerge – confident and generous, expansive and inclusive. Until recently, for example, few St George's flags were seen in trendy North London, home to political and cultural elites. In 2012, Labour leader Ed Milliband adopted the cause of Englishness, a cause previously mistrusted by his party. And he is a dynastic North Londoner. In a speech he made at the Royal Festival Hall that June, he said: 'We should embrace the positive, outward-looking version of the English identity . . . I am proud to be Jewish, I am proud to be English.' British political leaders habitually praise and declare allegiance to Britain. Rarely, if ever, do they make avowals of Englishness. But times are changing.

Migration and Integration

TO ENGLAND WITH LOVE

'The trouble with the Engenglish,' says the stuttering character S. S. Sisodia in Salman Rushdie's *Satanic Verses*, 'is that their his hiss history happened overseas so they do do don't know what it means.' He speaks a big truth. Large-scale postcolonial migration brought that history home. It started with the Caribbeans who arrived on the *Empire Windrush*, which docked in Tilbury on 22 June 1948, most of whom settled in England. The imperatives for both the immigrants and the receiving country were not disputed, even by Enoch Powell. Those who sailed over needed work, and workers were urgently required for post-war reconstruction. Other motives can only be sensed or speculated.

In 1982, Salman Rushdie delivered a coruscating TV lecture on the imperial mindset: '[The British] have chosen to import a new empire, a new community of subject people of whom they think and with whom they can deal in very much the same way their predecessors thought of and dealt with the "fluttered folk and wild".'[28] The broadcast caused a storm, particularly in the hearts of the English, and elation among us people of colour who felt alienated in Margaret Thatcher's Britain. I can now see why his words must have hurt.

Did the migrations from the ex-colonies give Englanders further opportunity to lord it over swarthy natives? Or was it that, having known the world, they could not stand a safe and monotonous life? The same questions can be addressed to the migrants. And were there reasons other than economic need that brought the migrants here? Did they miss contact with England and its rich culture?

Since 1990, flows of migration have increased from places with few links to England or Britain. It makes sense, says Neil MacGregor, if you take a long view: 'In earlier centuries, objects came to London from all over the world. In the last century, people of the world have been coming to England. We now have a complete equivalence.'

But a different climate is sweeping over England. It's as if its sons and daughters finally sobered up after one, long, fantastic party and now wish they had stayed at home, not been so wayward, not brought strangers to their shores, had just been sensible. Like those unchanging Italians in Tuscany, who stayed steady, passing on through the generations the same food, family stories, music, olive oil, old stone homes and values.

In the spring of 2011, David Cameron delivered a controversial speech. He gave a desultory nod to hard-working immigrants and then clipped their optimism: 'Real communities are bound by common experiences . . . forged by friendship and conversation . . . knitted together by all the rituals of the neighbourhood, from the school run to the chat down the pub.' No pub, no way we can belong – according to this English prime minister who projects an affable inclusivity. His own, genuinely open attitudes were sacrificed to placate petty chauvinists. Other party leaders and bigwigs do the same, partly for expediency, mostly because they feel they must.

But all is not lost. England can never become parochial and insular. It was, is and will be fascinated and constantly altered by its encounters with the 'Other'.

THIS CAPRICIOUS, COLOURFUL NATION

In the autumn of 2011, trouble and strife broke out in East Coker in Somerset, immortalized by the poet T. S. Eliot in *Four Quartets*. Inhabitants vociferously opposed council plans to build new homes in the village. They didn't want internal or external migrants spoiling their perfect little corner of England. Is it, was it ever, that? T. S. Eliot was an Anglicized American, an unexcavated Roman villa stands in East Coker, and crusaders lie in the old churchyard. In 1669, Andrew Elyot, the local vicar, sailed off to Salem, Massachusetts, and played a part in the witch trials. Another villager, the sea captain William Dampier, circumnavigated the globe three times. In 1709, he rescued the castaway Alexander Selkirk from a desert island. That story inspired Daniel Defoe and Coleridge. Then there is an old mill where sailcloth was made for the Royal Navy.[29] East Coker is a perfect symbol of outgoing, multifarious England. But, in a very English way, it doesn't think it is.

Like Neil MacGregor, the Labour MP and historian Tristram Hunt traces the beginnings of this epic saga to Tudor times: 'With the Reformation a heroic mindset develops. England is Jerusalem, special, blessed. It is confident, can absorb other cultures and identities. You don't get the blood-and-soil patriotism of the Celtic nations, the ethnic exclusivity.'[30] True, though commendably the Celtic nations were never quite as vain as Anglo-Saxons.

Gaze upon the paintings of Elizabeth I, all postcards from elsewhere. Rich Elizabethans were bedecked with oriental clothes and jewels, their tables laden with world food, just as ours are today. Heston Blumenthal recreates some of those dishes and usefully links past and present English cosmopolitanism, its inescapable destiny.[31]

Shakespeare became and remains the supreme diviner of a certain kind of Englishness, the speech by John of Gaunt its anthem:

> *This other Eden, demi-paradise,*
> *This fortress built by Nature for herself*
> *Against infection and the hand of war,*
> *This happy breed of men, this little world,*
> *This precious stone set in the silver sea,*
> *Which serves it in the office of a wall,*
> *Or as a moat defensive to a house,*
> *Against the envy of less happier lands;*
> *This blessed plot, this earth, this realm, this England.*[32]

England is portrayed as precious and fiercely protective, geologically and wilfully distanced from her neighbours.[33] However, the noblest of wordsmiths did not restrict his plays to his blessed homeland. He probably never travelled abroad,[34] but his plays took off – to France, Venice, Egypt, Rome, Athens, and beyond, to supernatural spheres. His audiences would have been thrilled by the faraway, magical places and bewitching characters. Think of Bottom (a local, illiterate artisan) and his drug-induced sojourn with a sexy fairy Queen, or the drunks Trinculo and Stephano on Prospero's weird and terrifying island. Anthony and Desdemona are helpless before 'otherness' and Cleopatra is, arguably, the most enticing Easterner in the whole of Western literature. Shakespeare empathized with despised outsiders. Caliban's grotesqueness is offset by moving reminders of his enslavement, of broken promises. *The Tempest* is both a manifesto for colonialism and its most savage critic.

A hundred years later, Daniel Defoe, in *Robinson Crusoe*, also reflected ambivalent attitudes to colonialism.[35] And in *The True-Born Englishman: A Satire in Verse*, he reminded his fellow countrymen they were crossbreeds:

> *Thus from a mixture of all kinds began*
> *The het'rogenous thing, an Englishman*
> *. . . A true born Englishman's a contradiction*
> *In speech an irony, in fact a fiction.*

A subsequent explanatory preface delivers the same message but in a more placatory tone: 'I confess myself somewhat surpris'd to hear I am taxed with bewraying my own nest, and abusing our nation, by discovering the meanness of our original, in order to make the English contemptible at home and abroad, in which I think, they are mistaken . . . had we been an unmix'd nation it had been to our disadvantage . . . those nations which are most mix'd are the best and have the least of barbarism and brutality among them.'[36]

The histories of England and the East – Empire and its aftermath, the Commonwealth and migration – are explored further in the next two chapters. Here they appear briefly as key elements in the formation of the English identity, past and present.

Rudyard Kipling's loyalties were divided between England and the East. Born in India, he went to English public school, then returned to India as a young adult. He was an inbetweener, a combination of conceit and diffidence, conflicted. His most famous refrains are enigmatic. Did he really mean 'East is East and West is West, and never the twain shall meet'? Or was that a poignant projection of himself, a man who was of both and of neither? The 'white man's burden' is his appalling condescension, but is it epitomized or mocked in Kipling's poem? Just as mysterious are the lines:

> *Winds of the World, give answer! They are whimpering to and fro –*
> *And what should they know of England who only England know? –*
> *The poor little street-bred people that vapour and fume and brag . . .*[37]

But, for all these dilemmas, Kipling was a man of the empire.

G. K. Chesterton, on the other hand, was resolutely not. His unflattering response to Kipling included the lines: 'What can they know of England who only know the world?'[38] Throughout the colonial era, there were prominent Englanders who proselytized for smallness and were against 'abroad' and expansionism. Among them was the Edwardian writer H. V. Morton, who drove around his beloved homeland and penned a bestselling travelogue entitled *In Search of England*;[39] it was nostalgic, anti-urban, anti-modern, racially protectionist, tender. The book was an atonement for leaving his homeland in 1923: 'I solemnly cursed every moment I had spent foolishly wandering the world and swore that if I ever saw the cliffs of Dover again, I would never leave them.'[40]

England to such naysayers was a perfect parish, not a ruthless, global landlord. They were a minority. Most Englanders were behind the overseas venture lasting several centuries. So too, of course, were the Scots, Irish and Welsh. When Britannia no longer ruled the waves, the Scots had plenty to fall back on, but the English had no alternative narrative and found the loss of power hard to bear. (Some still can't believe it happened.)[41]

TOWN, COUNTRY AND SUBURBS

One fine day in 1713, Joseph Addison went to the Royal Exchange in London and was overcome: '[it] gratifies my Vanity as I am an *Englishman*, to see so much an assembly of Country-men and Foreigners consulting together upon the private Business of Mankind, and making this Metropolis a kind of *Emporium* for the whole earth'.[42] And so it is today. For instinctive internationalists such as the Scottish journalist Andrew Neil, the capital 'is where England meets the world, to their mutual advantage. Tradition and tolerance, two great English virtues, have combined with foreign diversity, dynamics and exotica to create a twenty-first-century city state.'[43] I agree with him. Millions don't. They are shamed, inflamed by the sleepless, ever-expanding, Technicolor Mephistophelian metropolis.

The actor John Cleese is one of those doomsayers: 'London is no longer an English city, which is why I love Bath. That's how they sold it for the Olympics, not as a capital of England, but as a cosmopolitan city. I love being down in Bath because it feels like the England I grew up in.'[44] Wrong, wrong and wrong again. London was never monocultural. It was founded by foreign occupiers, has forever fed England's vast appetites and absorbed global wayfarers and dreamcatchers. Bath, too, was a Roman spa town and in Jane Austen's day, the clothes worn by the middle and upper classes, their wealth and domestic dramas, were inextricably linked with 'abroad'. Today the city's sounds, tastes and smells are a medley, as are its residents.

Midsomer Murders, a hugely popular, long-running TV crime series, is set in the picturesque English countryside. Non-white characters have never featured in the stories. Its producer, Brian True-May (what a resonant English name), explained why: 'It is the last bastion of Englishness . . . We just don't have ethnic minorities involved because it wouldn't be an English village with them. It just wouldn't work. Suddenly we might be in Slough.'[45] True-May was forced to apologize. I hope the English will forgive him.

The Archers, on Radio 4, long ago understood how inaccurate and irrational it would be to deliberately whiten the rural milieu, to render it colourless. *Major Pettigrew's Last Stand*, a hugely successful novel by Helen Simonson, tells the moving love story between a stiff, retired English major and Mrs Ali, a Muslim widow running the village corner shop.[46] No reviewers or readers seemed to think the relationship was improbable in a white parish. When Kate Middleton married Prince William, she invited the Asian couple who ran a corner shop in the village where she grew up to her wedding. That's England for you.

What about the English suburbs, where people escape to from the bedlam of city centres? I walked around some leafy streets on the outskirts of London one day in 2011. A white man in his sixties called out from his manicured front garden. Was I looking for something? Had I bought that house at the end of the road that was up for sale? There was panic in his eyes. I told him I was writing about England. His riposte: 'None of your business. The only thing I *will* say is that our politicians have betrayed England by letting immigrants flood in.' As I walked on even the trees seemed to sway away from me.

The very next day I went to another, contrasting suburb, Southall, in west London, a busy, noisy neighbourhood, known as 'Little Punjab' because most of the local stores sell Asian products and there is an profusion of Indian and Pakistani restaurants. In a clothes shop, I met three white women from Warwickshire, a grandmother, mother and daughter, who was choosing an outfit for her wedding. She had seen Gurinder Chadha's film *Bride and Prejudice*[47] and wanted 'a Bollywood wedding'. Chadha was raised in Southall and her film was a pastiche of Jane Austen's famed novel. I helped the women negotiate the price and they, sweetly, invited me to the wedding.

Mr and Mrs Williams are from Rotherham. They left in 1999, because there were too many Asians there, and moved to Pinner, which also changed too much too fast. The next move was to beautiful Bournemouth, but that seaside escape, say the couple, was 'overrun with Eastern Europeans'. So they are migrating to Brittany. Neither speaks any French. 'What will you miss about England when you finally move?' I asked. 'Nothing. Nothing but the curries, and London. We'll go there once a month to catch musicals, and all the world's there, isn't it?' Brittany will not keep this pair long. They cannot escape from themselves, or from England.

Defining England

In 2000, Andrew Marr wondered why the English discourse on nationhood was insubstantial and inchoate: 'Whether it is because of guilt, post-imperial and post-war exhaustion or the bland contentment of a basically secure and prosperous majority, the English seem to have dropped the politics of identity and self assertion . . . novels have been the most important ways a literate part of any community imagines itself. There are, clearly, lots of novels coming out of England . . . but there are very few gripping, mainstream ones about what life is like in England today. And when we do get novels with a strong, fresh sense of England today, who are the authors? V. S. Naipaul, Timothy Mo, Indira Singh, Vikram Seth.' The country, he concluded, 'seems to have a very thin sense of itself'.[48]

A year on from those observations, many detected a thickening, a quickening of that sense: 'For some, being English is an embarrassment – a shame – associated with empire, imperialism, stoicism, stiff upper lips; others feel uncomfortable taking pride in being English because of associations with nationalism, yobbishness and an inability to hold our drink. But this England, this Englishness is changing. No one can seriously deny that . . . we live in a country which is restless, uneasy, questioning and devolving.'[49]

The huge countryside demonstration in 2002 and the fox-hunting ban two years later unexpectedly turned into an expression of generic English frustration. In 2010, there were widespread protests against the threefold rise in university fees for students at English universities. In the summer of 2011, young people of all races and classes rioted in many of England's major cities (not in the rest of the UK). They stole stuff, wrecked buildings, used violence, terrified the nation with a new kind of nihilism.

When there was a possibility of an independent Scotland, the *Guardian* journalist Madeleine Bunting confessed that the idea affected her deeply: 'Why does that make us shiver? What is it about Englishness that, in some contexts, makes polite society nervous? We're happy to talk about the wonders of the English language, the delights of the English landscape and English rock or pop, but definitions of English nationalism have been abandoned to football hooligans and the far right. There is a curious and debilitating disconnect between the rich and cultural traditions of Englishness and its political expression.'[50]

Ideas and visions, traditional and modern, are added to and fermenting in the pot, bubbling away. Sweet and stinging aromas waft out. Smoke gets into the eyes. I still don't know what this new England will be.

Tentativeness can be a virtue, argues culture watcher Sunder Katwala: 'Far from being weakened by a lack of definition, the fact that we can't define Englishness means we can still create it depending on what we want it to be. That very nebulousness has enabled the English to absorb new cultures and influences with fluid ease.'[51] That may or may not continue in the future if a clearer national entity materializes. If it does.

Portraits of the nation are half-sketched and sometimes incongruous. (Perhaps such a portrait can never be completed and that will certainly be true of this book too). Paxman finds the English in the 1950s endearing: '. . . stoical, homely, quiet, disciplined, self-denying, kindly, honourable people who would infinitely rather be tending their gardens than defending the world against a fascist tyranny'.[52] That contained temperament underpinned by Anglican bourgeois values is still present in parts of the country. However, the folk tending their peonies support wars and assume international influence. Domestic pottering and epic adventuring are essential aspects of Englishness. Alan Titchmarsh, the gardening guru and one of England's favourite sons, would have made a very good empire builder.

For the environmentalist writer Paul Kingsnorth, Englishness is innate, an inherited attachment: 'England matters to me. Not because I am a "patriot" in the old-fashioned sense of the word. Not because I think it is better than everywhere else . . . Simply because it is the place where I was born and grew up and it is the place where I belong. I know its landscapes and its history, and feel connected to both. I couldn't write about Scotland or Wales in anything like the same way, because I am not part of them and they are not part of me. For better or worse, I am English.'[53]

To immigrants, claims of genetic belonging and authenticity can often feel like exclusion, but Kingsnorth's is a very moving English voice. His country, he warns, is 'being eroded' by big business, the wealthy, urban bourgeoisie and, most reveal-ingly, 'a very English reluctance to discuss who and what we are as a nation'.[54] Truth to tell, the beatific version of England he seeks to resuscitate mostly consists of romantic musings of the mind or utopias painted or embroidered on canvas. The cultural analyst Jonathan Rutherford is a perspicacious observer of that prelapsarian tendency: 'The past has been depicted as a magical place, and history as a reverie in which the English can affirm our conservative soul. Its mythology has shaped how we think of ourselves and who we think we are.'[55]

Yet there *is* a green England, an arcadia meaningful to millions. It is real and preternaturally beautiful. Places like Warwickshire, the Yorkshire moors, Thomas Hardy's Dorset, the Lake District have inspired some of England's best poets, artists, novelists, dramatists and filmmakers.

That England is also turned into useful political propaganda. For Stanley Baldwin, Englishness was the sound of hammers on anvils, corncrakes on dewy mornings, wood smoke.[56] As prime minister, John Major, himself raised in a tough, urban habitat, re-evoked Baldwin's folksy ruminations for electoral purposes in 1993. His was 'a country of long shadows on country (cricket) grounds, warm beer, invincible green suburbs . . . old maids bicycling to Holy Communion through the morning mist'.[57]

Such evocations are meant to reassure and promise continuity – harvests and pubs, hearty farmers and their earthy wives, hunting for some, old crafts and lordly mansions, *Upstairs, Downstairs, Downton Abbey*, the royals, the National Trust, Ascot and so on. You only have to unpick a few stitches of the needlepoint and it all unravels. The royals have absorbed German, Russian and Greek blood-lines; Stephen Fry, the perfect personification of Wodehouse's Jeeves, is half Hungarian-Jewish; and traditional English grub includes spicy pickles and chutneys. Way back in 1933, J. B. Priestly enthused: 'The England admired throughout the world is the England that keeps open house.'[58]

In her anthropological romp *Watching the English*, Kate Fox examines the manners and 'grammar' of Englanders and pronounces them 'reserved, inhibited, privacy obsessed, territorial, socially wary, uneasy and sometimes obnoxiously anti-social people'.[59] Though these are some enduring traits, they are contradicted by converse tendencies, as was pointed out in an acerbic review: 'Fox seems to lack the energy or invention that would be required to reconcile her theory of an inhibited "dis-eased" nation with the evidence of increasingly unbuttoned, cultur-ally diverse and unpredictable forms of Englishness.'[60] One thing we can all agree on is that nobody agrees on what the English character is. It accreted over centuries, before and after invasions, through immigration and emigration, travel, trade, exchange and irrepressible libertarian impulses.

HYPER-DIVERSITY AND HYPERTENSIONS

The final decades of the twentieth century turned out to be as transformative as the early age of exploration, the Empire, the world wars and the 1960s. Black and Asian MPs – all elected in England – changed the colour of politics; the media, pop culture, the arts and sports began to reflect England's glorious multiplicity;[61] the first millionaire Asian businessmen showed their faces; mixed-race families grew in numbers and visibility. And though tough laws were passed to keep them out, immigrants just kept coming and coming so the ground under England trembles.

Neo-Fascist ideology touches nerves and offers simple solutions – ethnic and political clean-ups. Just before the 2010 election I had coffee, at his request, with a young Englishman, a member of the British National Party (BNP), who was considering moving to the English Defence League (EDL). He wore a good suit and shades, wouldn't tell me what his job was but said I would be surprised. After the first sips of cappuccino he went off, like a just-lit Roman candle. He tried to torch me, I felt the burn. In sum, his beloved country has been too easy, a whore open to 'coloureds' and Europeans. Just before we parted, he took my hand and admired my Indian bangles. *He admired my Indian bangles*, in spite of himself and his cruel racism.

The critic Patrick Wright has peered into the body of England and found Chesterton's ominous lines festering there: 'Smile at us, pay us, pass us – but do not quite forget;/ For we are the people of England, that have never spoken yet.' (English Defence League members have memorized that short couplet.) Wright believes this Englishry 'finds its essence in an adjustable sense of being opposed to the prevailing trends of the present. It is a semi-instinctive theory of encroach-ment that allows even the most well-placed man of the world to imagine himself a member of an endangered aboriginal minority: a freedom fighter striking out against "alien" values and the infernal works of a usurping state'.[62] These 'kippered' views now appeal to millions. The journalist Andrew Gimson, for example, warns: 'Englishness is a very deep, though usually dormant emotion. Once roused we can become ferocious, a point often discovered too late by our enemies.'[63]

Whatever happened to the nation which was so sure of itself?

Opposing and conflicting ideas of Englishness seem to be in constant argument. Jeremy Paxman now describes himself as 'English' rather than 'British', but what he means by it would appal the young man from the EDL: 'I keep meeting lots of black and Asian people who describe themselves as English. So it's certainly not a racial identity. Englishness is a way of looking at the world. A Sikh friend of mine describes herself as English. She loves Jane Austen. We understand each other. I'm never quite sure in that way about being "British". It strikes me as being noisy. Englishness is gentler, not when it is roused of course.'[64]

Well, sometimes it can be gently excluding too. In 2011, I met Alia and Stu. Her Muslim family came over from Kenya in 1968; Stu is white English, born and raised in Norfolk. They married in 1999. She is happy, she told me, but can't get close to her in-laws: 'They are lovely people. They have welcomed me. But all the time, there is this thing that makes me feel I'm an outsider. They tell our kids stories about the war and how they, the English, won it. When I remind them that Indians, Africans, Americans helped them in that war – they look as if I am failing a test. They don't say anything. I have joined a club, their club, with their rules.' Stu tried to explain: 'It's like this. England dissolves differences, adapts them, colonizes, if you like. But it isn't a plot. We hardly know who we are. This false pride is just a walking stick we use as we walk to look for answers somewhere, we don't know where. It's much worse now that there are so many different types of immigrants. It just feels as if we will drown. Alia doesn't try to see things from our point of view. I never had these feelings before.'

Their marriage was in trouble.

Richard Bean is one of England's foremost contemporary playwrights. We met up to talk about the country and his plays. He is proud of his people, of his birthplace, Hull, of those who abolished the slave trade, plus 'old-fashioned fair play, the rules of cricket', liberal, enlightened values. That was fine and admirable. Less so was Bean's loathing of '*Guardian*-reading liberals' and 'leftie local authorities' that kowtow to multiculturalism (and even have 'ethnic' names of roads and estates!): 'It's good to be tolerant, but also to know what you would not tolerate, like Sharia law. There should be one law for all.' Though Bean's cantankerousness was off-putting, I do agree with much of what he had to say on the limits of tolerance and was very grateful to have met him. He is a remarkable animator of modern England and its clashing, crashing emotions, its mind both closed and open.

CROSSING BRIDGES

Englanders of all classes travel. Some are nervous, a number behave obnoxiously – excessively ebullient football fans and drunk trippers tumbling along the punished streets of Spanish resorts – but most appear to harbour no fear or loathing of abroad and are at ease with multiracialism at home.[65]

Gerry owns a cafe in a seaside town. His mum was widowed young and never married again. She took in clothes to wash. Gerry was single until he was in his late forties, when he found himself a Thai wife while on holiday in Bangkok. Just like that, he said, over one, fun-filled evening. They have two children, and live frugally so they can go to Thailand every year. 'My mum loves Maria – never had any doubts for a moment. Her parents were more worried. I'm proud to be English because we welcome the world, the best of us do.'

In June 2004, my son Ari married Elizabeth, from Cheshire, in a Unitarian church in Wilmslow. My Asian friends and family mixed cheerfully with the bride's side. An unselfconscious warmth soon circulated among them. It felt natural, even though, I suspect, there aren't that many mixed marriages in Cheshire and this one was also bringing Londoners to the countryside, the south to the north. Two grandmothers – my mum Jena, in a red sari, and Dorothy, looking splendid in blue – drank champagne together and enjoyed smoked salmon as well as samosas.

What then of the workless and working-class white English? Again, the picture is mixed and inconsistent. With globalization, job losses caused by modern capitalism, xenophobia is on the rise among those who have lost out. Lynsey Hanley, author of *Estates: An Intimate History*, describes, with rare honesty, her own kith and kin: 'paranoid, suspicious, mistrustful, misogynist and racist'.[66] Frustrated and politically disengaged, they turn on migrants and asylum seekers, terrorize them in the name of England, their England, a mean and mingy place. However, on the most divided of housing estates, so-called 'baby-mothers' of white, working class stock have children with black, Asian and Arab men and there is little white disapproval, certainly much less than in the decades between the 1950s and 1980s. Friendships here know no race.

Empire and migration have led to intimacy, not always between equals, but an instinctive, unarticulated connection. As Maria found out when she came here from Thailand: 'I married Gerry because I had no work back home and wanted to have some chance. So, for me, it was like a business. But he really loved me and now I love him also. I see so many English people like that. Maybe some not so kind. I think most are like Gerry. I am lucky.'

'NEW' ENGLANDERS

As a modern English identity comes together slowly and with difficulty, there are thinkers and writers who are assembling the positive, progressive attributes of Englishness.[67]

The novelist Tim Lott is one of them: 'I am from England made . . . I identify with the ancient nation of Shakespeare and Dickens and Orwell and, for that matter, Linton Kwesi Johnson, the Specials, Zadie Smith and Steve McQueen . . . it is a deep, barely describable sense of a particular way of being . . . pomp and circumstance is not my England; this is an England imposed by Tory romantics.' He calls for 'this most imaginative and clever and individualistic and inclusive and artistic and rebellious country' to be one 'for all to embrace and no longer recoil from'.[68] Though not English myself, I would sing this song with feeling.

So too, I imagine, would the black British journalist Gary Younge, born and raised in Hertfordshire: 'The apparently seamless link between Englishness and whiteness has been broken. Even though nobody would question that England is, and most likely will always be, predominantly white, it remains almost impossible to imagine it without black and Asian people as part of it . . . The black experience is now intimately interwoven into the fabric of English daily life in a way that is not so obviously the case in Scotland and Wales.'[69]

Mark Perryman, an original thinker on these challenges of new nationhood, agrees that the 'combination of Englishness and migration is virtually indivisible' and to drive a wedge between the two is well-nigh impossible.[70] Jon Cruddas, MP for Dagenham and Rainham, has his own, different take on English extroversion. Though part-Irish himself, Cruddas is messianic about virtuous, just, internationalist, fraternal England and 'the infinite capacity of the English to deal with demographic changes, things that are thrown at them'.[71] With this optimistic narrative he gets the votes and respect of white working-class constituents, including those attracted to Fascist parties.[72]

Indigenous folk are of course bound by many centuries of shared values, history and legends. England's culture, though, is staunchly protectionist, and also pliable, supple and stretchy. That is unlikely to change, says the Tory MP

Jesse Norman, author of a superb biography of the iconic traditionalist Edmund Burke: 'I exemplify the same ambiguities of other English-British mongrels. We are at once welcoming and forbidding and cold to people who come here.' What about extremism on the rise in England? It will implode because 'the English are moderate, conservative. Most regard national purity as phoney.'[73]

The Future

In 2011, I went around many parts of England and talked to white, ethnic Englanders about devolution and England's future. James Clarkson (mid-thirties) reflected the views of many interviewees: 'Being English means I am not Scottish, Irish or Welsh. It's ingrained in me. But as much as you celebrate pride in your own nation – England in my case – it is quite divisive in its own way as well. I don't want the UK to break apart.' Overt nationalism still makes many English people uneasy. For Jacqui Lane (mid-fifties): 'I always think of the Scots as being overly nationalistic. And the Welsh too. We English don't have to be so and now it is thrust upon us.' An A-level student in Lancashire said: 'You don't have healthy pride here in England. There's a bit of stigma attached to that. To hang an English flag in your window is regarded as racist and I don't think that is right. But I know some members of my family want England to be white again. So it's really hard.'

There was a big, lively group discussion in Luton about whether Englishness was inclusive or exclusive. Here are replies from some of the young white people (aged sixteen to nineteen):

'The only way people can celebrate Englishness is by shunning other cultures.'

'I have actually felt jealous of other peoples' cultures.'

'England is so diverse but these Muslims are killing all that, wanting their Sharia and that.'

'When I go to France and Italy I realize how much I love my country, England, and how it is always changing. We are the world.'

Longer one-to-one interviews with adults produced more detail.

Mark Edgar, a teacher from Lincolnshire, strongly believed that 'Some white English people will never accept people from other cultures. There are some foreign people in Lincoln but we are fifty years behind the times.' Yet Jacqui Lane, quoted above, a Conservative voter, confessed it made her smile when 'people who are Indian or Caribbean have a strong Yorkshire accent'. These views were widespread.[74] Brenda, who worked in a bakery in Leeds, said: 'I know they say the terrorists came from here and that. But look at Leeds. I go to a pub and a bloke from Krakow buys me a drink, or someone starts talking about Kashmir – I didn't even know where that was. They love Leeds. That's great, that is.' Her boyfriend is half Pakistani, a quarter Irish and a quarter English. In contrast, Patrick, Brenda's co-worker in the bakery, a quiet, polite guy, wanted his country to banish all other Europeans, Scots, Welsh and Irish and 'coloureds'. They had to go back home so the English could get their country back: 'I am not racist. I think everyone needs to get back their countries. The English should also come back here and give Australia back.' There will not be any agreement between these two patriots about their English nation.

According to Omar Khan from the Runnymede Trust think-tank: 'Every constituency, probably every ward in England, has ethnic-minority people living in them and projections suggest more and more diverse people will live in the countryside, especially as the ethnic-minority population ages. There's nothing worrying or shocking about this unless we think that the captains of the English football, cricket or rugby teams are unable to wear the full mantle of Englishness or reside in its green pastures.'[75]

More than a decade ago Billy Bragg wrote and sang his song 'England, Half English', in which he sang that he was a fine specimen of an Essex man who knew India well because his neighbours were half English and he was half English too. Bragg is a pioneer nationalist reclaiming England so that it can meaningfully belong to all those who live within its boundaries: 'For too long the left allowed English nationalism to be owned by some of the most unpleasant people on the right or, even worse, extremists. It was part squeamishness, part neglect. If we want to beat them, we have to articulate a more inclusive sense of Englishness. If we don't do this, the more belligerent Englishness will take control, especially in times of economic hardship. We have to work through the baggage of Empire – bad and good – and embrace that. The reason why so many black and Asian people want to come here is because they know there is racism but that England will try to understand them, accept them, even love them in the end. That's who we are, that's who you are, though you won't say you are English. You are.'[76]

I don't feel it, though I may one day. It depends on how the nation shapes up in the future and whether we migrants feel safe, appreciated and content within Albion's new imagined borders. Our suitcases are half packed. Just in case.

2 England and the Other Abroad

'From the court life of Tudor and Stuart England to the radical clubs of eighteenth-century London to the Victorian port economies of Liverpool and Cardiff, our internal history has been a global story of forced and unforced multiracial exchange, migration and trade.'[1]

Tristram Hunt

THE NOMADIC SPIRIT IS universal and immanent, makes us who we are, moved the first Homo sapiens off the African plains. People rove and migrate. When they do, they change, and the places they leave and where they arrive also change.

European exploration, mercantilism and ensuing paramountcy was spectacular and aggressive. That history left ineradicable imprints on the victors and losers. 'New' England, as it marks out its distinctiveness and imagined boundaries, needs to process that past. For Professor Gerald Maclean, studying the encounter between English travellers and Islamic civilizations 'is necessarily an enquiry into the global formations of Englishness itself . . . Each traveller, all native to England, represents Englishness in the making.'[2]

Imperiums succumb to the cultural caresses of those they overpower. The English encircled the world with a steely grip and the steel warmed up when touched. They who went out to anglicize the world did so, but in the process were mystified and transformed, more of them than we will ever know of. Anglo-Saxons are made that way.

Fascinatingly, most compulsive English wayfarers seemed emotionally tethered to their homeland too. Explorers, buccaneers and empire builders were pulled by discrepant, elemental forces. Those urges are present among today's internationalist Englanders. One day they might colonize the moon and open an olde worlde teashop up there.

The Scots, Welsh and Irish too were players in the blockbusters of exploration, slavery and colonialism, but were subsumed under England. The Acts of Union of 1707 and 1800 officially brought them into the imperial venture. Yet, even now, they are missing from the storylines.

Early Exploration, Conflicts and Trade

Indians, the Chinese, Persians, Arabs and Phoenicians were sea traders long before the main European countries.[3] In 1430 the Portuguese reached the coastlines of Africa and eventually found a route to India. Spain and the Netherlands followed. In 1527, John Rut, an Englishman, sailed west and returned home. Fifty years later Francis Drake circumnavigated the earth and the English were up and away.

Let us imagine those times. Strong Queen Bess was on the throne; Protestantism was in, Catholicism out; the country was pulsating, edgy, full of vitality and dangers. You wonder if anyone ever slept then. Wayward fortune seekers and impetuous adventurers went forth. The acquisitive and inquisitive sovereign gave them her blessing and expected high returns.

Richard Hakluyt's *The Principal Navigations, Voyages, Traffiques and Discoveries of the English Nation (1598–1600)*[4] became England's foundational epic, extolled and sentimentalized over the centuries: 'As it was in the days of the Apostles, when a few poor fishermen from an obscure lake in Palestine, assumed, under the Divine mission, the spiritual authority over mankind, so in the days of our own Elizabeth, the seamen from the banks of the Thames, and the Avon, the Plym and the Dart, self-taught and self-directed with no impulse but what was beating in their royal hearts, went out across the unknown seas fighting, discovering, colonizing, and graved out the channels, paving them at last with their bones, through which the commerce and enterprise of England has flowed out to the world.'[5] England would procure the globe, make its own small plot so big it could never be measured.

Several historians see the Reformation as critical to this expansionism, as does the theatre director Michael Boyd. The nation was 'traumatised, the value system was smashed, dishonoured. There was a search for an alternative utopia, a new beginning. Like the end of *The Tempest*, reconciliation and a new start . . . Every membrane that breaks is a luminal experience, escape from claustrophobia, fear and thrill.'[6]

The crusader spirit was waning in Elizabethan England.[7] Professor Nabil Matar and Professor MacLean are among those who repudiate the idea of perpetual enmity between Islam and Britain: 'Attitudes were never uniformly hostile as we have been led to believe . . . by linking crusading rhetoric with millennial literalism, a powerful tradition of Protestant thought has perpetrated the belief that there can be, and indeed must be, only conflict with Islam.'[8] In fact England's relationship with Islamic states was complicated, more a wave than a hard line.

English Christians did undoubtedly curse Islam and its devotees. (Muslim hatred of Christianity came much later.) For example the sixteenth-century Cheshire poet Thomas Newton warned: 'this Babylonian Nebuchadnezzar and Turkish Pharoeh are so near our noses, they are even at our doors and ready to come into our Houses . . . this raging Beast and bloody Tyrant . . .'[9] Othello, a Moor himself, remembers how:

> *. . . in Aleppo once*
> *Where a malignant and turbaned Turk*
> *Beat a Venetian and traduced the state,*
> *I took by the throat the circumcised dog*
> *And smote him thus.* '[10]

These attitudes, though, were not fixed. The queen coyly slipped off her own bigotries when necessary. The Ottoman Empire was the dominant power and a vital ally in England's bitter battles with Catholic Europe; knowing the balance of forces, Queen Elizabeth sought out advantage. Although English and Muslim sea dogs fought each other, Elizabeth often ordered the release of Muslims captured by Spaniards. Her captains were pleased to 'apparel them, and furnish them with money' and give safe passage.[11] Raleigh and others defined themselves as the 'human liberals' against the monstrously dogmatic Spaniards.[12] When Drake and his crew arrived in Mogador, in Morocco, he lavishly entertained their Moorish equivalents on his ship and offered 'such giftes as seemed to be most glade of'. He noted that his guests drank wine, abundantly but stealthily.[13] They understood each other, bandits together on the oceans, sometimes friends, often ruthless foes.

RAIDS AND CAPTIVITY

From the sixteenth century, Muslim pirates operating from the Barbary Coast in North Africa took English vessels, raided England's coastal areas, abducted and enslaved men and women. By 1616, Algiers alone had taken 450 English ships. In 1625, in a single year, 1,000 sailors were taken from Plymouth. Most were treated as subhuman. Many died of food poisoning, heat stroke, illness and torture, some of shame and despair.[14] Survivors' testimonies reveal terror, forced labour, physical and mental torment, forced circumcisions and conversions. However, the historian Linda Colley indicates that in some cases Barbary captivity could 'involve only a brief stay, being reasonably well cared for . . . [captives] might learn new languages and attitudes, or adjust to Muslim households where they were treated less like servants and more like family members or convert to Islam out of conviction or in order to marry a cherished Muslim woman, or enter into well-paid employment as mercenaries, medical experts, architectural advisors or armourers'.[15]

The Adventures of (Mr T. S.) An English Merchant Taken Prisoner by the Turks of Angiers, published in London in 1670, is a swashbuckling account, some of it improbable, but much of it truthful to a fault. The author confirmed the brutality of the infidels – molten lead poured into the gullet, the first extermination ovens and much more. That said, he also found the captors 'very polite and well bred . . . affable, hospitable, courteous, kind and very liberal'. Like a number of other captives, he neither demonized nor romanticized his Muslim captors, displaying sophistication rare in our twenty-first century.

Fifteen-year-old Joseph Pitts was taken to Algeria in 1678 and only made his way back home when he was in his thirties. Though forced to convert to

Islam, he grew to appreciate aspects of Islamic societies: 'I was in a much fairer way for honour and preferment in Algiers than I would expect ever to have in England.'[16]

English slaves 'turn'd Turks' to survive – or perhaps because the cushions were soft, the sex inventive and life more amenable. During Elizabeth's reign, 5,000 English converts were living in Algiers alone. Later, when King Charles II sent Captain Hamilton to the Barbary Coast to secure the release of hostages, not one agreed to return. They were 'partaking of the prosperous Success of the Turks', wrote the disgruntled Hamilton, '[and] are tempted to forsake their God for the love of Turkish women. Such Ladies are, in general, very beautiful.'[17]

Despite the terrifying tales of returning captives, England's economy needed young men to carry on venturing abroad, whatever the dangers. In 1702 the Dean of St Paul reminded his flock: 'These are men who make you rich . . . who bring the Indies home to you and clothe you in all the bravery of the East. These [men are] the great strength and glory of this island.'[18]

Colley argues that 'Barbary captive taking . . . not only exacerbated pre-existing hostility to Islam . . . it also increased the volume and variety of information available about it in Britain.'[19] In the 1630s embassies from Muslim lands appeared in London and the first chairs in Arabic were established. In 1734, a remarkably accurate translation of the Koran by George Sale was published on the very day 150 redeemed, wounded English slaves walked in slow procession through the streets of London. Though English Protestants were the chosen ones, Sale felt Muslims were 'emphatically civilized, and they were no less emphatically flourishing'.[20] English ships transporting pilgrims to ports near Mecca learnt about hajj and Islam. These chronicles comprehensively dash the presumptions of a perpetual crusade and 'clash of civilizations'.[21]

AWESOME CIVILIZATIONS

From the sixteenth century to the early eighteenth century, travellers to the East recorded its delights: a gentle welcome, their hands washed with rose-water, feasts, magnificent horses, civility and dancing girls. Admiration, collaboration, commercial envy and espionage were part of the heady mix.

Snoopers were dispatched 'to note all kindes of clothing in Turkie and all kinds of their labour', and London weavers sent spies to Persia.[22] Talent went abroad. In 1604, Captain John Smith, a mercenary who later married the American-Indian Pocahontas, saw many 'English goldsmiths, plummers, carvers, polishers of stone and watchmakers in Morocco'.[23] Canny merchants imported Eastern goods, knowing well the Anglo-Saxon hunger for novelties. Scientists, doctors and apothecaries went east to learn about ancient Muslim discoveries and remedies.[24] Then there were adventurers, ambassadors and their wives, fervent messianic Christians too. All turned up in the lands of the infidels.

Sixteenth-century English Christians set out to convert 'heathens' and discovered they were deeply civilized. Jesuit Thomas Stevens, rector of a college in Goa, observed: 'Like a jewel among pebbles, like a sapphire among jewels, is the excellence of the Marathi tongue. Like the jasmine among blossoms, the musk among perfumes, the peacock among birds, the Zodiac among the stars, is Marathi among languages.'[25]

So impressed were some English travellers that they couldn't themselves tear away. Some surrendered completely to the Islamic life. Among them were two English musicians sent over to entertain the Mughal Emperor Jahangir, who became his courtiers after embracing Islam. And William Hawkins, envoy of Elizabeth I, who failed to get trading rights in India, took a Muslim wife and 'used altogether the customes of the Moores or Mohameddan, both in his drink and meate and other customs'.[26] In 1591, John Anderson visited Istanbul and noted: 'Many Englishmen old and young have, in my remembrance, turned Turkes, as Benjamin Bishop, George Butler, John Ambrose and others'.[27]

Samson Rowlie, from Great Yarmouth, son of a Bristol merchant, was captured in 1580, castrated and taken to the court of Hassan Bassa, King of Algiers, then part of the Ottoman realm. There he became the immensely powerful Hasan (or Assan) Aga, treasurer, man of cunning and influence, who dressed in gold brocade robes and finery, was feared and admired. A picture thought to be of Aga shows him as a man of high status, knowing and haughty.[28] The playwright Phillip Massinger included an English eunuch slave in his play *The Renegado* (1624), a character thought to have been based on Rowlie. William Harborne, the first English ambassador in Istanbul, sought Aga's help when trying to secure the release of captured Englishmen in parts of the Ottoman Empire and assured him he would always be thought of as a true Englishman.[29]

And so it has been through the centuries. Even when the English went abroad to pillage and conquer, the most resolute individuals could find themselves diverted, their world views swayed. In the nineteenth century, the archaeologist Sir Charles Fellows, who went scavenging through the Ottoman Empire for the British Museum, spoke for such men and women before and after his time: 'I was strongly biased against the Turks; and it will be seen in the course of the narrative how this unfavourable idea of the Turkish character was gradually removed by personal intimacy with the people.'[30]

MEN ON A MISSION

English churchmen in the Ottoman Empire were expected to stick to their mission and script. Many couldn't. Henry Maundrell, a cleric sent to minster to the Syrian Levant Company in 1695, was lost in ecstasy: 'Certainly no place on earth can promise the beholder . . . greater voluptuousness.'[31] Even William Biddulph, a dry clergyman in Aleppo at the turn of the seventeenth century, saw some virtues in Arabian heathens: 'The Women keepe their tents and spend their time spinning or carding or knitting or some household housewifery not spending their time in gossiping and gadding abroad from place to place and from house to house from ale house to wine taverne as many idle housewives in England doe.'[32] He came to a sticky end when he was found in flagrante with a 'strumpitt' on his way back to England.[33]

Other travellers found themselves questioning their own civilization and suppositions: 'The Ottoman Empire was striking for its tolerance and cosmopolitanism – a reality which lived ill with all the blood-curdling claims about the Islamic threat to Christians.'[34] Unlike in popish Spain, Muslim rulers permitted freedom of worship. Sir Henry Blount embarked on a rationalist, impartial inquiry into the Muslim empires; in *A Voyage into the Levant*, published in 1636, he wrote: 'he who would behold these times in their greatest glory, could not find a better scene than Turky for the Turkish way may not appeare absolutely barbarous as we are given to understand or rather is another kind of civility, different from ours but no lesse pretending'.[35] No less pretending.

The Portuguese and Dutch had been present in the Mughal courts since 1595; when England's urbane ambassador, Sir Thomas Roe, showed up in 1614, he charmed the vain and greedy Emperor Jahangir. In his diary Roe wrote that the emperor 'wore more jewels than any other monarch in the world'.[36] Some compliment from a man of the extravagantly splendorous English court. Roe was seeking permission to set up a trading base in Surat. In 1615 he delivered to James I a gushing letter from Jahangir: 'Let your royal heart be as fresh as a sweet garden . . . Let all people make reverence at your gate. Let your throne be advanced higher. Command your merchants to bring in their ships of all sorts of rarities and rich goods fit for my palace.'[37] So started British ascendancy in India.

A mural in the House of Commons shows English emissaries at the opulent Mughal court. No other Western parliament has such visual memorials on their walls.

The Atlantic Slave Trade

This book is primarily about the English and the Orient, but when it comes to England and the Other, the enslavement of Africans was a definitive part of the story and cannot be overlooked. Slavery and colonialism were entwined and both histories remain divisive and contested. Most English people seem reluctant to dwell on the fortunes that were made by investors and plantation owners. Abolition rightly raises fulsome national pride and the campaigners are alive in the national consciousness as if that noble crusade was won but yesterday. Slavery, on the other hand, induces either ennui or indignation because it is thought to be mainly an evil executed by Americans and Africans and in any case was 'a long time ago'.

John Hawkins, the second cousin of Francis Drake, was the first known English slave trader. His business took off in the mid-1500s with royal approval, backing from the City of London and rich capitalists in the West Country.[38] The English expanded the trade to the West Indies and by 1650, more than 800,000 Africans had been captured and sold. Britain became the brand leader and the number of victims was to reach 'dizzying heights'.[39] The abominable business that made the nation rich remains a deplorable and unacknowledged part of England's history.

When English men and women were taken and sold into bondage to be used and coerced, the fury of their proud compatriots was indescribable. Few of them questioned their own slave traders or cared to know much about Albion's seafarers who held Moorish and Turkish captives, far away from the streets and lanes of England.

Admittedly, Arabs and the Portuguese have let their guilty slave history dissolve into almost total, collective amnesia. Their ancestors were the first to get into human trafficking in Africa. Then came the other European nations, cashing in big time.

The wretched cargo was taken across the perilous and terrifying ocean. Men, women and children were manacled, packed below deck, given half a bowl of uncooked millet or corn flour and water and left untreated when ill.[40] The slave traders didn't look in on them because of the stench and fear of contamination. 'Problem' slaves were thrown overboard, their limbs fettered so they couldn't even swim, not that it would have saved them. Sharks followed the ships to dine on delicious human flesh and blood.[41]

In 1781, 142 slaves were dumped in the sea from the *Zong*, a slave ship owned by a cartel in Liverpool. The owners put in an insurance claim for the 'lost' lives. Lord Chief Justice Mansfield presided over the case, the same judge who had pronounced in the 1770s that slavery was an infringement of the liberties guaranteed to all in England and had ruled that slavery was unlawful on English soil. In his court, the Solicitor General for England and Wales argued that the dead were no different from horses and cattle when they were thrown off the ship. This story shocked parliamentarians and aroused their sleepy moral sense. Over time slaves were treated better on the transatlantic voyages for economic reasons – dead slaves made no money.

Slaves were bought and sold, used and abused across England. Churches betrayed those who tried to escape and sent them back to punishment and captivity. Coffee houses did brisk business in shackles, 'travelling' chains and slave collars. The port cities of Bristol and Liverpool built monuments to honour the profiteers. Jeremy Paxman characteristically cuts through the cant and lies accumulated over the centuries: 'You would have to be wilfully deaf and blind to remain ignorant of the profound change the slave trade was working in England during the seventeenth and eighteenth centuries. It was, in the words of one apostle, "the mainspring of the machine which sets every wheel in motion", making possible the network of enterprises which brought tea and coffee to the sideboards, oils and wines to the lunch table, Chinese pottery and Persian silks to the drawing room.'[42] The Society for the Propagation of the Gospel branded the slaves they owned with their logo; Oxford's All Souls College was built on this blood money, as were many of our museums and galleries.

Quakers in the USA and Britain had been agitating for abolition since 1670 with little effect. The Trinidadian Marxist historian Eric Williams maintains that slavery ended not because good guys opposed it but because it stopped being profitable. The revolutionary spirit unleashed in the US and France also had an impact. Revolts by black male and female chattels in the Caribbean brought on severe retaliation and an awareness that the system would one day have to end.

Resistance was part of the English story too. It seems to me incontestable that English women and men of conscience fought inestimably hard against the abominable trade, changed attitudes and used the law to eventually abolish the grotesque commodification of Africans. In 1786, a young Cambridge graduate, Thomas Clarkson, wrote a persuasive, powerful essay against slavery. It was published by abolitionists and the movement started to gain momentum. Once more Quakers were among the leading activists. One of them, Josiah Wedgewood, the famous maker of fine pottery, created medallions with a cameo of a supplicant slave claiming his brotherhood with all men. They were widely distributed. Petitions were gathered from around the country and delivered to Parliament; anti-slavery lectures and public meetings were packed out. Ordinary women took up the cause, and stopped using or eating sugar. The Anglican playwright and poet Hannah More penned a moving poem on slavery in 1788 and made her readers weep. William Cowper's 'The Negro's Complaint' (1788) and Blake's 'The Little Black Boy' (1789) embraced black people as brethren.

Ex-slaves Ignatius Sancho and Olaudah Equiano were relentless crusaders, supported by a staunch network of enlightened English men and women. Their best-selling books, authentic and vivid, affected hearts and minds, and built up the case for anti-slavery laws. The Slavery Abolition Act of 1833 ended slavery throughout the British Empire, but colonial dominance carried on for another century.

Economic Colonization

Early English trading companies petitioned for and obtained royal charters from the late sixteenth century to the mid-seventeenth century. The Levant Company

(1581) and Royal African Company (1672) were among the most gainful, but it was the East India Company, founded in 1600, that changed the course of history. Its profits were vast, its methods suspect, its men – too many of them – wickedly avaricious. By the eighteenth century the firm's methods were roundly condemned by several Englishmen of substance. The *Gentlemen's Magazine* decried the 'imperious company' of East India Company merchants.[43] Horace Walpole was a fearsome critic.[44] The Anglo-Irish playwright Richard Sheridan was another: 'The company combines the meanness of a pedlar and profligacy of pirates, wielding a truncheon with one hand and picking pockets with the other.'[45] Edmund Burke was mortified that 'every rupee of profit made by an Englishman is a rupee lost forever to India', and Britons there were more uncivilized than previous invaders.[46]

Clearly not all company men were blackguards: 'For some [being in India] meant sticking to the ex-pat bars and dreaming of Surrey over yet more drink. But for many that meant genuinely getting to grips with the local culture, the local people, the local women. You were as likely to shed prejudice as to gain it. You might even have kids, put down roots and think about it as home. Meanwhile your Indian neighbours would have little reason to resent your presence. They were friends and lovers. Others were business partners, clients or suppliers . . . You were in all this together.'[47] Even when commerce led to the Raj, the British-Indian writer Zareer Masani contends that 'the British were essentially traders, serving the East India Company, for whom territorial control was subordinate to commercial profits'.[48]

Merchants chasing lucre were not more benign than empire builders – they could be even more monstrous – but it is perverse to conflate the various and changing motives of Englanders who went east, or to claim that trade was the Trojan horse that allowed Britain to dupe naive nations. Empire was not something Britain just fell into,[49] but nor was it the result of a cleverly calibrated strategy.

Various modern historians have verified that Western merchants didn't all suppose that Eastern lands were asking to be subjugated, swindled and saved.[50] (That came much later, when colonial carve-ups needed to be justified.) They knew about the wonders and sophistication of the Ottoman Empire, of China and India before the European presence. When the British started grabbing Indian kingdoms, records show some of the English abandoned their side. William Whiteway was just a boy when he was captured during a battle between the company and Tipu Sultan, who refused to accept foreign domination. The sultan was demonized by the British, who cast him as a tyrannical and corrupt ruler.[51] But young Whiteway was educated, taught several languages, grew to admire the maharajah, a 'noble encourager of learning', and was persuaded that the most incompliant Indian rulers had reason to hate the occupiers because 'aggression provokes retaliation'.[52]

Those at the head of the East India Company were not of a type either. Major-General Robert Clive (1725–74), who became known as Clive of India, was a supremacist and corrupt capitalist. A company official when he arrived in India in 1744, in time, using private armies, he took vast areas of the subcontinent. In Indian villages, even today they have puppet shows and festival parades where the evil monster is Robert Clive.[53]

Though flawed, Warren Hastings (1732–1818), the first Governor-General of Bengal, was relatively enlightened and judicious. He warned it would be wanton tyranny if the British did not rule with consent and within the norms of Indian society. Company officials, he insisted, had to be multilingual and conversant with the cultures of occupied territories. Colleges were set up to revive Sanskrit, old

Indian histories and languages.[54] Like other virtuous Orientalists, Hastings strongly opposed missionary activity in India and went on a 'pilgrimage' to Varanasi, to the ghats by the River Ganges where bathers prayed and bodies and corpses floated in a watery grave. He confessed: 'I love India a little more than my own country.'[55] No wonder such men were seen as enemies within.

Back home, Lord Clive was lauded and rewarded in Britain for his foul deeds; Hastings, who took over the East India Company in 1773, was impeached and denounced for 'venality, unnecessary violence and wholesale corruption'.[56] Though acquitted, his name was mud. Today he has prestigious, vocal defenders, among them Simon Schama and Jeremy Paxman.[57] He was not Satan's creature and, on some matters, might have been a saint.

Empire Builders and Expansionists

The British Empire is a ceaseless argument. It was black, white and several shades of grey. It was more than a story of power and submission and, even at its zenith, there were famous English disbelievers such as Edward Gibbon, the salubrious eighteenth-century English historian and MP: 'The history of empires is the history of human misery . . . A more unjust and absurd constitution cannot be devised than that which condemns the natives of a country to perpetual servitude, under the arbitrary domination of strangers.'[58] The historian Sir John Seeley (1834–95) was tortured by 'barbaric' colonial presumptions: 'It is a mistake to suppose that the Empire is standing proof of some vast superiority of the English race over the races of India.'[59] The colonial mind preoccupied E. M. Forster, one of the greatest English writers of all time. In one essay he wrote of his countrymen: 'They go forth in a world that is not entirely composed of public school men or even of Anglo-Saxons but of men who are as various as the sand of the sea; into a world of whose richness and subtlety they have no conception. They go forth with well developed bodies, fairly well developed minds and underdeveloped hearts. And it is the underdeveloped heart that is largely responsible for the difficulties of Englishmen abroad'.[60]

George Orwell made typically incisive observations about the Empire's disreputable scaffolding: 'Seen from the outside British rule in India appears benevolent and indeed it is . . . but it is not possible to be part of such a system without recognizing it as an unjustifiable tyranny. Even the thickest-skinned Anglo-Indian is aware of this. [Anglo-Indian means British.] Every "native" face he sees in the street brings home to him his monstrous intrusion.'[61]

The 'natives' must have sensed those quivers behind English certainties; maybe that helped humanize their rulers.

Empire builders themselves were divided and inconsistent. Take the Taj Mahal as an example. William Bentinck, who was Governor-General of India from 1828 to 1835, was a modernizer who banned suttee (widow burning) and saved lives. But his reformism rose from contempt, not care. It is said that he wanted to break up the dazzling memorial and sell off the marble.[62] Lord Curzon, of Anglo-Irish stock, was appointed Viceroy of India in 1899. He too was arrogant and ruthless, yet he spent a fortune on restoring the Taj: 'We are not so rich in originality ourselves as to afford the memorials of an earlier and superior art or architecture to fall into ruin.'[63]

Between the rulers and subjects, the relationship could be symbiotic and frequently mutually appreciative. This, one of millions of encounters, exemplifies that mutuality perfectly. In 1930, the gifted writer R. K. Narayan penned his first work set in a small, fictional Indian town called Malgudi. The British then were deeply unpopular, Gandhi was leading massive marches against the Raj, but Narayan sent his manuscript to Graham Greene, one of his favourite writers, who helped to get it published. The two authors became friends.

By the time Delhi became the symbol and power base of the Raj, there were fewer British officials running the Indian subcontinent than there were Austrian officials in Prague.[64] Class affinities were useful, and captured perfectly in one photograph taken in 1899. Curzon and the Maharajah of Gwalior were photographed with their slain tigers. The two strike the same pose; their haughty faces tell us that they understand each other rather well and share the same violent passions.[65]

For colonialists, 'Quite simply, it was often far more effective to negotiate deals with the Mughals or with local potentates than to rush in with guns blazing and swords flashing. Statecraft, and the patient playing-off of one group against another, was often an excellent and economical way forward. So was the encouragement of collaboration between a variety of Indian elites and groups with the English authorities. Indeed, it is arguable that, even at the height of its power, the Raj relied upon the collaboration of the ruled with the rulers just as much as upon military strength.'[66]

That is not to say that these tactics were wholly clean or honourable. Indians today say the deviousness of English traders and politicians was worse than plain battle and conquest.[67] However, as blinkered is the widespread notion that the entire enterprise was driven by control-freaks and men of bad faith.

Mr B. K. Amin, our history master at Kololo Secondary School in Kampala, owned a gilt-framed picture of Winston Churchill. Sometimes he lit incense in front of the picture. Clouds of strong scent rose over the adipose tissue and unyielding eyes. Mr Amin told us about Churchill's tender paintings of Moroccan scenes – old gates, desert landscapes and enigmatic inhabitants;[68] how on one trip he met Hassan El Glaoui, the artist son of the Berber Pasha, who wanted his boy to wield sabres, not twiddle with paint brushes. Churchill persuaded the father to indulge the boy, who went on to become a celebrated figurative painter. In Uganda, Churchill's words are still used in their tourist brochures: 'Uganda, the Pearl of Africa . . . from end to end a beautiful garden . . . the exuberance of the vegetation scarcely describable'.[69]

Churchill was doubtlessly a bigot too. He despised Hindus, and Indians, backed apartheid, was indifferent to the poor and starving in the colonies.[70] Old Indian war veterans retired in Britain told me that when they were fighting in Burma during the war, he ordered that they be given smaller rations than white men. His paradoxes make Churchill an authentic symbol of England.

Aspirational Indians collaborated with the British Empire, were helpful stooges or simply pragmatic. The long list includes soldiers, merchants, nautch girls and brothel keepers, moneylenders, factory owners and royals. Cooperation was common, deals were struck, and double deals executed.

As time went on, British occupiers turned more overtly racist. Those in charge began to believe in innate white supremacy. The Earl of Moira, Governor-General from 1813 to 1823, declared that Hindus had no more intelligence than a dog, an elephant or a monkey; Lord Cornwallis and the Earl of Dalhousie habitually disparaged natives. These grandees squandered the goodwill built up by some of their more conscientious (maybe canny) predecessors. Commoners took their cue from those in charge.

In his memoir written after 1857, Sita Ram Pandey, a loyal soldier in the armies of the East India Company, and later the Raj, recalled the times when the British understood they had to mix with the locals: 'in those days the sahibs would speak our language much better than they do now . . . The sahibs often used to give nautches for the regiment, and they attended all the men's games. They also took us with them when they were hunting . . .'[71] Intimacy was pushed out by racial conceit. That shift made a morally dubious project morally indefensible.

THE HIDDEN EMPIRE

For its many champions, the Empire was a chivalric, picaresque tale of English pluck, moral courage and noble sacrifice. Some of this pride is justified, but they surely must know that dirty deals and deeds were thrown into a vast pit of state secrets. The murky side of the Empire, at long last, is being excavated by modern historians.

Colonized subjects were infantilized or bestialized in order to justify their subjugation. In the 1870s, famines killed between 21 million and 27 million Indians while cheap grain continued to be exported to Britain. Charitable donations to the starving were outlawed. Drought and famine caused havoc in the Gujarat in 1899, yet food surpluses elsewhere in India were denied to the dying.[72] Amartya Sen, winner of the Nobel Prize in economics, points out that such famines have not blighted India since independence.

Lord Bentinck himself observed: 'the bones of cotton weavers were bleaching the plains of India'.[73] Elsewhere, too, trade was skewed so cheap raw materials would flow to the UK and manufactured goods would be forced on colonials. After 1769, the East India Company imposed trade restrictions on Indians and forced weavers into working for British factories. Those who disobeyed were imprisoned or flogged. Many had their thumbs chopped off. British-made cloth was forced on Indians, killing off their own industries.[74]

India was required to supply £250 million worth of goods for the two world wars. Between 1891 and 1935 the 'largest budgetary expenditure continued to be the military'.[75] After the First World War, 17 million Indians fell victim to a flu epidemic and many starved because national coffers were depleted. Indian soldiers fought with the Allies and thousands died fighting for liberties they did not enjoy under British rule.[76] In 2001, the English writer Roy Moxham set out to find out why a hedge was planted in British India of spiny Indian plum and acacias, 2,300 miles long. It was in fact a customs barrier: 'I had been looking for a folly, a harmless piece of English eccentricity. It had been a shock to find that the great hedge was, in reality, a monstrosity; a terrible instrument of British oppression.'[77]

Most Britons have been taught some facts about the 'Indian Mutiny' of 1857, known in India as the First War of Independence. Unrest was spreading though the parts of India controlled by the East India Company, which was getting ever more expansionist and hubristic. Rulers, even popular ones, were summarily removed. Indian sepoys were underpaid and starting to get restive. Some believed there was a plot to Christianize India. New cartridges provided to them were greased with cow or pig fat, forbidden to Hindus and Muslims respectively. When army chiefs learnt of the unacceptable grease, the cartridges were replaced but the suspicion remained. On 10 May a small group of sepoys rose up against the commanders and within a month the revolt had spread across north central India.

The maiming and killing of officials, soldiers, families, missionaries and educators was truly atrocious. But British reprisals were even more savage: 'Entire villages were burnt down; mutineers were smeared in pig fat before execution, tied to the muzzles of cannons and blown to pieces.'[78] In his incisive book *From the Ruins of Empire*, Pankaj Mishra, an outstanding British-Indian intellectual, uses the sharpest of tools to dissect Empire and post-imperial righteousness.[79]

In Africa too the British were guilty of land larceny and other crimes. Indigenous smallholders were dispossessed, trading licences denied to 'Hindus, Greeks and Chinamen'.[80] In Rhodesia, the most fertile farming land was reserved for white people and interracial sex was a punishable offence. The British there 'aimed to ensure and perpetuate privilege and control. They dominated access to all resources – land, education, health . . . Inequality was enforced by the settler-controlled parliament and reinforced by social segregation.'[81] Robert Mugabe is a frightful autocrat, but his anger is not baseless.

During the Mau Mau insurrection in Kenya between 1952 and 1960, suspect Kikuyus were tortured and killed.[82] In the Middle East, Britain wanted 'control of the oil fields of Northern Iraq, control of the Suez Canal, and control of the oil pipelines . . . Indeed the whole project of planting a Jewish emigrant population in Palestine can be seen as no more than a project to help guard both the oil pipeline and the Suez Canal'.[83]

These commentaries are about the British Empire in the South and East. However, although the English were the top chaps in most outposts let it not be forgotten that the smaller UK nations were wholly engaged in Britain's global project. By the end of the nineteenth century, 'seven of the eight large Indian provinces were headed by Irishmen, while the chief justices of Bengal and Hong Kong were both Welshmen'.[84] The Scots were, like the English, rapaciously greedy for profits amassed from overseas trade and Empire.

THE SCOTS: SLAVERY, EMPIRE AND DIVERSITY

Prominent Scots were keen slave traders. The poet Jackie Kay, part-African, raised by adoptive Glaswegian parents, used to think that 'Scotland was not nearly as implicated in the horrors of the slave trade as England. Scotland's image is one of a hard-done-to wee nation, yet bonny and blithe.' In 2007 she began researching the interred truths. When Richard Pococke, Bishop of Meath, visited Glasgow in 1760, he remarked that 'the city has, above all others, felt the advantage of West Indies trade which is great, especially in tobacco, indigo and sugar.'[85] More than a third of the Caribbean plantation owners were Scots. The poet Robert Burns was offered a job in Jamaica. Penniless, his life full of scandal, he almost went to be, in his own words, a 'poor negro driver'.[86] Though he had sporadically expressed sympathy for the enslaved, his conscience wasn't unduly troubled when he decided to go and seek his fortune on a plantation. He didn't get on the ship because a collection of his poems published around that time turned him into a local hero.

The Scots were unreserved colonists. *Blackwood's Magazine* of Edinburgh published news of global expansion and missionary activity; Glasgow and Dundee were Empire boom towns; their missionaries ranged far and wide.[87] Linda Colley puts forward the thesis that: 'A British Imperium . . . enabled Scots to feel themselves peers to the English in a way still denied to them in an island kingdom.'[88] It gave them status, a big part in the imperial drama. William Jardine and James Matheson, both Scotsmen, masterminded the unlawful export of opium from India to China and persuaded the British government to go to war when the emperor tried to stop the drug trade. By the 1830s, addiction rates in China were reaching 90 per cent. In devolved Scotland, this, one of the worst abuses of white power, causes no shame.[89]

When David Livingstone embarked on his explorations in East Africa in 1849, he was aided by Indian merchants, yet was repelled by the 'Jews of Africa', as he called them.[90] He feared too that 'degraded' black men were unnaturally aroused by pure, white females.[91] None of this features in the telling and retelling of

Scottish history by its people. Troublesome facts are also doctored in the annals of England's heroic deeds, but, off stage, persistent men and women subvert the narrative and reinsert absent truths.

Get Jeremy Paxman started on this subject and a gale blows up: 'The Scots failed spectacularly with their own imperial adventures in the new world, were bankrupted by it. They were envious of the English. Estimates say that between a fifth and a third of the wealth of Scotland was thrown at the ventures in South America. The Act of Union was grasped at partly as a chance to join the English Empire.'[92]

As prime minister, Gordon Brown, a true Scotsman, decided Britain no longer carried guilt about its great Empire and, in a very imperial way, directed Indians and Africans to get over it.[93] That guilt bypassed Scotland altogether. Scottish revivalism needs to initiate a long period of reckoning with this history. It is true that a number of Scots in India and elsewhere did 'assimilate aggressively'.[94] William Dalrymple's monumental tome *White Mughals* contains enthralling tales of some of these men who married local woman and happily adapted Indian lifestyles. Today a growing number of Scots are instinctively cosmopolitan.

The Scottish novelist Andrew O'Hagan reflects on the two nations: 'The ambience of Empire has made a curiously small imprint on Scotland, despite the Scots' energetic cooperation and sometimes aggressive lead in foreign adventures. The Scottish nationalists of today are able to exploit a ridiculous pretension: that their country is an occupied territory, occupied by a devilish England bent on colonization. Anyone who knows anything about tobacco and cotton will need no convincing of Scotland's part in exploiting the Empire, but England carries the can and the English seem perfectly willing to do so.'[95]

I think they are mighty tired of carrying the can.

GOING NATIVE

Rory Stewart, the Conservative Anglo-Scottish MP, acknowledges that England is uniquely susceptible to Eastern civilizations: 'There is something in the English culture – you'd have thought the Italians, French, Spanish would find the East irresistible . . . doesn't happen. There was no French equivalent of the kind of hero worship of someone like Lawrence of Arabia. In such places the English found cultures interested in food the way the English were not, interested in sex the way the English pretended not to be, [these places] had sunshine and much more – this island race could not hold back.'[96] For some the connections went deeper.

In Barnsley, Yorkshire, they are proud of Hudson Taylor, an evangelical missionary who went to China in 1853. Exceptionally, he has been honoured with two plaques, one in English, another in Chinese. The British in China were engaged in unholy ventures and politics, but Taylor was a rebel with his own cause. He wore Chinese clothes and sported a pigtail, spoke local dialects, adopted a Chinese child, died in China, as did his first wife. Both are buried near the Yangtze River. This Christian soldier embraced the Orient. How should we judge him, or those whose souls wandered between England and the East? The Indian MP and diplomat Shashi Tharoor is still intrigued by Raj officials who created 'little islands of Englishness, planting ferns and roses and giving their cottages names like "Grasmere Cottage" (in Ootacamund) and "Willowdale" (in Darjeeling).' And when they returned home and settled in Cheltenham or Kensington, they surrounded themselves with the reminders and artefacts of India. One administrator named his suburban English house 'Quetta', a frontier Pakistani city; another set his watch to Calcutta time, eating breakfast at teatime in England.[97]

Alfred Lyall arrived in India in 1856, joined the Indian civil service, was caught up in the 1857 Uprising and wrote profound poetry. His poetic observations on Indian life and Hindu religious philosophy are marvelled at by Indians today. One poignant poem, 'The Land of Regrets', expresses the English exile's pain. However, back in England, Lyall found himself yearning for India. There were others, too many to be described as eccentrics.

Some were disoriented individuals or drifters who never acclimatized to the iciness of their own societies. The novelist Lawrence Durrell stayed abroad to escape what he called 'the English death'.[98] William Beckford's novel *Vathek*, about the 'dark, sinister and macabre orient',[99] is a distasteful fantasy, but he confessed that 'English phlegm and frostiness nips my slight texture to death. I cannot endure the composed indifference of my Countrymen . . . The island is lovely without doubt – its woods and verdure unparalleled. But such inhabitants! Ye Gods!'[100] When in Fonthill, his abode in Wiltshire, Beckford would 'ride out every Morn, and translate Arabic every Night . . . I often fancy myself in the catacombs of Egypt and expect myself to stumble over a Mummy.'[101]

It wasn't all clever fakery or orgiastic self-indulgence. Englishmen and women often discarded the role assigned to them by history. They deserve to be better known. Men like Wilfrid Scawen Blunt, a poet, horse breeder and traveller, who was married to Lady Anne Noel, Byron's granddaughter. In the 1870s they went to the Middle East, bred thoroughbreds, and became avid anti-imperialists. Blunt defended Islam, keenly backed Arab nationalism and railed against the 'inequitable and criminal relations between the Englishman and native'. His unorthodox views landed him in a great deal of trouble, but he carried on annoying those in power till he died.[102]

And Glubb Pasha, John Bagot Glubb, a Lancashireman who was one of the great Arabists of the twentieth century. When the Ottoman Empire was collapsing and Israel was created, Glubb – probably a double and triple agent – made himself indispensable to all sides in the Middle East. He lived among Bedouins, promoted literacy in villages, pushed for modernization and helped build the Arab legion. The last is considered one of his greatest achievements. He started with men who were unused to allegiances beyond their ethnic or religious tribes. He lived in the desert, slept in his old Buick automobile and built up a squad, and eventually an army. In the end he was thrown out by King Hussein; to this day, old Jordanians feel both guilt and anger at the way Glubb was treated, and talk of him as though he is still riding around Jordan, wheeling, dealing, smoking, drinking.[103]

When the British-Asian show *Goodness Gracious Me* was first broadcast on BBC TV in 1999, the actress Meera Syal received letters from wistful old Englanders with ruminations of loss and memories of times when they were out East.[104] Though the English were satirized in the programme, viewers laughed and rekindled an old relationship, more subtle and indefinable than the caricatures and stereotypes that have come to represent that past.

EDWARD SAID'S 'ORIENTALISM': FOR AND AGAINST

Professor Terry Eagleton neatly summarizes Edward Said's exposition: 'Orientalism . . . habitually represents the East as indolent, treacherous, passive, inscrutable, devious, feminized and inferior . . .'[105] It was an exposé of the systemic cultural collusion with political and economic dominance.[106] Said fundamentally shifted paradigms and challenged established ways of looking at the past; this was both necessary and overdue, provocative and, in the final analysis, unsustainable. His followers see only one shape, one pattern, one track in East–West relationships; they replicate the thought processes of those they censure.

The most genuine and true Orientalists 'contributed far more to Indian nationalism than they did to British colonialism'.[107] Think of William Jones, the Anglo-Welsh philologist and polyglot, fluent in Arabic, Sanskrit, Bengali, Hindi, Turkish, Tibetan, Pali, Pahlavi, Dari, Syriac, Ethiopic, Coptic, and other, even more esoteric tongues. He is described by the Indian historian O. P. Kejariwal as the 'Copernicus of history', who looked at the East without Western bias.[108] Jones (elegantly) described his compatriots as 'savages, who thought that the sun rose and set for them alone and could not imagine that the waves, which surround their island, left coral and pearls on any other shore'.[109]

The voices of opposition to Said can be intransigent and mulish. The historian and novelist Robert Irwin denounced Said's text as 'essentialist, racialist, patronizing and ideologically motivated' and 'a work of malignant charlatanry'.[110] Rage, almost hate, overwhelms reasonable argument. Such fierce detractors came out after Said died of cancer and so couldn't fight back. We need more nuance and less bias on both sides.

To discuss these quandaries, I went to meet William Dalrymple at his farmhouse outside Delhi. In his view: 'Said's book was very important. It changed the way we saw the relationship between East and West, but was also a book which needs a huge amount of refinement. Young Indians wholly buy into it. It was broad-brush, and has become the only keyhole through which to look.'

Contemporary scholars and critics no longer look only through that restrictive keyhole. Take, for example, Gamal el-Ghitani, one of Egypt's greatest writers: 'There is no absolute Occident or fixed Orient. There are sensible voices in the Occident who know the richness of humanity is found in the intermingling of its cultures and the complementariness of its elements, not in building one sole culture and smashing all the others.'[111] Several modern Western histories have demonstrated the 'permeable and constantly shifting boundaries' between East and West from the sixteenth to the eighteenth centuries and the cultural reciprocities resulting from England's identification with Islam.[112]

That openness is detectable even in the age of Empire. Brian Sewell's observations on this history are finely tuned and incontestable. He is persuaded that having been exposed to other cultures, religion and people, English engagement was deeper and wider than those of any other Europeans; 'Kipling's poem "Mandalay", for example, is brilliant: a soldier from the East End saying there is a better land, a dream, a place called Mandalay, that hope was behind so much. So too the seafarer's psyche.'[113] There was a 'thread of wistful identification and affection' within the English abroad. It was real and still is.

NEO-COLONIALISM

Margaret Thatcher hyped the British Empire in her speech in Bruges in 1992; Tony Blair delivered the same eulogy in 1997 and acted as if the 'third world' was his to take. Uninhibited imperial hubris continues because there has been no proper reckoning with the damage that was done then.

The *Guardian* columnist Seamus Milne, a Scot and man of the left, is unusually and brutally honest about the legacy: 'many of the world's most intractable conflicts are in former British colonies or protectorates. From the West Bank and Gaza, Iraq, Kurdistan, Yemen and Somalia to Pakistan, Sri Lanka, Afghanistan and Sudan . . . modern Britain has failed to recognize the empire for what it was – an avowedly racist despotism, built on ethnic cleansing and ruthless exploitation.'[114] To his credit, and my total surprise, Prime Minister David Cameron seems to agree with this analysis. While on a visit to Pakistan in 2011, he acknowledged that Britain's colonial policies significantly contributed to many of the world's most entrenched economic and political problems.

Over the last decade, a new posse of retro-chic revisionists of British imperialism have got on their high horses. They either argue that the Empire was a historical inevitability or aggressively reclaim its reputation, insisting it was a largely benign mission that brought on 'backward' natives, primed them, spruced them up, got them ready for modernization and industrialization.

British rule did bring some progressive developments and we natives are duly grateful, truly we are. But the Romans brought great systems and style to England too. That didn't stop the English from hating their presence.

For example, the popular historian Dominic Sandbrook maintains that, unlike the wicked French, 'Britain's empire stands out as a beacon of tolerance, decency and the rule of law'.[115] The most established (and establishment) Empire celebrant is Andrew Roberts, considered by some to be Churchill's heir. Even revisionism gets a bad name when Roberts concludes that the murder of hundreds of Sikhs in Amritsar, India, in 1919 was a good move because 'it was not necessary for another shot to be fired throughout the entire region.'[116]

And then there is Niall Ferguson, the star rehabilitator of colonialism, a dazzling showman who carries people away on the most exciting of rewoven magic carpets. Understandably, post-colonial critics just won't fly with him. As the *Guardian* journalist Priyamvada Gopal points out, 'Ferguson's "history" is a fairy tale for our times which puts the white man and his burden back at the centre of heroic action. Colonialism – a tale of slavery, plunder, war, corruption, land grabbing, famines, exploitation, indentured labour, impoverishment, massacres, genocide and forced resettlement – is rewritten into a benign developmental mission marred by a few unfortunate incidents and excesses.'[117]

England and the Other: A Magnetic Field

Many English folk still go east or south for political or economic reasons and get absorbed into Eastern cultures, just as their ancestors did centuries back. That can happen even during wars and their aftermath, despite clever state propaganda and mind manipulation. Peter, an ex-soldier from Swindon, who had been on service in Iraq, told me: 'You go out there trained to shoot and kill. But then I started knowing the Iraqis, how kind they were, shared food, smiled. And when the call to prayer started I felt calm inside, like God had got into me. I started looking at their history and their culture, what we destroyed.' These sympathies appear 'abnormal' to his father, a military man through and through: 'My father thinks he is a true Englishman. But so am I. Being English means so many different things. To him it's control, to me it's being open-minded, free.'

Brigid Wadham is a travel writer and campaigner for Palestinian rights. Her husband was a European Union ambassador posted to the Middle East and central Asia. Like Orwell and Kipling, Wadham was born in India. Spending her early, formative years there meant her inner codes were set differently and made her feel 'very, very un-English'. As an adult, she felt most at home in Damascus, where she restored an old house and held soirees for the 'amazing' Syrians she befriended. For her, life has never again been as vitalizing and pleasurable: 'Contrary to what everyone says, I know Arabs genuinely like and respect women, even women older than thirty-five. I felt at home there.' This woman with her plummy accent reflects the best part of Englishness: its semi-permeable membrane, sophisticated interactions, wide vision and capacities (some devilish) to insinuate itself into various cultures.

A point comes when delusions about the unsafe 'other' melt away, when enemies, rulers and the ruled, East and West are pulled together.

The writer Mihir Bose was born and raised in India; he remembers the mythology of Empire surviving long after the British had crept back to their cold isles: 'I was brought up to think every English person dressed for breakfast and dinner. My father was very keen on English breakfasts. The newspapers wanted to look and sound like the great English newspapers, had offices in London. After the British left, Indians were still riveted by Yorkshire cricketers and Pudsey Cricket club. When *Wisden* came out we would pore over it.'[118]

Derek Walcott, the Caribbean Nobel poet laureate, is unforgiving of slavery and colonialism, but he revered English literature as a boy. His mother taught Shakespeare in St Lucia: 'When I come to England I don't claim England. I don't own it. I feel a great kinship because of the literature and landscape. I have great affection for Edward Thomas and Phillip Larkin.' England cannot be extracted or bled out of him.[119] Nor out of me and millions of other subjects. The master nation left a part of itself inside us. Ex-colonial elites became proficient cultural navigators, people of many parts. Their descendants even more so.

History doesn't abruptly turn or end when flags pass up and down poles. I travelled around India and some Middle Eastern countries to find out what people thought and felt about this once overweening and still irrepressible nation.

INDIA

An Indian academic I met in Mumbai[120] is impatient with his colleagues: 'They blame the British for everything. They stole our resources and routinely treated us badly. That is incontrovertible. You think Indians don't do that? Look at Indian businessmen in Singapore, Malaysia, Kenya, South Africa. We just don't do it under a colonial flag. Until the Brits came, we neglected our long history – relics, archaeological sites, antiques, stories . . . Even today in Delhi, precious monuments have become shitholes, literally. The English treated servants one hundred times better than we treat them.' His grandfather worked as a servant for a Mr Hodgekin, a minor official, who left him some money. The money paid for the education of three sons and a plot of land on which the family planted a rose bush to remember Hodge sahib, who always wore a freshly cut rose on his lapel.

The author Gitanjali Prasad is angry about the Raj and yet inordinately fond of the English, partly because they accept her criticisms with such good grace. When on sabbatical in Cambridge in 2009, she didn't hold back: 'They don't like sycophancy, so I tell them that they demeaned and exploited us. But you know, if you have to be a colony, it is better to be under the English.' Her grandfather once sat on and boxed his English boss who had accused him of stealing a pen. He was not sacked. Her grandmother, a nationalist, mocked an English official for not learning an Indian language. He went off and did just that.

Charles Dickens is revered in India as a literary genius who spoke for the poor and desperate. In 2012, the two-hundredth anniversary of Dickens' birth, I was invited to a small Mumbai apartment for a special evening where enthusiasts read aloud from his books. A small picture of the Victorian author was garlanded with fragrant white jasmine flowers, as if he had been admitted to the pantheon of Hindu gods. It would have been cruel to remind them that after the 1857 Indian Uprising an enraged Dickens wanted the 'the Hindu race' to be exterminated.[121]

Bengali intellectuals, including communists, can't break away completely from the nation they saw off. Brits visiting Kolkata often find themselves in crumbling grand homes or tiny local teashops engaged in highly literate conversations about

English culture, language, political sophistication and even honesty! And in Delhi one evening in a smoky journalist's club, we talked about this indestructible, incomprehensible bond. The columnist Shastri Ramachandaran is volubly critical of British imperialism and Britain's growing disavowal of multiculturalism, but hugely admires 'the *New Statesman*, journalistic objectivity and ethics, England's predilection for radicals – from Marx to the ANC'. Others added to the list: the Westminster model, fair elections, Malcolm Muggeridge, the libraries, railways and the wonderful English language.

Indians today find it hard to be judgemental about the past because the present is so disorderly, speedy and out of control. University students I met, though born in free India, felt the pain of broken political promises and yearn for an orderly state. For Mina, studying business management, 'The English left no Taj, but they deepened the way we think. And had more integrity than our guys.' Sharmila added: 'Listen to us – we are debating in English. Everything we are is shaped by the language.' The past has left young Indians permanently questioning what was and is. No bad thing.

In a hip club in Delhi I talked to high-flying professionals in their twenties. For them, England is passé and America rules. I asked them for names of talented Westerners they admired. Top Hollywood stars were chosen but so too were Amy Winehouse, Paul McCartney, the Rolling Stones and Adele, Elton John, Martin Amis, Ian McEwan, Jeffrey Archer, Nick Hornby, Douglas Adams, Robert Fisk, Damien Hirst, Stella McCartney, Robert Harris, Judy Dench, Victoria and David Beckham, other English footballers, Colin Firth, Emma Thompson, on and on. Prakash, a youngish IT expert, was an unabashed Anglophile: 'When I read English novelists, I recognize their thoughts and characters. Like they are in my DNA, inside me. My dad never stops talking about the world wars.

When he was in London he saw the play *War Horse* three times, blew his entire budget on it. I had to FedEx him more cash. Michael Morpurgo is his latest hero.'

The more things change, the more they stay the same, according to the Indian-born writer and filmmaker Timeri Murari: 'Despite the onslaught of Americanism . . . India still retains the Englishness I grew up with. It lurks beneath the patina of change . . . . the harder we try to purge Englishness, the closer we remain stuck together for an eternity. Parliament still convenes with British pomp and cere-mony, newspapers still use quaint English phrases, and regiments beat the retreat. My school retains its very English traditions and the old clubs are even stuffier than in the Raj days. England itself may have become a mini-America, but if Englishmen want to explore their past, it lives on here. And they do keep coming back, even those backpackers who have no sense of history find India a familiar country. It's as if they too feel this strange land in their bones.'[122]

Murari is right about the thriving sanctums of snobbery. In one resplendent colonial club with old leather wingchairs and mahogany coat stands, they took away my shoes and polished them before letting me step in. We ate soggy fried fish and mash followed by a slippery pink pud named 'Queen Victoria's Petticoat'. This was in 2006.

There is no end to this affair. Deconstruction and reconstruction goes on and on. The winning British TV show *Who Wants to Be a Millionaire?*, presented by Chris Tarrant, was copied in India and attracted inconceivably high audience figures. The apotheosis of the relationship was the film *Slumdog Millionaire*, based on a novel by an Indian diplomat, Vikas Swarup, directed by Danny Boyle, an Englishman, with co-director Loveleen Tandan, an Indian woman. Most of the cast was picked in India, but Dev Patel, the hero, is a British Asian from London.

The creative heat of the film was produced by the synthesis of two disparate cultures. In 2012, Freida Pinto, female star of *Slumdog*, played the main role in *Trishna*, based on Thomas Hardy's *Tess of the D'Urbervilles*. It was set in Rajasthan and directed by Michael Winterbottom, who is, yes, English.

EGYPT, JORDAN AND IRAQ

I was in Egypt and later in Jordan in 2011, just after the Arab Spring, when the region felt liberated and tentative, hopeful yet fearful of what lay ahead. In these two very different countries, I found that feelings about England were even more complex and contradictory than in India. On the subcontinent the grief surrounding Partition is still detectable, but in the Middle East, colonial wounds are open, festering. Time does not heal them and they cannot be sutured. Ask any Arab about England and you have to be ready for an outburst of sorrow and rage about the 1917 Balfour Declaration and dispossessed Palestinians. After that unburdening, real conversations can begin.

I met the journalist and novelist Gamal el-Ghitani, mentioned previously, who was imprisoned in the 1960s in independent Egypt for his 'seditious' views. His apartment in Cairo is a den of books and magazines, the air itself thick with words and thoughts. 'Our relationship with England is contradictory. Imperialism – look what it did to us. English plotters, they put in place all the fundamentals for our problems. We resisted them. But Egyptians looked and still look to England as a minaret of civilization and culture. We speak a lot about the Magna Carta and the struggles of the English people. To our minds English culture is very important for our instruction.'

As Arabs break free of dictatorships, post-independence clarity has been replaced with uncertainty. The Cairean writer Mahmoud El Wardany, born in

1950, cannot forget the Suez crisis or forgive Britain's duplicities: 'But I read English literature – Chaucer, Shakespeare. I learned about England's great heritage, freedom especially. So I was torn. Blair was a monster but his people did not agree with him and his war. Americans drink in propaganda, not so much the English. And I think your countrymen understand our pain better than our Arab brothers.' I had not thought England would today be the prism through which Arabs judge their leaders and rights.

A conversation with three eminent Jordanian academics was almost embarrassingly pro-English. Professor Mohammad Al Masalha, Dean of the Faculty of International Studies at the University of Jordan, was effusive about English statecraft, the rule of law, administration, tax systems and order: 'They were more civilized and more acquainted with the nature of the regions than the French. It was not good to be ruled by any outsiders, but the English were better than the French, no doubt about that. I have translated their great political writers. We still think it is the most legal country in the world.' Some of them had studied in England and raved about English landladies. One remembered Mrs Berry: 'She was wonderful, helped me not to feel homesick, looked after me so well.' More praise, and more still, poured out. A professor of sociology commented, 'Colonialism was not all negative. They were very advanced and had vision. Our education today doesn't enlighten. Then it did, at least the elites. Look how divided we have become.' Someone informed me that President Nasser, an irreconcilable anti-colonial leader, had on his wall English landscapes of haystacks and thatched cottages.

I was invited to lunch by urbane Dr Kamel Abu Jaber, formerly Jordan's foreign minister and director of the Royal Institute for Inter-Faith Studies. It was at his farmhouse near Oman, where Romans once dwelt and cultivated crops. The

English, he said, 'were at the forefront of Western people who were fascinated by Arab cultures and values. You know it is in the English imagination – the romantic English imagination – flowing robes, the camel or horse, man against nature, in the wind and sands, ultimate symbols of freedom. A Bedouin in his tent can make an educated man from England feel small and insignificant. It is a fantastic attraction and a fatal one.'

The former Iraqi diplomat Wissam al-Zahawie now lives in Amman. He remembers Iraq as a place of artists, architects, archaeologists, photographers, painters, musicians, poets and writers. Foreigners, many of them English, brought creative ideas and intellectual excitement, 'not bombs, like now'. As a young man, he met the historian Arnold Toynbee and dined with the English archaeologist Sir Max Mallowan and his wife, Agatha Christie, who knitted contentedly after dinner. In 2011, some beautiful ivory treasures from the Assyrian city of Nimrud were exhibited at the British Museum; they had been dug up by Max and tended by Agatha, who had used expensive face cream to rub off scorch marks – not very successfully![123]

At the Egyptian Museum of Antiquities in Cairo I spoke to the senior curator, Hisham el-Leithy. In the summer of 2005, he had been on a course at the British Museum. Did it make him angry to see all the Pharonic objects and embalmed mummies in London? 'No,' he replied calmly, philosophically. 'I am happy they have them. The English people are our good ambassadors and they take care of these precious things.' What about the grasping Egyptologist Howard Carter? 'OK, he damaged a mummy, but we honour him. I know you are surprised to hear this. But he really loved old Egypt. We have completely repaired his small rest house in the Valley of the Kings and Lord Carnarvon's and Carter's descendants came to the ceremony in 2008.' I was more than surprised. For this young man, colonialism happened and has left its mark, but it cannot indelibly colour the present and future.

Millions of Arabs feel at home in England. For Ayisha, an Egyptian belly dancer who fled after the Muslim Brotherhood came to power, 'No other country will have a place like Edgware Road, a small Arabia for us to eat, speak, smoke shisha and just be ourselves. In our countries, we had Jewish people, but we pushed them out. You think the English can have their own street in Cairo today? No. They will be beaten up and pushed out.' She now lives near her beloved Edgware Road; settling in England has been harder than she expected, but she still loves London.

English émigrés to the Middle East feel the same convoluted love for their adopted lands. In Cairo, an upper-class Englishman and his Egyptian wife with the sweetest of smiles invited me to their home for dinner.[124] He had converted to Islam; their children looked and sounded Arab, the décor was pointedly Egyptian. In England his family own a country mansion and farmland. 'I hate the pettiness, the coldness, the way they kill your spirit with a raised eyebrow, the class shit, the lifelessness of England.' I asked his wife what she wanted for her country: 'I want my country to be like England, fair, free.' Later she confessed that for a very long time she had wanted to move to England with her children, but her husband would never agree.

At the Dead Sea, I bumped into another English migrant, around fifty, in a white suit, straw boater and cigarette holder, straight out of a movie. He was a businessman, the son of a county-town butcher. 'My childhood, even in the 1960s,was colourless. My mother never cried or expressed any emotions even when her parents died. She was a wooden doll in black. My father, well, he never left the 1950s, wore to death smelly tweed jackets. Boiled cabbage – that was the smell of my life till I came away.' So, was he not viewed with suspicion in Jordan?

'Not at all. I now speak Arabic, so all differences melt away. England means nothing to me. If there was a war, you know which side I would be on.'

In his book on Empire, Jeremy Paxman tells the stories of other restless men and women for whom 'little islands are all large prisons'.[125] His own young daughter went on holiday with her mother to the Sinai, where they mingled with Bedouins. The young woman was so intoxicated by it all she later decided to study Arabic in Cairo.

Upright, uptight England and the emotive and mystifying nations of the East will never be able to turn away and part from each other whatever the politics of past and present.

3 England and the Other at Home

'People don't make the journeys to come and die, they make them to come and live. And to live you transform the place.'

John Akomfrah, black British filmmaker and artist[1]

SEAL, HENRY OLUSEGUN OLUMIDE Adeola Samuel, the soul and R&B star, has no existential qualms about his identity: 'I see myself as an Englishman.' He was born in Paddington, London, and is of Nigerian and Brazilian parentage.[2] Though not rich and famous, Manish Gajjer of Hastings, son of East African Asian parents, is another proud Englander and avid supporter of English rugby and cricket teams.[3] Julian Alexander Kitchener-Fellowes, the Tory peer who created the TV series Downton Abbey, is a virtuoso storyteller of the English upper class, where he seems naturally to belong, yet he was born in Cairo and his father, Peregrine Edward Launcelot Fellowes, was a passionate Arabist and good friend to Ethiopia's Emperor Selassie.

The footballer David Beckham, born in Leytonstone, east London, has covered most of his skin with tattoos, like a gorgeous African nomadic warrior. His wife Victoria's name is tattooed in very dark ink in (misspelt) Hindi script, and an enigmatic saying in Chinese runs down one side of his torso. I doubt very much that a Spanish player for Real Madrid, say, or an Italian footballer would choose tattoos in Arabic. Yet like France, Spain and Italy were seafaring, commercial nations, and Spain was ruled by the Moors for centuries. Of course traces of those histories remain, but they are faded and discarded, unlike in England, where the colonial past is alive and kicking.

Jemima Goldsmith, daughter of the millionaire Sir James Goldsmith, when married to the Pakistani cricketer-turned-politician Imran Khan, joined his extended family in Lahore and consented to strict rules governing female behaviour, rules discarded by us modern Muslim women. Over lunch I asked her about those years. 'I was twenty years old, totally unintimidated, never a moment's doubt. I thought, I can do this. I was curious and it was enhancing, exciting, adventurous. That life I led is a part of me, 100 per cent. It was the making of me. I learned to see things through the eyes of others, to think in a very different way.'

These are all England's people, formed by their nation's ceaseless contact with the world. That internationalism is deeply embedded and explains why, in spite of strict immigration controls, outlanders still want to come to England.

Much has changed since 1972, the year we Ugandan Asian exiles landed in England. Or has it, really? Just when it feels safe to assume the nation no longer begrudges immigrants *that much*, rancour breaks out and elegies are intoned. In our times, Eastern European migrants are raising alarm and angst among many Englanders. Most migrants have lived through such cyclical trouble and strife. Most sense too that there is more to these people than meets the eye or accosts the ear. Many of us have been touched by the way the English eventually open up to foreigners. We have then often been unnerved by the limits to the intimacy offered. Conditions are inscribed in small print and catastrophe follows if these are transgressed. And they are still transgressed daily. As the Indian Anglophile Ranjee Shahani put it in the 1940s, 'The English soul, like the English language, is a patchwork. We see this or that bit, but the whole escapes us . . . Behind a correct and cold exterior they hide a warm and sometimes a fierce heart . . . They do not burn slowly but blaze like a torch.'[4]

Every ethnic group which came and stayed in England has its own, mostly undocumented, memories of hard times caused by economic vulnerabilities, disorientation, powerlessness and, hardest of all, prejudices. The hostility gets into our bones. That explains the thick cardis and woolly hats on our heads even when the sun is shining. Most migrants have also found natives who understood, helped, became champions, admirers, allies, lovers and friends. The Englander and the foreigner create synergy and energy, make things happen. Most of all in London.

A RAINBOW METROPOLIS

The Shard in Southwark was part-opened in 2012. It is the tallest building in Western Europe, crystalline, with a sharp peak piercing the clouds, as if to say the sky cannot be the limit. Renzo Piano, the main architect, is Italian and most backers were wealthy Arabs. Modernists found the glass tower thrilling, while traditionalists griped about Arab money and the unsuitability of 'Dubai-style buildings' in their capital.[5] I share their criticisms of the Shard, but not their crabbiness about uppity foreigners. The building has become a contentious landmark. Close to this glass structure is Roast, a restaurant serving excellent traditional roasts and stews. The founder, Iqbal Wahhab, is of Bangladeshi origin. When it first opened, Anglo-Saxon critics decried the venture as impertinent, presumptuous. Wahhab fought back: 'Perhaps it takes someone from another culture to step back and say British food can be great.' Twenty nationalities work in Roast to produce food that brings back memories of old English family dinners.[6]

London has never been a bland white sauce. It has known conquest and occupation, trade and wars, had folk washing in and taking off. Sediments of this long history lie beneath our feet and are all around us. Mosey through the older parts of the capital and you almost hear the exhalations of émigrés, those who stayed for a while, set up holy houses of worship for this faith or that, worked hard, made it big and moved, or just survived – or maybe didn't, passed on.

Wordsworth, best known for his philosophical poems on nature, mused on the various occupants of the metropolis in *The Prelude*: the Jew 'with basket at his waist' and the 'slow-moving Turk, with freight of slippers piled beneath his arm',

> *And every character of form and face:*
> *The Swede, the Russian; from the genial south,*
> *The Frenchman and the Spaniard; from remote*
> *America, the Hunter-Indian; Moors,*
> *Malays, Lascars, the Tartar, the Chinese,*
> *And Negro Ladies in white muslin gowns.*[7]

An inventory of immigrants in London would never be finished. The novelist Peter Ackroyd, who knows London's body, heart and soul, is sure that 'it was the city itself which seemed to summon them, as if only in the experience of the city could their lives have meaning'.[8]

They Came, Saw, Conquered and Were Conquered

Mihir Bose, quoted earlier, is a British-Indian author and journalist. As a child in Bombay, his head was filled with pictures of England. He even memorized train times from Paddington Station. In 1969 he came to London and never left. 'I have no regrets. In India today I could be a rich partner in an accountancy firm, but here, in London, you can be yourself, you can achieve all sorts of things you never dreamt of.'[9]

That self-fulfilment can be found in other parts of England too.

Prince Hassan bin Talal of Jordan is an erudite and thoughtful Arab leader. At his posh English prep school some kids called him 'the camel driver's son' and stoned him. He got out fast; 'You can slit my throat,' he told his mother, 'but I'm not going back.'[10] He was happier at Harrow, though he found the august public school self-reverential. But it was at Oxford, under those timeless spires, where he was intellectually stimulated and found his voice. He would not be what he is today had he not left his homeland to study in England.

Prince Hassan married Sarvath Ikramullah, whose parents and grandparents were part of the political elite which oversaw the birth of Pakistan after Partition, a period of bitterness and much bloodshed. In spite of the turmoil, her family did not break its long links with England. Her grandfather opposed British rule and decolonization strategies but decamped to London's Carlton Hotel in the hot season, mingled with the colonial establishment, and led prayers in the Woking mosque. Her mother, one of Pakistan's first female MPs, was adored by English high society. The princess knows her history, but, like her forebears, is not trapped in it. 'There is so much more in this incredible country, so much between us.'[11]

Of course, her social status is an entry visa into class-obsessed England. The historian Tony Kushner has explored in detail which 'groups have been allowed into and which have been excluded from the nation's borders . . . how constructs of race, religion, ethnicity, place, gender, age and class have been employed in selection processes both at the level of immigration procedures and within the stories Britain tells of itself.'[12]

Many of us are here because the British were there, in our countries of origin. We have a history between us and a deep, sentimental attachment that neither time nor painful experiences seem to weaken. Fadia Faqir is a Jordanian novelist and academic at Durham university. She doesn't trust British politicians or even Arabists: 'Among the most educated lovers of the Arab world you find the worst racism.' So why, I asked her, was she content to live in their land? 'I have been here so long. They have been so hospitable, in so many different ways. And they care. They say they don't like immigrants, but they care.'[13]

Simon Schama perceives the same paradoxes: 'The word "immigrant" sets off all kinds of alarm bells, yet there is in England an extraordinary amount of porousness. Just look at the day-to-day business of living together and mixed-race marriages. America boasts it is an immigrant nation but neighbourhoods even in New York are segregated.'[14] That porousness doesn't just happen; it is desired, consciously and unconsciously.

For all the English people who believe the best they can offer foreigners is reluctant tolerance, there are also those, as the literary critic Maya Jaggi notes, who are 'open and curious, not least about why their neighbours are who they are'.[15] And that was happening long before the large-scale post-war migrations from the old colonies. What follows is a very short history of that receptive, impressionable England.

THE EARLY CENTURIES

During the Roman occupation of Britannia (AD 43–410), people from all around the vast Roman Empire were recruited to control and govern the unruly island. In

Stratford-upon-Avon, the heart of England, a skeleton was dug up in 2011 of an African male which was 1,700 years old.[16] Other African remains have been found in York and elsewhere. Hadrian's Wall was patrolled by African militia, prompting one historian to write: 'There were Africans in Britain before the English came here.'[17] Anglo-puritans might be affronted by that indisputable truth. These dramatic archaeological discoveries don't disconcert nationalist storytellers. Think of it as strict immigration control of inconvenient facts.

In the British Museum a coin dating back to the Kingdom of Mercia (AD 773–96) has King Offa's regal mark and, in Arabic, proclaims the greatness of Allah, like the gold dinars of the Muslim Abbasid dynasty in Baghdad. In the words of Billy Bragg, the coin shows that, back then, 'All groovy things came from the Caliphate.'[18]

According to the *Anglo-Saxon Chronicle* Vikings arrived in England around AD 787. We know all the gory tales of rape, pillage and slaughter, but in fact the Vikings were also into fine things – silk, gold, glass and jewels. They sailed to and traded in North Africa, the Black Sea, central Asia and around the Arabian sea.[19] The locals must have been impressed with and influenced by the seafarers who had been far and wide, who brought splendid objects and fabulous tales.

In 2009, the Anglo-Saxon Staffordshire Hoard was unearthed. Historian Tristram Hunt was thrilled by the objects, which revealed 'the unexpected inter-nationalism of seventh-century Mercian trade, with some of the precious stones hailing from today's Turkey and Sri Lanka'.[20] OK, so Anglo-Saxons liked pretty gems from here and everywhere. Hardly news. But it *is* because it shows England was never content with domesticity, with the small life. Today's trendy localism would have seemed dreary to the earliest intrepid Anglo-Saxons.

The prodigious consumerism of Anglo-Saxons pulled merchants and producers from all around mainland Europe. By the thirteenth century, market towns bustled with French, Venetian, Flemish and other buyers and sellers. Dutch and German brewers supplied beer to gluttonous drinkers; wool was sold to European cloth-makers, many of whom moved to England. Locals, then as now, wanted new, foreign goods but not brassy foreign traders and makers. Then as now, the ruling classes tried to both placate the masses and ensure the merchants from abroad stayed so that the state could benefit from their skills and taxes.

In the early twelfth century Jews in England had been banned from other occupations and trades and so became moneylenders. Adventurous capitalists, prospectors and English monarchs needed cash for their wars, so gave them special, if erratic, protection, which would sometimes be withdrawn. During the good times prosperous Jews helped fund prestigious public buildings – strategic moves to secure the future. The endowments didn't protect them from the bad times, but laid down markers of permanence.

Jews were collectively maligned, most of all in the most high-church English cities, and individuals were frequently framed, tortured and killed. From 1220 onwards Jews were repeatedly persecuted and set upon and after 1253, their degra-dation intensified. Communities were banished from local areas, their property confiscated. In 1264, hundreds were massacred in London. In 1272, King Edward I made all Jews wear a yellow patch (Nazis upgraded that to a yellow star), and in 1290, Jewish settlers were expelled en masse. Except for a few who stayed behind and hid their identities, England's Jews had to leave. They did not return. Finally, after hundreds of years, in the mid-seventeenth century, Cromwell readmitted

Jews, partly because he needed to borrow money. Throughout English history, Jewish escapees from pogroms in Eastern Europe came into antipathy as thick as fog. And so it has gone on.[21]

The Black Plague of 1348 killed off nearly a third of Britain's population, so workers from abroad arrived to fill labour shortages. They were needed and begrudged, usefully employed yet reviled. That pattern would repeat itself over the centuries. In 1573, a survey of 7,143 migrants recorded that most had found England indescribably hard.[22] Dramatists stoked up antipathy in their plays. In 1590, Robert Wilson, for example, had a self-pitying character complaining about migrant workers:

> *I would gladly get by living by mine Art*
> *But Aliants chop up houses so in the Citie*
> *That we poore crafts men must needs depart.*[23]

One can imagine the reactions of the audiences.

Exiles fleeing religious oppression were more benignly treated, but again, goodwill could vanish without warning. In the late sixteenth century, Huguenots fled to England from Catholic France to escape the persecution of Protestants. They brought fresh energy and skills to the production of goods and textiles – paper, pins and needles, glorious hats, coats and beautiful watches. They too had to go through the usual baptism of fire. By 1694 successful Huguenots could provide capital funding for the new Bank of England. Seven of the twenty-five directors were Huguenots, as was the first governor: 'a drop of Huguenot blood in your veins, the saying went, was worth a thousand pounds'.[24] They had arrived. And were grateful destiny had transported them to England.

During the reign of Elizabeth I, and for some time after her death, luminaries from the Islamic world were welcomed to the English court. They were allies in England's bitter battles with Catholic Europe, and, undeniably, there was mutual attraction between the cultures. The queen and her courtiers fostered trade, flattered and were flattered, fascinated and were fascinated. The queen even ordered fancy Turkish clothes.[25] In that muscular age Elizabeth was a cunning player.

These political dalliances with Muslim rulers provoked grave displeasure. King James VI of Scotland swore no other Christian ruler 'ever had in a Turk suche high estimation' and the Pope warned the queen was becoming a 'confederate with a Turk'.[26]

Muslim envoys dazzled London with their style, opulence, exaggerated decorum and 'Araby' horses.[27] One of the Moroccan dignitaries, Abd el-Ouahed ben Messaoud, had an exquisite portrait painted – he is dressed in black and gold, looking at once dangerous and tantalizing.[28] For six months he and his entourage were the guests of the alderman at the Royal Exchange. One observer recorded: 'They kild all their own meate within their house, as sheepe, lambes, poultrie and suchlike and they turne their faces eastward when they kill any thing.'[29]

Spectacular events were hosted to welcome these emissaries. In 1637, when Alkaid Jaurar bin Abdella, the Moroccan ambassador, disembarked at Tower Hill, dignitaries greeted him in 'scarlet gowns' and 'chyanes of gold'; thousands lined the streets and a procession of 600 torches escorted him to his quarters.[30]

The historiographer Thomas Rymer (1643–1713) concluded that the English, unlike the Venetians, did not feel 'hatred and aversion to Moors' and were even willing to marry them.[31] Some Turks moved to England in the late seventeenth century and worked as button-makers, tailors and even as solicitors.[32] By 1742 there were nearly eighty English coffee houses, inspired by Ottoman cafes, mostly in London.

There was real intimacy between the English and the Moors as they worked, lived, socialized together, sometimes fighting, sometimes making love. It wasn't, of course, all sweetness and light. Tensions were ever present. Halal slaughtering methods revolted local Londoners, while some visitors were ungracious about the city's sexual mores, although the sternest Islamic puritans did sometimes surrender to the open charms of London women. Continuing sea wars, piracy, the enslavement of thousands of Britons by Barbary pirates made total trust and respect well nigh impossible.[33] All sides played dirty – that makes the concomitant attraction even more extraordinary.

DIVERSE PLEASURES AND PAINS

From the sixteenth century onwards, slaves, servants, chancers, performers, prostitutes, musicians, itinerants and others from the South and the East came to England. One painted panel shows Elizabeth I and her courtiers being entertained by African musicians and dancers.[34] Greg Doran, artistic director of the Royal Shakespeare Company, told me that blackness was a popular fantasy in the Tudor and Stuart courts. In 1605, Anne, queen consort of James I, invited Inigo Jones and Ben Jonson to plan an African-themed masque. Players 'blacked up', as did Anne herself, who was criticized for the frivolous racial swap. It was performed in the Banqueting Hall of Whitehall Palace on Twelfth Night. Other masques enacted voyages and exotic encounters.

In 1663, contemporary accounts describe 'two Negroes, habited very costly after their manner, seated on the backs of two leopards richly set out'. Each held banners, one with the arms of the City of London and the other with the arms of the Skinners' Company.[35] At a pageant in 1687, two 'beautiful young negroes' rode on 'the excellently carv'd and painted' golden unicorns of the Goldsmiths' Company.[36] (Today a good number of migrants are silent cleaners.)

During the late seventeenth century, the satirist Ned Ward published *The London Spy*, sharp, witty annals of London, which noted a black female at St Bartholomew Fair: 'a rope dancer, half acrobat, half posture girl', who had much 'art and agility', moving her 'well proportioned limbs to the satisfaction of the Spectators'.[37] One can almost feel the crackling heat in the atmosphere.

Although dark-skinned emigrés and entertainers were popular, they also caused native disquiet. (They still do.) As early as 1596 Queen Elizabeth had decreed: 'Her Majestie understanding that there are of late divers blackamores brought into this realme, of which kinde there are allready here to manie . . . those kinde of people should be sent forth from this lande.'[38] Other such edicts followed. All were ignored, but following such official statements, migrants must have felt desperately insecure. The lucky found men and women who were fond and appreciative, such as Samuel Pepys, who recorded his thoughts on their new cook in 1669: 'a black-moore of Mr Batelier's . . . who dresses our meat mighty well and we mightily pleased with her'.[39] The rest helped each other or had to find ways to survive in a country with inclement weather and some rough citizens. Destitution, illness, attacks and killings were fairly common and got worse during bad economic times.[40]

Soon after the East India Company started trading in 1612, Indian servants and ayahs were brought back to England by company men and their families. One picture by Sir Peter Lely, from 1674, tells a thousand stories. It is of little Lady

Charlotte Fitzroy, daughter of King Charles II and his mistress Barbara Villiers, with her Indian pageboy. Who was he? Was he treated well? Was he happy? Indian lackeys usually went back when no longer needed, but some stayed on, too poor to pay for the journey home. Dozens of Indian seaman crewing East India Company vessels 'jumped ship to escape maltreatment' and were stranded in English ports.[41] We don't know much about these dispossessed Indians; their stories died with them.

By the middle of the eighteenth century, concern was being raised about impoverished Indian ayahs, servants and lascars in English cities. In 1786, reporters found Indian and black beggars 'on the point of perishing'. That led some to feel compassion, others to demand they be punished or deported.[42] A good number of Chinese sailors, too, were homeless and destitute. More fortunate were the 'coloured' performers, healers, intellectuals and members of the aristocracy, seen as fascinating orientals by all classes.[43]

HYBRID ENGLAND

These were centuries of intense racism as well as inexorable racial mixing. White women paired up with 'blackamores', causing moral panic. The lusty maidens carried on regardless. In 1578 one George Best recorded his outrage: 'I myself have seene an Ethiopian as blacke as cole broughte into Englande, who, taking a faire English woman to wife, begatte a sonne in all respects as blacke as the father was.'[44]

Cross-racial sex flourished mostly in port cities. Such carnal mixing was the ultimate horror for national purists such as Philip Thicknesse. In a best-selling memoir published in 1778, he proclaimed that black men, possessed by an 'unnatural' craving for white women, would populate England 'with a race of men of the very worst sort under heaven . . . a race of Mulattos mischievous as monkeys but infinitely more dangerous'.[45] He had spent time in the colonies and came away hating and fearing black masculinity.

Six years earlier, Edward Long, a historian and apologist for slavery, had published the same dire forewarning about miscegenation: 'a venomous and danger ulcer, that threatens to disperse its malignancy far and wide, until every family catches infection from it'.[46] (Long was not concerned about despoiled black bloodlines on plantations where masters and their henchmen habitually raped and impregnated female slaves.) At the turn of the nineteenth century, the radical anti-poverty campaigner William Cobbett issued further alerts: 'Who, that has any sense or decency, can help being shocked at the familiar intercourse, which has gradually been gaining ground, and which has, at last, got a complete footing between Negroes and the women of England? . . . Amongst white women, this disregard of decency, this defiance of the dictates of nature, this foul, this beastly propensity, is, I say it with sorrow and with shame, *peculiar to the English.*'[47]

Slavery in England

Slaves were traded in England throughout the eighteenth century, a fact that is rarely acknowledged.[48] African and Indian adults and children were offered for sale in coffee houses, in newspapers and fashionable magazines. To take one example, an advert from 1769: 'A well made and good tempered Black Boy; he has lately had the small-pox and will be sold to any gentleman.'[49] The commodification of dark-skinned people was normal. Guilt, if felt, was soon quietened, as in this poem by William Cowper (1731–1800):

I Own I am shock'd at the purchase of slaves,

And fear those who buy them and sell them are knaves;

What I hear of their hardships, their tortures and groans,

Is almost enough to drive pity from stones.

I pity them greatly but must be mum,

For how would we do without sugar and rum?[50]

If this was irony, I wonder how many would have understood it.

The slave trade delivered vast profits, coveted luxury commodities and grandeur. That there were Englishmen and women of conscience who fought inestimably hard to end the grotesque commodification of Africans is all the more impressive. The abolition of slavery was a cause taken up by Christians and humanitarians, including William Wilberforce; Thomas Clarkson; Lady Middleton; Georgiana, Duchess of Devonshire; Ann Yearsley, the milkmaid poet from Bristol; and many others. The roll of honour is long. In 1768, the magistrate Sir John Fielding complained that the London 'mob' often protected runaway slaves, and helped them escape.[51]

The Englanders who campaigned against the slave trade were profoundly affected by the burning stories of ex-slaves. Two of them, in particular, helped changed the course of that ignoble history. The first was Ignatius Sancho (1729–80), who talked and wrote about his years as a forced labourer in cruel captivity. His book, published after his death in 1782, was a bestseller; it was the first work by a black author to appear in Britain. Gainsborough painted his portrait, almost as a symbolic plea for redemption.

Sancho's mother died after giving birth on board a ship crossing the Atlantic, and his father committed suicide. The orphan was gifted by his owner to three spinsters in Greenwich, London. They named him 'Sancho' after the uneducated, gullible squire in *Don Quixote*, because they believed that black helots had to be kept illiterate for their own good. Sancho's revenge was a dish served cold. He taught himself to read and write.

Nearby, in Blackheath, lived the Duke of Montagu. He gave the bright, assiduous boy books and encouragement. When Sancho turned twenty, he ran away from his mistresses and sought refuge with the Montagus. The old duke was dead and, after some persuasion, the duchess grudgingly took Sancho on as a butler. Thereafter he thrived, penned poetry, stage plays, composed music. One of his pieces was rediscovered and broadcast on the BBC in 1958. He was soon taken up by London's fashionable literary and artistic circles and was befriended by David Garrick, Samuel Johnson and Laurence Stern. Sancho's story prompted key figures to agitate against the slave trade.[52] He married Anne, a black Caribbean woman, and opened a grocery shop in Westminster. Charles James Fox dropped in, so did the Duchess of Queensbury and various aristocratic ladies and gentleman.[53] As a property owner, Sancho was the first black man to get the vote in Britain.

Compunctious Englanders went on to support the tireless campaigner Olaudah Equiano (1745–97), who also wrote a book about his life as a slave.[54] When a small boy in eastern Nigeria, he was seized and thrown on to a ship carrying human cargo. The child survived the horrors of the Middle Passage and was sold to a Virginia plantation owner whose black cook had to wear an iron muzzle to stop her tasting the food she made. Michael Pascal, a British naval lieutenant, bought Equiano, then aged twelve, renamed him Gustavus Vassa, and sailed with him to England. After that came many adventures, changes of owners, travels, wars, and ceaseless lobbying against slavery. By the time he was in his forties, he was 'a capable and energetic publicist; a fluent writer and speaker, a campaigner who was prepared to travel wherever he was invited to present the abolitionist case'.[55] His public profile and compelling arguments made him enemies, who tried to slander him and undermine his mission, and sometimes got under his smarting skin. When Equiano's memoir was published in 1789,[56] most reviewers were profoundly touched by the narrative and cause: '[The book] seems to have been written with much truth and simplicity . . . The reader, unless perchance he is either a West Indian planter or Liverpool merchant, will find his humanity severely wounded by the shameless barbarity practised towards the author's hapless countrymen in our colonies.'[57] Over a dozen editions were printed and sold. Equiano did not live to see slavery outlawed.

Black and White in it Together

Around 20,000 black people were recorded as living in London in the mid-eighteenth century, many of them free men and women.[58] At that time there was relative ease between whites and blacks. (A century on, most had merged with the nation's genetic pool, melted into its bloodstream.) The tales that follow demonstrate that multi-ethnic England existed long before the mass migration of the twentieth century.

The atmosphere was open enough for black servants in London to meet and air their grievances. One such meeting took place in the home of the great Dr Johnson, hosted by his black manservant Francis Barber. Barber was brought to England by a plantation owner, the father of one of Johnson's close friends. Though Barber often ran away and was trouble, his master was fond of him and paid to have him educated at Bishop Stortford Grammar School between 1767 and 1772. In a letter, the paterfamilias commends the young man and offers advice: 'I am very well satisfied with your progress, if you can really perform the exercises which you are set . . . Let me know what English books you read for your entertainment. You can never be wise unless you love reading. Do not imagine that I shall forget or forsake you . . .' The relationship had a profound impact on Johnson. Invited to a formal dinner Oxford, he proposed a toast: 'Here's to the next insurrection of the negroes in the West Indies,' which caused dyspepsia among the 'grave men'.[59]

Eventually Johnson came to depend on his protégé, who was exceedingly popular with the ladies. Barber married an Englishwoman, Betsy, had four children and moved his family in with the writer. Snoots and racists disapproved, but Johnson didn't care. When he died, he left Barber a hefty annuity and a gold watch.[60]

Julius Soubise's life reads like a Thackeray novel. Born in St Kitts, the son of a slave woman, he travelled to England with a naval captain who presented him to the beautiful and eccentric Duchess of Queensbury in 1764. She withheld nothing from the boy and later the man, who was possibly one of her lovers. Lady Mary Coke, a great gossip and letter-writer, reported that when visiting the duchess, she found her parading before Soubise 'half undressed'.[61] He was taught to fence, ride, sing, act, orate – the last two by the great David Garrick himself. Gainsborough sketched the black man, a fop among fops. A larger-than-life character who titillated London, Soubise became known as 'the black Othello' and a 'black Don Juan', with willing maidens lining up to be pleasured. In 1777, fearing some sexual scandal, he fled to India and opened a riding school in Calcutta. Two days after he departed, the duchess died after eating too many cherries. Some years later Soubise fell off his horse in India and died of his injuries.[62]

Born in the West Indies, Dido Elizabeth Belle was the daughter of John Lindsay, a naval captain, and Maria Belle, a slave. In 1760, the girl was sent to live with her father's uncle, the Earl of Mansfield, in Kenwood House on Hampstead Heath. Mansfield was the Lord Chief Justice whose legal judgements were significant milestones on the road to abolition. Defenders of slavery 'feared that she "ruled" the Lord Chief Justice's household. Visitors to Kenwood noted how attentive he was to her words and opinions.

Dido was indeed treated well and Mansfield left her a substantial inheritance when he died.[63] This beautiful daughter of a slave woman became an heiress, enjoyed liberties and luxuries in the mansion in Hampstead, but probably never felt she could belong. The Mansfields were childless and had adopted another child, Elizabeth, an orphaned female relative. In a painting of the two young women by Johann Zoffany, they seem close but not equal.

In the eighteenth century, black people were integrated into metropolitan London life.[64] In 1764, newspapers carried reports of a pub in Fleet Street where black men and women danced and played violins, entertaining themselves away from white eyes and ears.[65] Black dance halls, even then, were thought funky and cool. In one 'black hop', as they were known,[66] Sally, a white prostitute, beheld 'A lovely African, blooming with the hue of the warm country that gave him birth . . .'[67] Impromptu concerts by the 'negroes' drew huge crowds. An early rapper was Joseph Johnson, who wore a homemade model of a ship on his head, which rocked as he sang sailor's ditties.[68] Military bands often had black musicians – there was a time in the eighteenth century when all the drummers of the 7th Royal Fusiliers were black.

Hogarth's sketches show blacks and whites intermingling, and paintings of the time feature gorgeously attired black children and adults.[69] These precious snippets, whispers of that multiracial England, have sadly receded in the mists of time.

VICTORIA'S REIGN

The Victorian era was noticeably different, less laid back, more moralistic. Dark skin tested values and manners, represented temptation and provocation.

As the trade in slaves declined, so too, apparently, did the number of black people in England and Britain as a whole. But that is only conjecture. The census of 1841 did not include details of race or ethnicity and, as the names of many ex-slaves and foreign servants were Anglicized, the records of births, marriages and deaths are of little use. Information about them is gleaned from reports in the press and entries in books, published testimonies, recollections and tracts.

The relatively fluid racial boundaries of the previous age hardened, and scientific racism took root. Doctrinal experts expounded and validated theories of racial gradation, Anglo-Saxon genetic supremacy, Celtic 'inferiority', and the irredeemable nature of dusky peoples. Darwin's theories were requisitioned by those who were seeking rational justifications for slavery and colonialism.[70]

RECEPTIVE ENGLANDERS AND TALENTED FOREIGNERS

Even during times when social mores were strictly enforced and emotions confined, rules were often broken. Myriad rebels challenged the values of Victorian England.

In 1842, Captain Frederick Forbes, commander of HMS *Bonetta*, was patrolling the West African coast around Benin to stop local rulers taking captives to sell into slavery. Perhaps to distract him from his purpose, he was given a gift, a captured African girl, aged eight. He adopted the child and renamed her Sarah

Forbes Bonetta. She turned out to be a 'perfect genius', learnt English fast and had a talent for music. Queen Victoria and Prince Albert paid for her education. The National Portrait Gallery owns a photograph of her at twenty, in demure Victorian garb. She married another freed African, Jim Davies, a businessman. Their daughter went to Cheltenham Ladies' College.[71]

Pablo Fanque, the first black circus owner in England, had an extraordinary life. In pictures he has a full face, big manly moustache and eyes which look at the camera with absolute confidence. Born William Darby, in Norwich, to an English mother and African father, he was apprenticed to the circus owner William Batty. Then with the famous clown W. F. Wallet, he set up a new circus, which became phenomenally popular. His breathtaking acts, none too risqué or outrageous, were loved by audiences and sanctioned by church leaders. The press declared him an unsurpassed performer and operator. He married Susannah Marlaw, daughter of a button-maker in Birmingham, who tragically died when a circus pit collapsed.[72] After his death, Thomas Horne, chaplain of the Showman's Guild, eulogized the circus star: 'In the great brotherhood of the equestrian there is no colour line.'[73] Fanque's circus is remembered in the Beatle's song 'For the Benefit of Mr Kite', on the album *Sergeant Pepper's Lonely Hearts Club Band*, and with a blue plaque in Norwich.[74]

Samuel Coleridge-Taylor (1875–1912) was the illegitimate son of Daniel Peter Hughes Taylor from Sierra Leone, who became a surgeon, and Alice Hare Martin, an Englishwoman. She raised the boy on her own, a musical prodigy. A Croydon choirmaster, among others, nurtured Coleridge-Taylor's talent and at the age of fifteen he joined the Royal College of Music. He was encouraged and admired by Elgar and became an illustrious composer. His greatest composition, *Hiawatha's Wedding Feast*, was rapturously acclaimed by audiences and critics.

One found the work: 'brilliant, full of colour, at times luscious, rich and sensual'.[75]

Dr George Rice was another aspirational black man who made good in Victorian England. He ran several hospitals and his daughter became head of a prep school. In 1852, William Brown, a runaway American slave, expressed astonishment at how many 'coloured' men from various colleges he met in London and how free they were. Joseph Renner Maxwell, a black student who graduated from Oxford in 1879, maintained that none of his fellow students was ever racist towards him. The Africa Society was founded in 1897, a statement of extraordinary confidence.[76]

The success of these individuals is not just a black but also a white story. They thrived despite the prevailing prejudices. As Victoria's reign went on and the Empire expanded, more people from the empire of many colours turned up in England – sailors, royals, students, entertainers, itinerants, entrepreneurs and flunkies. None would have found life easy, yet magazines reproduced the prevailing prejudices: 'Foreigners are, in fact, deceitful, effeminate, irreligious, immoral, unclean and unwholesome.'[77] They still kept coming; they never gave up on their second motherland. Charitable Christians and their own wits and resilience got them through the toughest times.

In his monumental study of the poor in London, published in 1861, Henry Mayhew described Indian 'tom-tom' players, tract-sellers and lascars on the streets: 'One performer was a handsome lad . . . He had a copper skin and long, black hair . . . on his head was a turban'; he was 'sentimental Othello looking'. This appealing chap spoke perfect English, unlike his companion, an Indianized Arab who missed his own language. Mayhew tried to repeat their Indian Hindustani songs and they laughed at him.[78] Both had 'turn'd Christians', a smart move to make them seem less alien and win over brethren. Another tom-tom player from Bengal was a 'most handsome man . . . his teeth were exquisitely white and his laugh or smile lighted up his countenance to an expression of great intelligence'. The musician complained of racist abuse and attacks. His wife was English, 'but dere is no work for her, poor ting'.

Black musicians were hugely popular across England. A print shows an Ethiopian band in top hats and tails entertaining passers-by, and there were black 'time beaters' in the Worcestershire Regiment in the 1830s, dressed in turbans, Turkish pantaloons and carrying Ottoman scimitars.[79]

Most marvellous of all, for the English, were the visiting Indian royals. Ostentatious, bejewelled, glamorous, immaculately snobbish and yet ingratiating, they embodied English fantasies of 'the pomp and grandeur of empire'.[80]

BREAKING IN: ASIANS, JEWS AND BLACKS

Remarkably, between 1892 and 1922, when the voting population was almost totally white, propertied and male, three Indians became MPs, all representing English constituencies. Dadabhai Naoroji, Liberal, an eloquent anti-imperialist, won Finsbury Central in 1892 with a tiny majority. Right-wingers vocally denounced the MP and the culpable electorate. Tory Mancherjee Bhownagree won the seat in Bethnal Green North-East in 1895 and again in 1900. He was a somewhat compliant character, but still a big deal for the Conservative Party. In 1922, Shapurji Saklatvala, from a wealthy Indian family, took Battersea North for the Communist Party of Great Britain. The fact that these three were outsiders made them more, not less, attractive to voters.

London's East End has always been a multi-ethnic crucible, inhabited by revolutionaries and anarchists, industrious natives and economic migrants, arty types, criminals, the poor and desperate, the cunning and ambitious. Prone to flashpoints and flare-ups, set off by crimes, policing tactics, mutual mistrust and xeno-phobia, the early years of the twentieth century were especially volatile and violent. The *Morning Post* blamed all trouble on incomers, described as 'typhoid bacilli, aliens of the worst type – violent, cruel and dirty'.[81] The *Daily Mail*, too, was vigi-lantly xenophobic: 'Even the most sentimental will feel the time has come to stop the abuse of this country's hospitality by the foreign malefactors.'[82]

Anti-black race riots were common in major British cities from 1918. Those attacked included soldiers who had fought in the First World War and loyal seamen. The worst eruptions were in Cardiff, Liverpool, South Shields and London in 1919. Black residents were stabbed, scapegoated and terrorized, and further maltreated by the police and authorities. The *Liverpool Courier* printed racist explanations: 'You glimpse black figures beneath the gas lamps and somehow you think of pimps, and bullies, and women, and birds of ill omen gener-ally . . . One of the chief reasons of popular anger behind the present disturbances lies in the fact that the average negro is nearer to an animal than is the average white man and that there are women [who go with them] who have no self respect.'[83] Other papers echoed the same sentiments. Politicians did not feel any compunction to intervene. Mob scapegoating of outsiders went on right through to the 1960s.

By the 1930s, several English cities were becoming multi-ethnic while others were becoming less so. J. B. Priestley found Bristol 'Not one of your museum pieces, living on tourists and the sale of bogus antiques, but a genuine city, an ancient metropolis . . . and not far from the docks it still has a West Indian flavour.'[84] Bradford, however, was no longer 'a haven of intelligent aliens . . . the war changed all that. It seems duller and smaller now . . . [the foreigners] acted as a leaven. These exchanges are good for everybody'.[85] Priestley criticized the miserable meanness of 'leader writers in the cheap press . . . yelping again about keeping the foreigner out'.[86]

The persecution of Jewish refugees in England continued in the nineteenth and twentieth centuries. Beatrice Webb wept when she witnessed one ship unloading its wretched human cargo, foully treated by boatmen and dockers, robbed of the little money they had and of all dignity.[87] By 1914 some 150,000 had arrived in London, Hull and Manchester. Established Jews helped the new arrivals as much out of charity as fear that the bedraggled would provoke and justify a fresh surge of ever-present anti-Semitism. When Nazism was on the rise across Europe, the *East Anglian Daily Times* acknowledged that Jews coming into England were met with: 'a vague, unfriendly toleration not far removed from dislike . . .'[88] And the *Daily Mail* campaigned to stop the 'flood' of refugees.[89] Descendants of those hounded refugees had to melt England's resistance and racism. And they did.

Simon Schama recalls his life growing up in an immigrant Jewish community: 'I don't know if my father experienced anti-Semitism. What I saw was the extreme Englishry of the dignitaries in the synagogue [with their] top hats, bowler hats, and that still goes on. My father was romantic about Parliament, spellbound by the Thames and always insisted we should go to Greenwich to eat whitebait.' The immigrants' enthusiastic embrace of the grudging 'host' country paid off. Imagine English life and the Establishment without the Freuds, Lawsons and Saatchis, Jewish writers and actors, scientists, media and parliamentary figures, jewellers, bankers, lawyers, business leaders.

SOLDIERS AND CIVVIES FIGHTING FOR BLIGHTY

Few tourists or Londoners ambling around Trafalgar Square stop to look closely at the plinth of Nelson's column. If they did, they would see black sailors and soldiers in the carved frieze. In a painting of Nelson's death by Daniel Maclise (1859–64), black fighters are by his side. The artist studied the records of the warships and confirms those men were really there, playing their part in the legendary battles.[90]

Around a million and a half men and women from the non-white colonies perished in the two world wars. Photographs show Indian and African volunteers who joined up and those who were injured.[91] A rare picture has even been found of a black Tommy in uniform.[92] In France, during the Great War, nearly a third of British troops were Indian.[93]

Surviving letters from various fronts and sickbays are revealing: some colonial troops claim they were used as cannon fodder, others feel a brotherhood with British soldiers. Their bravery and patriotism shine though; British sergeants and soldiers describe the Indians as 'tigers', inordinately brave, patriotic, decent and always honourable. Englishwomen were admired by the Indians for their stoicism as well as their sexiness. One wounded Brahmin soldier, recuperating in the Brighton Pavilion hospital, wrote to a friend in Indore, India, in November 1915: 'This place is very picturesque, and the Indians are liked very much here. The girls of this place are notorious and very fond of accosting Indians and fooling with them.'[94] Soldiers of colour were admired – pushed forward in queues, kissed by girls, and much praised. But if seen talking to white women, they were threatened and sometimes attacked. Inconsistency is a consistent part of this story. In 1921, on the South Downs, Edward, Prince of Wales, unveiled the Chattri memorial to these extraordinarily brave soldiers. Future generations, said the prince, would not forget. They did forget.

A Sikh veteran of the Second World War, Ranjeet Singh, remembered English nurses asking to touch his long hair when he was recuperating: 'So I did, my dear,

I let them comb it. Until this man stopped it – I think he was a commander. He banned the beauties from coming to see me. I missed them.'[95] Andrew Shepherd, a Caribbean RAF pilot, told me of his humiliating experiences: 'They used to say that Blacks would corrupt white women. We were examined for special infections and the WAAFs were told if they slept with black men they would have mulatto children and harm themselves. They couldn't stop the ladies.'[96] When these loyal fighters later migrated to Britain, they were not welcome. Mr Fairweather, from Jamaica, a war hero in 1943, was one of them: 'Things had changed. They hated the very sight of you once it was over. But I say, if I am good enough to die in your wars, then I am good enough to live with you.'[97] Today around 40 per cent of Caribbean children have a white parent or grandparent. Love and hate wrestle in this unending black and white epic.

POST-WAR IMMIGRATION

The *Empire Windrush* docked in Tilbury in June 1948 with 492 passengers from Jamaica, and so began a small tidal wave from the Caribbean. Andrea Levy's evocative narrative, *Small Island*,[98] imagines the encounter between the resistant English and the expectant, naïve incomers, who thought they had sailed home. Deeply affected by the loss of Empire, the English couldn't adjust to the new world order.

Caribbeans were black Englishmen and women, well mannered, smooth dancers and talkers, Christian, educated, skilled, impeccably turned out. None of that was good enough. Their labour was required for the post-war welfare state, but they had to endure discrimination, a price not previously agreed.[99] Worse than abuse was sly, insinuated, polite bigotry. A black character in a novel by the Jamaican writer A. G. Bennett wryly observes: 'Once I walked the whole length of a street looking for a room and everyone told me that he or she 'ad no prejudice against coloured people. It was the neighbour who was stupid. If we could find the "neighbour" we could solve the entire problem. But to find 'im is the trouble! Neighbours are the worst people to live beside in this country.'[100]

Politicians have been playing the race and immigration cards for so long it can be described as a national game.[101] A small number have refused to play. One of them was Winston Churchill, who held unsound views on 'coloured' subjects[102] and yet, in 1904, opposed anti-immigration colleagues and condemned the police for harassing the 'simple immigrant, the political refugee, the helpless and poor'.[103] Enoch Powell was the most effective, if inflammatory, defender of genetic nationalism: 'The West Indian or Indian does not, by being born in England, become an Englishman.'[104] He was a hero to millions who felt the same.

C. L. R. James, the Trinidadian Marxist historian, was also an eloquent cricket analyst. With this cricket card, the black leftie was enthusiastically admitted into the club. He predicted that the struggle for equality would be fought by both whites and blacks.[105] He was right: fair Englanders, with black, Asian and Jewish activists and lawyers, have fought together against racial injustice and inequality. Their persistence and England's relative amenability ensured that post-war immigrants were given the right to vote from the moment of landing, and race discrimination laws were introduced in the early 1960s. That didn't happen in other European nations, where acquired citizenship is still an argument.

Unlike elsewhere in Britain and the Continent, human bonds and intimacy between the races have been woven into the fabric of English society. Old photographs catch the easy, warm rapport. One of my favourites is of two black and two white schoolgirls in the sun, hugging, chatting and smiling. It was taken in

Liverpool in 1949. Dance and music halls were not segregated as they were in the USA, and again photographic evidence reveals fluidity and pleasures largely untroubled by race.[106]

THE BROWNING OF ENGLAND

Indian and Pakistani professionals, entrepreneurs and students had been in England since Victorian times, but in small enough numbers. In the 1950s, manual workers from the Indian subcontinent arrived in northern English towns where labour was needed for heavy industry. Factory bosses actively encouraged them to come, and to bring fit and willing relatives. This labour inflow raised nativist fears and umbrage, more so than with previous migrants. Asians were physically identifiable and, unlike Caribbeans, were culturally non-European. (What a thin line there is between the 'exotic' and 'alien'.) As always, some found acceptance, but most learnt to put up, shut up, and make good. They too had expected better from their old rulers – at least some of those famously English good manners.

Suchdev Singh, from Wolverhampton, still can't get over the insolence. 'They asked us to come, the factory bosses. We are good workers. Then when we came, the people insulted us. One man in the factory told me I smelt. He had a dog. I asked him if my smell was worse than his dog. He hit me. I hit him back. I lost my job. They would not eat with us because of our spicy food. Look how much spicy food they are eating now!'[107]

England's thin patience was tried again when thousands of us Ugandan Asians crowded around its formidable portal after being expelled by Idi Amin. We were admitted, reluctantly, by Ted Heath, the huffy Englishman. That lost him the leadership of the Conservative party. Some Ugandan Asians have framed pictures of 'Gentleman Heath', who sacrificed so much for them. Heath never regretted his decision, believed the enterprising Asians dispensed economic vigour, 'like vitamins' to an old country when it was on its knees.[108]

The late Mr Mehta, a Ugandan Asian jeweller, was typical of these vigorous exiles: 'My dear, these English love deluxe things, the more expensive the better. So we will sell them those. They will not like us at first. They didn't like the European craftsmen when they came. Then they did. When we have real money, they will like us very much. That way they are fair.' He did get rich and was well liked and envied by his English neighbours.[109]

Most Asians I know believe that the hardships they endured were worth the life they are able to live in England. Amir Khan, a Pakistani-British engineer, was laid off in 1981 and set up a small delivery company in London. A particular white customer racially abused him whenever he was late. One day Khan punched the man. He was spared prison, but he fell into a deep depression and died three years on. Even so, his wife says, he believed England gave him an education, new eyes, cars and words, and faithful English friends too: 'Every Thursday he went to pub with his English friends. Drank juice and they drank beer. He said that was the happiest part of the week.'

The Story Continues

The journalist and author Robert Winder believes that animosity to immigrants 'is balanced by acts of routine kindness between the races. Individual open-mindedness has often defeated our nastier streaks, though it is much less recorded . . . inspiring no shocked headlines, no urgent documentaries.'[110]

Sam King came over from Jamaica in 1940. He served with the RAF in the war, worked for thirty-three years for the post office, became mayor of Southwark, and was awarded an MBE: 'God has been good to me, and so has this country.'[111] My mother's words exactly. My own life would never have been as exigent in Uganda, nor this full, exciting, stretching and utterly unpredictable.

More groups from all over the world have since arrived – refugees from Arab and African nations, from South-east Asia and the Far East too, economic migrants from every corner of the globe. Again, most have worked hard and asked only for a chance and for respect, yet are seen as problems and pollutants. Eastern Europeans, though white, have recently been added to the pile of the needed and unwanted. Immigrants should be seen as resilient and determined, not as pitiful wretches: 'it is amazing how often a migrant's life resembles a heroic escape – risky boat rides, midnight treks, cars nosing through dark woods, disguises, the barking of police dogs, hiding places, secret papers, close shaves, nail-biting escapes and whispers. Yet we habitually see immigrants not as brave voyagers but as needy beggars.'[112]

RACISM AND INTEGRATION

Race and ethnicity negatively affect third-generation black and Asian people, even in the supposedly 'post-racial' era. Reliable research by Omar Khan, from the Runnymede Trust think tank, shows that 'Though the experience of racism has changed . . . it still determines the life chances of too many citizens.'[113] A government-funded report by Business in the Community, published in June 2010, concluded that blatant and subtle racism was still stopping talented black and Asian professionals from getting the best-paid jobs in Britain.

In 2010, David James Smith, the respected *Sunday Times* journalist, wrote a shocking account of the racism his African wife Petal and their four children had experienced in Lewes, East Sussex. '[It] is like a cancer for black people, slowly eating away at you – you don't call people racist, because they don't like it, they get offended. They don't even like to think about it.' Subsequently some towns-folk burnt his effigy, while well-meaning local women invited Petal out for a drink.[114] Over this decade academics have considered the evidence for anti-Muslim discrimination. Few doubt that it exists and is active in British society.[115] Even mixed-race Britons, often described as the pride of modern England, can still face racism.[116]

The 'tolerance' of England is a silk scarf and easily falls away.

Evidence is mounting of anti-white attitudes among black and Asian people, as well as of inter-ethnic and inter-religious enmities. Islamicist terrorism has intensified generic apprehension and inchoate hatred and given succour to extreme English nationalists. The bombs in London in 2005 that killed many did not break Londoners apart but have burnt into the collective memory. Another pressing anxiety is religious separatism. Trevor Phillips, as chair of the Equalities and Human Rights Commission, warned in 2009 that the country was sleep-walking into segregation; it was a tad sensational, but not wholly inaccurate.

As a modernist Shia Muslim, I fear this drift. How then can we expect the English to accept Muslim obscurantism? Theirs is a history of slow progress towards freedom, autonomy, emancipation, and here come these righteous, ideo-logical reactionaries with no respect for any of those hard-won rights. Earlier Muslim migrants never behaved with such contempt for their adopted land, in spite of the racism they experienced.

The Web is both a buzzing marketplace of ideas and an outlet for demonic chauvinists. I have to stop myself reading the stuff for fear that it will fill me with a fatal pessimism about England's instinctive extroversion. We migrants are held responsible for the structural impact of late capitalism, growing income inequality and unregulated globalization. Newcomers are thought of as interlopers by under-standably troubled local citizens – including earlier immigrants. Their sense of place has gone.

It takes patience and impatience, work and imagination, resilience and doggedness, fight and faith to maintain the patchwork quilt that is England. It will always be a work in progress and there are times when it tears, or proves impos-sible to work on without dejection and a sense of futility. The hands and eyes tire. If migrants are poor and work for little money, they are accused of corrupting the labour market; on benefits they are scroungers; and if they succeed, they are robbing the true-born English of their inheritance. Stalwart Englanders who stand with migrants must sometimes feel it is a hopeless cause. Politicians always seem to think they have to swim with the tide or drown. Anti-immigration think tanks, academics, journalists and bloggers have successfully disseminated the idea that 'uncontrolled' immigration has weakened social bonds and mutuality. Scottish and Welsh nationalism can be as excluding and suspicious, but as only a small minority of migrants have moved to these parts of the UK, antipathy is sporadic and contained. Possibly because the Scots and Welsh aren't as tried and tested as the English are.

English patriot Mark Perryman remains upbeat: 'From pop to politics, cuisine to music, fashion to business, the "black" experience is now intimately woven into the fabric of English daily life, in a way that is not so obviously the case in Scotland or Wales.'[117] I think, or maybe hope, he is right.

DIVERSITY: THE GOOD STORY

Saadi Al-Timimi is an architect born in Iraq. He trained in Britain in 1958 and now won't leave his spot in west London. His English wife, to whom he has been married for forty-nine happy years, travels all over, but he stays put. 'I confess I am a bit of an Anglophile. I am fascinated by all things English. I absolutely adore it. I've read Agatha Christie, Dickens from start to finish. It took me a whole year to read one Dickens book. I so admire their understatement, self-possession. Of course that has changed a lot, but underneath it is still there. We Arabs are very hot-blooded. They are not. It is a good match.'[118] The Iraq War brought him low, but never turned him against England, because it taught him how to think and challenge, analyse and doubt. His Iraqi family witnessed the transmutation and realized he was lost to them.

Mo (short for Mohamed), an Egyptian, is another of those Arabs marooned in England after escaping oppressive dictatorships. He is a trained actor and used to work for the BBC World Service. Personally and professionally, he has not had an easy time, but he has never been tempted to go back, not even after Egypt was liberated: 'I cannot live in Cairo. Here I can disappear. I love many things about here, to be honest. It is a liberal nation. The politicians are relatively honest. You don't actually value it until you go elsewhere in Europe. In what other country would we find a wonderful politician like Shirley Williams?'[119]

I met innumerable such enthusiasts – Arabs, Africans, South Asians, East Asians, even a couple of Polynesians – of all classes. Some have moved out to quieter pastures and told me the London spirit is migrating to all of England, to the countryside and small market towns, bit by bit, irreversibly.

I spoke to young and old Englanders outside London about their nation. A large number – about half – were impatient with un-integrated fellow citizens and furious about unstoppable 'floods' of migrants. That was a given. The revelations were in the detail. The majority did not want their culture to be drained of colour, assorted voices and traditions – that pride, as one said, 'that the world is ours but in a good way now'. The number of cross-racial friendships and relationships was higher than even I had expected.

Author Katie Hickman is quintessentially English – she looks it too, with her creamy skin and the blush of rose petals upon her face. She would have fitted in nicely in Jane Austen's world, yet she says: 'I grew up not feeling English at all, at least not that little Englander who is completely introverted, very, very conservative, who doesn't like anything new, is emotionally cut off; I felt like a displaced person, because I never felt like them. But then, that too is a kind of Englishness, isn't it?' Yes, the Englishness that cannot be fenced in and enclasps, sometimes willingly becomes, the 'Other'. This is a deeper transformation than, say, the way South Asian and Far Eastern food has colonized the nation's taste buds, or the absorption of the East into fashion, the arts and popular culture. It is what happens most visibly in mixed-race families with one Anglo-Saxon partner, and, less obviously but as profoundly, in matters of faith.

An unprecedented number of Christian Europeans are converting to Islam. Exact figures are not available, but I would wager that more take place in England than elsewhere. Mosque congregations, Muslim help groups for converts, press stories and other anecdotal evidence backs this supposition.[120] Some of the names may surprise, or maybe not. This is, after all, England.

Yahya Birt, previously Jonathan, son of Lord Birt, erstwhile Director General of the BBC, converted in 1997 and has become one of the most effective and intellectual defenders of Islam and its enlightened messages; Lauren Booth, sister of Cherie Blair, had an epiphany in Iran, became a Muslim and said she found real peace; the Cambridge academic Tim Winter – Abdal Hakim Murad – an Englishman and Islamic scholar, was voted one of the most influential Muslims in the world in 2010.[121] My last example combines earthly love and religion: Adam

Osborne, aka Mohammed, brother of Chancellor George Osborne, became Muslim so he could marry his Bangladeshi sweetheart. This was in 2009, when the West had declared an unending 'war on terror'.[122]

London: The Twenty-First-Century Global Hub

All around London are haunts where exiles gather, some legit and others shady. They are dens of nostalgia, full of the fecund smell of fertile plans, shisha smoke and pain. I went to several while writing this book.

In a smoky Kurdish cafe all talk was about trade opportunities. The men wondered if artificial red roses would sell on Valentine's Day. One said his wife could make them and had a hand-painted poster with the slogan 'They Do Not Die'. I coughed while they smoked, sang and played their instruments. And more sounds were added to the infinite repertoire of the country.

In a Persian kebab house an old woman in black told me London had helped her to 'totally forget' Tehran. In a small Sri Lankan home in South London, they cooked hot curries every night and locals (up to six) happily came and paid for an authentic meal. The family was trying to get refugee status. Mary Alders, seventy, voiced her fears for them and the neighbourhood: 'Where will we gather if they go? Where can we get these curries and such smiles?'

Omari, a skilled and sought-after Somali carpenter, has taken the name Benn, after Tony Benn, his hero: 'I was in immigration detention centres where they treat us worse than animals. You think why I came to this place? But now I am legal. I go into their houses in Oxford and Windsor, and always there are the carpets, pictures, clothes, lights. Not made in England, made in the East . . . They like me better than people would like me in Kenya. Give me tea, biscuits. There – in Kenya – they think Somalis are cockroaches.'[123]

One summer evening in Clapham, I heard the music of West Africa, South India, German folk songs, Chopin being played by a young Chinese girl at the piano (she smiled and waved), American rock 'n' roll and reggae. It was a street of many melodies and voices, which were, inexplicably, harmonious. London is the main thoroughfare of our wondrous planet, a six-lane cultural highway.

In 2006, the *Guardian* announced 'The second great age of immigration . . . a wave of incomers has been sweeping across the country, scattering new cultures, languages and religions into almost every town and village.' The first wave, according to the paper, was in the 1950s and 1960s, when white Britons were really, really aggrieved; in the new millennium they appear to be much less so. Continuing racism gainsays such a buoyant assessment. However, there is, as always, a dynamic and uplifting immigration and diversity narrative in England. Both trajectories are concurrent. The harder it gets, the better it also gets.

At the end of 2011, when economic conditions were perilous across Europe, a survey of more than 160,000 foreign job seekers in a range of sectors found that more than half would choose to work in London if they decided to move abroad. New York came second, with 28 per cent, and only 15 per cent chose Paris.[124]

When I interviewed the well-connected and upper-class Geordie Greig, then editor of the *London Evening Standard*, he rapturously proclaimed London as 'the greatest city in the world. There is no competition. You ask anyone from any nationality where they would live outside their own countries and it is always London. Its colours change, its shapes change, the population too. They find freedom here, institutional stability, creativity, cleverness . . . It has depth, echo. It leads in culture, sports, business, fashion; no American city has the breadth or depth. Not even New York. London is a mosaic but its colour and shape changes all the time. . . . People want to feel part of it.'[125] It made me giddy with pride and also a little wary. It can be too easy to get carried away by the capital's pizzazz and to forget the forces of conservatism.

England can't simply muddle along through the next phase of her turbulent history. Who can and can't be English, who wants to be or declines the option (politely) – these are looming questions. Migration tests Christian charity, English socialist ideals, the welfare state, cohesion, national identity and the natural instincts for self-preservation and protection of culture. It might help if political leaders reminded England of its real mixed heritage and the incalculable economic and cultural wealth brought or generated by immigrants past and present. To ignore that perspective is profoundly unfair to the English, and steals from incomers the sense that this is their place too, and has been for a very long time.

Future generations must not be betrayed and deceived by biased historians and storytellers. A more truthful, holistic story about strangers within England's shores needs to be told again and again and again, both by the 'Other' and by the English.

PART II

4 Trade, Things and Appetites

'I'll have [spirits] fly to India for gold,

Ransack the ocean for orient pearl,

And search all the corners of the new-found world,

For pleasant fruits and princely delicates [spices].'

Christopher Marlowe,

Doctor Faustus Act 1, Scene 1 (1604)

T RADE WAS THE FIRST and strongest link between the English and Arabian, Turkish, Chinese, Indian and other oriental makers, sellers and buyers. It still is. Imports and exports come and go, even during periods of mutual suspicion or stormy political fallouts.

An innovative London company makes tandoori ovens and sells them to India. The exceptionally malleable and durable clay is from Stoke, and higher-end tandoors are bedecked with shimmering mirror tiles.[1] In a posh hotel in Delhi, a proud chef with a handlebar moustache showed me one of the bling ovens: 'Made in England, so must be best. Our people here don't know about quality. Yes, they can make things, but village quality.' To appropriate an ancient Indian cooking appliance, add value and sell it back to the originators is a ballsy and an entirely English thing to do.

An Englishman and his Chinese wife export well-chosen items of Worcester and Spode china to, well, China. She explains: 'It's to new millionaires. They want Gucci clothes, Milan furniture and English china. They think it gives them class. They want class after so many years without class.' England, in turn, imports vast quantities of consumer goods from these two economic super-nations.

All civilizations have their restless merchant classes. Overland trade routes, such as the busy Silk Road, have been traversed for over two thousand years. In the *Anglo-Saxon Chronicle* it is noted that King Alfred the Great (AD 848/9–99) sent a devout Christian, Sighelm, on a pilgrimage to the Indian subcontinent in AD 883. The pilgrim, presumably an ascetic, still brought to his king 'many strange and precious unions [pearls] and costly spices'.[2]

Also recorded in the chronicle are the early Viking arrivals and battles in England. The first of these, it is believed, took place in Dorset in 787. These men were traders as well as raiders, who we now know loved silk, spices, wine, jewels, glass and other luxuries. They must surely have induced envy and covetousness in the tribal folk of old England.[3] The crusades, from 1095 to 1291, were bloody, ideological and territorial. Islam was the enemy. Even so, those who went out to proclaim Christian victories were enthralled by the goods made by the enemy. They came back with coffee, tea, silks, ivory and jewels. And got rich.[4]

The Middle East was once a vast souk for European men on the make. In the fifteenth century, Venice and Antwerp were buzzy hubs for weird and wonderful goods. A Venetian galley which docked in London in 1481 carried barrels of oil, several carpets, pepper, silk, two apes, camlet (cloth made out of camel hair), Moorish wax, sugar, mace, green ginger, a vulture's egg and glass beads.[5] However, by the sixteenth century, the two seaports seemed spent, exhausted, and couldn't handle international business. After Vasco da Gama reached India in

1498, sea trade opened up unimaginable opportunities. Portuguese and Dutch speculators rushed off, grabbing territories and brawling over business. England was late joining this cut-throat fraternity but rapidly became leader of the pack.[6] Its engagement with the East was bigger, longer and more intense.

Conspicuous consumption defined the Elizabethan age, writes social historian Linda Levy Peck: 'Luxury commodities circulated throughout society, from the merchant who imported them, to the retailer who sold them, to the purchaser who bought them, the client who presented them to his patron, and the poor who wore them as second-hand goods . . . [T]he English became enamoured of foreign wares . . . appropriated artefacts and skills from abroad in ways that transformed their economy and culture.'[7]

In 1570 English potters obtained a licence to produce 'earthen vessels with colour . . . after the manner of the Turks'.[8] A sixteenth-century Turkish Iznik jug was brought to England and further embellished by an English jeweller in 1592. A stunning blue and white Iznik ewer, made in 1570, had an eagle beak and floral designs in silver mounted around the original by an English craftsman.[9] The embellishments show irreverence, and yet the reworked objects are a perfect metaphor for the relationship between England and the Orient: a mixture of greed, lust and respect.

Proto-Capitalists without Frontiers

From the sixteenth to the eighteenth centuries, England wanted to know and cut deals with the world, not to own it, asserts James Mather, one of the most persuasive reappraisers of pre-imperial history: 'it was the thirst for imports, reflecting the burgeoning wants of English consumers, which, before all else, stoked the allure of Eastern Mediterranean routes connecting London with the Levantine world.'[10] European merchants in the Orient were becoming extraordinarily prosperous. Their English counterparts were envious. Entrepreneurs petitioned Henry VIII for permission to go and seize some booty for themselves and, of course, His Majesty. It was Henry's daughter Elizabeth who finally let them push out the boats. Imagine how the dynamic fortune hunters must have felt as they embarked on their daring, unpredictable adventures.[11]

Early in the sixteenth century, a few agents had turned up in Turkey, selling woollen cloth and buying silk, pepper and spices.[12] Some hung around Constantinople, looking for big breaks without much success. Backed by patrons, William Harborne went there in 1575[13] and five years later obtained 'a charter of privileges' from Sultan Murad III. In 1582, with Queen Elizabeth's blessings, the Turkey Company was formed and soon after renamed the Levant Company.[14] The company's merchants knew English shoppers would pay good money for Ottoman products like 'sylke, spyces, of all sortes . . . cotton woole and yearne . . . Woormseed . . . Sope . . . Oyles . . . all kinds of drugs for potycaries . . . Lynnen cloth . . . Carpetts . . . quyltes . . . Indigo for dyers . . . Gotes Skynnes . . . dates and anyseeds'.[15] For his part, the sultan saw the advantages of bestowing commercial favours on an anti-Catholic nation.[16] Besides, his traders coveted English tin, bronze, lead and weapons. All sides profited.

Enterprising Englishmen also turned up in Aleppo, Smyrna, Istanbul, Damascus and other bustling bazaars. Had these men not ventured forth as far and freely as they did, England would have remained smaller, safer, more hidebound, and less prosperous, competitive and cosmopolitan.

In 1583 John Eldred, Ralph Fitch, John Newbery, jeweller William Leach and others[17] set out carrying letters from Queen Elizabeth for the emperors of China and Mughal India. Newbery spoke Arabic and Eldred had spent time in Syria. He remained in Basra to trade while the rest travelled through Aleppo, Baghdad, Fallujah, and reached the Persian Gulf. Crossing the Strait of Hormuz, their ship, the *Tiger*, was attacked by the Portuguese and the men were imprisoned in Goa, India. One of the witches in *Macbeth* rasps about a woman whose 'husband's to Aleppo gone, Master o'th' Tiger'.[18] It was clearly still a big story in 1623, when the play was printed in the First Folio.

Fitch and the others eventually escaped and reached Akbar's Mughal court, where Leach stayed on, earning a fortune making jewellery for the royal family. Newbery went his own way and was never heard of again. Fitch opened a shop in Goa[19] and provided excellent service: 'They alwaies respected Gentleman, specially such as brought [sic] their wares, shewing great curtesie and honor unto them, whereby they wonne much credite and were beloved of all men so that everie man favoured them, and was willing to doe them pleasure'.[20]

These early globetrotting opportunists learnt to 'negotiate a place at the table', put aside Christian chauvinism, obeyed unfamiliar rules, won over people of diverse faiths and ethnicities. '[They] came as guests into a world of open trade that was not at all of their own making, governed by an Islamic polity, which, as some admitted, outshone their own . . . Not until the later eighteenth century, when a fully fledged territorial British Empire appeared, was this older pattern of Middle East trade to melt away, together with the mode of accommodation between Britain and the Islamic world which it had nurtured . . . There was a big difference between these "pashas" and the brash "nabobs" of India.'[21]

In 1599 Richard Hakluyt paid homage to the pioneering merchants: 'Theirs was the onerous task of exploration and reconnaissance, of showing the proper road to wealth and mapping out of markets where trade could yield prosperity to the English nation'.[22] Ambassador Thomas Roe, Essex man, though mistrustful of orientals, was the kind of pragmatic, commercial Englishman Hakluyt so admired: 'war and traffique [trade] are incompatible . . . if you will seek profit, seek it at sea and in quiet trade'.[23]

That is exactly what British businessmen – a disproportionate number of them English – want today. In the Middle East I met several who have never forgiven Tony Blair for the war on Iraq, which destroyed trust and badly affected their ventures.

HEAPS OF CHARISMA AND PRESENTS

Roe's magnetism wasn't enough to swing the deal with spoilt Eastern potentates. Luxurious gifts and proper supplication were needed to lubricate negotiations. (Nothing really changes. Now, an *embarras de richesses* passes between British rulers and big businesses and their Arab counterparts to smooth weapons and oil transactions.) Roe presented choice items to the Mughal Emperor Jahangir and in return received a gold chain and locket with a miniature painting of the emperor.[24] The envoy returned home with many splendid presents – including indigo, cotton and silk, an opulent bed and quilts, cabinets and carpets.

History would have taken a very different course without the shared greed and vanity of English and Eastern monarchs.

In 1583, when he arrived in Constantinople, William Harborne had given the sultan 'thirteen dogs, a mass of silver plate and a silver clock studded with jewels'.[25] But the ultimate gift for a spoilt ruler was made by a humble English craftsman, Thomas Dallam, from Warrington, Lancashire. In 1599 Queen Elizabeth I ordered him to make an organ of sublime beauty, take it apart, reassemble it in Istanbul and present it to Mehmet III. The ship arrived after many perilous, stormy months.

On board with Dallam were carpenter Michael Watson, Rowland Buckett, a painter, and John Harvey, an engineer.

How daunting and elating it must have been for these working-class men given the task of delivering English exotica to the capital of the exotic Orient. Author Katie Hickman imagines what it was like in her novel *The Aviary Gate*.[26] As they worked on this gift of gifts in the Topkapi palace garden, gossip swirled and feverish anticipation rose. The organ, when finally unveiled, astounded the Turks. How could it not? Made of oak, it was gilded, had black metal birds fluttering among holly, piped songs, angel trumpeters, planets revolving around a figure of Queen Elizabeth – an impudent touch.

The delighted sultan invited Dallam to join his court for a fat salary and a choice of obliging virgins.[27] The modest craftsman, the first Westerner to be shown the king's harem, politely declined and headed back. He later crafted another magnificent organ for King's College Chapel, Cambridge, subsequently smashed by Cromwell's Puritans. Dallam's Istanbul organ was also destroyed by Mehmet's successor, Ahmet I, an implacable Islamic puritan. Poor Mr Dallam.[28]

Occasionally the most lavish gifts could fail to impress Eastern monarchs. Lord George Macartney learnt that hard lesson in 1794. The Irish-born Scotsman, turned ersatz English gentleman, was sent over to woo China, which was refusing to trade with the West. Dozens of wagons, 2,000 horses and 3,000 men transported watches, mirrors, Wedgewood pottery and decorative scientific instruments. An eleven-year-old English boy in the entourage spoke Chinese to Emperor Qianlong and warmed the royal heart. The gifts, however, were unceremoniously spurned.[29] The Opium Wars of 1839–42 were perhaps punishment for that almighty rebuff.

Under British territorial control, presents became symbols of imperial entitlement. Emasculated maharajahs, who must have wanted to slay the usurpers, furnished British rulers with outlandishly expensive items. At durbars and coronations such bounties were presented and accepted, reminding the givers of their humiliation. Some gave far more than just things: the ex-Rajah of Coorg, stripped of his power, sent his favourite daughter, Gouramma, to Queen Victoria – a child given as an offering of appeasement. Imagine that. The 'gift', renamed Victoria and converted to Christianity, must have 'proved highly gratifying to the ex-Rajah', wrote one newspaper.[30] For a while, she was a pretty caged bird, a curiosity. But she was miserable, eloped with a servant, was forced to marry an old English aristocrat and died young. The bird never sang.

The East India Company

The predominantly English East India Company was set up in 1600 to get into a rich, commercially advanced territory. In the first decades it concentrated on cloves, nutmeg, pepper, cinnamon bark and cardamom 'that made unrefrigerated food and unwashed bodies more tolerable'.[31] But by the second half of the seventeenth century, the company was 'importing an expanding range of fine Indian textiles, as well as coffee from Mokha in Yemen, and tea and porcelain from China'.[32]

Between 1600 and 1850, over 5,000 voyages were made under company colours. Its profits and audacity were such that its London headquarters, in Leadenhall Street in the City of London, were bigger than a national museum. In 1648, the company took over an Elizabethan mansion on that site and by 1661 it was established as East India House. It was completely rebuilt between 1727 and 1729 and became a landmark, vast, with courtyards and gardens, Doric pilasters and other grand features. It made a statement. Today there is no sign of the building, as author and banker Nick Robins discovered: 'there was nothing, no sign, no plaque, nothing to mark the fact that this was the location where the world's most powerful corporation had once been'.[33] The East India Company overreached itself, turned nasty, died and is gone from national memory. The forgetfulness seems odd for a nation obsessed with its past.

The first company men who went out to India – Sir Henry Middleton, and Lawrence Femell, Sir John Banks and others, were ambitious businessmen, not land grabbers. Like the English traders in Arabia, they knew how to cultivate friendships and networks with locals: 'there was little racism for the first 150 years of the encounter and not much evidence that Indians were considered inferior . . . some fell in love with India as well as Indians'.[34] Indian middlemen, known as *banians*, were interpreters, book-keepers, secretaries, industrial spies, suppliers, account-fiddlers, guarantors of loans for the white traders. They were eager to do business with their British partners. 'In time *banian* fortunes would match those of their masters . . . Military muscle had not yet undermined the basic rules of fair trade . . . the company had no territorial ambition, no imperial strategy, quite the opposite: it wanted low costs, high profits and an easy life'.[35]

Sir Jamsetjee Bomanjee Wadia and his clan were not mere middlemen; they were prestigious industrialists. They built warships and merchant vessels out of Indian teak in Surat, the first site of the East India Company's factories. Without those ships, the British would have been sunk. Did the master shipbuilder worry he was aiding and abetting foreign profiteers? Not at all. He was proud of his products and the medals bestowed on him by the British establishment in gratitude.

A Gujarati doctor I met in Poona told me about her ancestors, who helped company agents, for the right price: 'We Indians don't speak about common interests between Indian and English business-wallahs. There was trust between them, they gave each other loans and tips. Those Indians weren't *chamchas* [suckers]. They were clever, understood they could gain by working with the English, not against them.'

But by the mid-eighteenth century the company got venal, forgot Thomas Roe's shrewd dictum, did not keep to honest, peaceful trade and instead created havoc, rampaged, played dirty and grabbed territories. Robert Clive turned a trading concern into a colonial corporation with tax raising and other illegitimate powers. Warren Hastings, appointed the first Governor-General of Bengal in 1772, knew this was unwise and self-defeating: 'If our people, instead of erecting themselves into lords and oppressors, stuck to trade on fair and equitable grounds, the English name, instead of becoming a reproach, would be universally revered.'[36] Conscientious voices back in England 'questioned the propriety of a private commercial company ruling swathes of territory and a vast number of people'.[37]

AVARICE AND AGGRESSION

Gluttony and conceit made the firm like a gorging, obese man, who could never have enough. Territories were grabbed, rulers unceremoniously ousted, in Bengal, Mysore, parts of the Gujarat, Delhi, Agra, Bombay, and on and on. As Sunil Dutta, an Indian history graduate put it: 'The nawabs and rajahs were bastards too, treated people very badly, taxing them highly and all that. . . . But they were our bastards, our problem. Under the pretence of justice and fair play, the whites stole everything, killed fair trade.'

The company was so frenzied and unrestrained, so destructive, even insiders recorded their disquiet. A letter written in 1769 by administrator Richard Bercher is revealing: 'The condition of the people has been worse than it was before . . . This fine country, which flourished under the most despotic and arbitrary governments, is verging towards its ruin while the English have so great a share in the Administration.'[38] The dissenters were not heeded.

During a famine in Bengal in 1770, the living fed on the dead, children were sold off, corpses festered. The nabobs partied and increased taxes by 10 per cent. Horace Walpole was sickened: 'The groans of India have mounted to heaven, where the heaven-born General Lord Clive will certainly be disavowed. Oh, my dear sir, we have outdone the Spaniards in Peru! They were at least butchers on a religious principle, however diabolical their zeal. We have murdered, deposed, plundered, usurped – nay, what think you of the famine in Bengal, in which three millions perished, being caused by a monopoly of provisions, by the servants of the East Indies?'[39] Clive, by then a very wealthy man and the uncrowned king of most of India, was called before parliament. A free vote on a motion of censure against him was defeated and instead he received praise and thanks 'for meritorious services' to his nation. Eighteen months later he slit his own throat. His statue stands outside the Foreign Office.[40]

MISSION CREEP

Historian Mike Davis has discovered shocking facts about thirty-four Indian famines and other 'holocausts' caused by colonial free-market extremists.[41] By the nineteenth century 'coloured' folk had been deemed hopeless and inferior. Iniquitous high taxes and trade restrictions were imposed, Indian artisans were persecuted. To sell its mill-made cloth, the East India Company had Bengal's best hand-weavers cut off their thumbs so they could not make fine muslin.[42]

The Indian Uprising of 1857 began as a sepoy rebellion in Bengal and spread across the northern and western regions. Pent-up rage against British occu-pation exploded. Indians felt unchained for a while and the British decided to tighten their hold on the recalcitrant, reluctant subjects.[43] Both sides were savage, both unforgiving. Much blood was shed. After terrible reprisals, the British regained control. Yet, even when attitudes towards Indians had hardened, Englanders could not deny themselves Indian goods and pleasures. Supercilious Victorian memsahibs simply adored Kashmiri shawls and rugs, entertainers and dancers who moved like cobras. Good, hot curries, made by local cooks too, of course.[44]

Though resistance to British rule was increasing, there were always helpful Indians around, happy to oblige their masters. Their descendants are still around all over India. Ram Naick's family, originally from Madras, were what we would now call 'collaborators'. We met in Mumbai in 2011. Naick seemed eager to explain away his own historical burden: 'I have looked at family business records and know that my relatives were treated very well by the English. And we are not even Brahmins. I have the set of silver forks they used when business partners came to have dinners. Those white men had more honesty than our guys now.'

British rule in India ended in 1947, but the business connections have never ended. A popular TV advert in India in 1999 had an Indian tycoon driving around London seeking to buy the East India Company, with the words: 'They ruled us for 200 years, now it is our turn to rule.'[45] In 2005–6, for the first time ever, the amount of money invested in the UK by Indian companies overtook the amount invested in India by British companies. Thirty Indian businesses are listed on the stock exchange and over 500 Indian firms are based in London alone.

A Nation of Shoppers

TEA AND CHINA

For his BBC radio series *A History of the World in 100 Objects*, British Museum director Neil MacGregor included a Wedgewood tea set. He pondered the ironies of tea becoming the British national beverage, made as it is from plants grown in India, Ceylon or China and often sweetened with sugar from the Caribbean.[46]

The Dutch and Portuguese were the first to get tea from China. In 1658, tea began to be served in London's coffee houses and four years later the Portuguese Princess Catherine of Braganza married King Charles II and introduced the drink to the British aristocracy. In 1664, the first bulk order was made by the East India Company for 100 lbs of tea. By 1672, the company was importing over 13,000 lbs from Canton.[47] Taxes on the drink were high (very lucrative for the state), so smugglers came, prepared to risk everything for that sweet, warm brew. Englanders, in particular, were hooked.

Next, porcelain mania spread through Europe's elite. Chinese suppliers couldn't meet the demand.[48] Industrial spies were desperate to discover how such translucent, exquisite objects were made. The secret was revealed by a French Jesuit priest in 1712. Several decades on, Josiah Spode the elder came up with a unique formula for bone china, which was almost as lovely as porcelain. He had started to develop the technique in 1788 and it took five years to perfect. By the nineteenth century perfect English china was being made by Wedgwood, Royal Worcester, Royal Crown Derby and other pottery companies.[49] Admiral Lord Nelson owned a delicate, lovely breakfast service, with a formal floral pattern. It looks Japanese, but was made in Worcester in Chamberlain's China Factory.

Modern designer Jasper Conran has created an exquisite collection of chinoiserie china for Wedgwood in jade green, with delicate blue and white flowers, pensive peacocks and songbirds. He continues what Josiah Spode started.

TEXTILES, FASHION AND DESIGN

Silk was another highly sought-after commodity in the West from the sixteenth century. The fabric, first made in China in 3500 BC, spread to India, the Ottoman Empire, then westwards into Europe. Initially, silk for English customers was imported from Italy. In 1608, James I had 1,000 mulberry trees planted. He thought the trees would nourish silk worms and enable his country to make its own silk.[50] Wrong trees – the precious pupae died and the King was lampooned. Though the plan failed, it epitomized a recurrent urge among the English – if they liked something made elsewhere, they found ways of producing it at home, thus badly damaging the foreign producers and sometimes national economies. In the seventeenth century, Huguenot weavers and garment-makers in Spitalfields made silk at a price affordable to the middle classes.[51] The makers and the fabric became part of England.

Chintz – associated, now, with middle England to the point of caricature – was woodblock-printed or painted calico from India. It was brilliantly coloured and didn't fade fast. India's cotton fabrics were thought to be the best in the world. The Dutch, Portuguese, French and others were also besotted with the textures and beauty of Indian materials. Early samples had been reaching London from around 1613. Savvy middlemen got Indian makers to produce chintz designs that were more likely to appeal to white eyes. By 1664 textiles accounted for 70 per cent of the East India Company trade.[52] Chintz patterns also appeared on English pottery. Popular, too, were flamboyant men's waistcoats in embellished Chinese silk and coat linings with oriental patterns.

European governments couldn't compete with the Indian suppliers or curb domestic demand. France banned the importation of chintz in 1686; England followed suit in 1720. Riots broke out, and in fact making the fabric illegal simply increased its desirability.[53] Regency ladies, in particular, loved these fabrics. (Those Jane Austen costume dramas are less 'English' than audiences think or know.)

As with pottery, the only way to beat the foreign producers was to learn their techniques and start domestic textile industries. Silk mills were opened in Macclesfield and Congleton in Cheshire in 1744 and 1753 respectively. By the end of the eighteenth century, British manufacturers were making faux Indian fabrics for home consumers and exporting surpluses to India. They even made loin-cloths in Manchester.[54] And soon the world market was theirs. The turnabout was achieved through ruthlessly uncompetitive trade rules and by manipulating tastes. This was when 'made in England' was turned into a top brand, a badge of class and quality. In India in the 1820s, one Mrs Fenton declared it was 'the extremity of bad taste to appear in anything of Indian manufacture . . . when I wanted to purchase one of those fine-wrought Dacca muslins, I was assured I must not be seen in it as none but half-castes ever wore them.'[55] Even Indians were persuaded that muslin and chintz made in England were special and highly desirable, far better than anything Indians could produce.

And so chintz and muslin and Indian motifs became as English as tea and china! Liberty, an up-market Eastern bazaar, opened for business in London in 1875, and has never looked back. As my mum lay dying in 2006, she hugged a hot-water bottle which she had covered in gorgeous Liberty cotton with peacocks and trees of paradise.

In the 1960s and 1970s the young got into tie and dye, cheap beads, crinkled Indian cotton, Moroccan velvet gowns, Palestinian scarves, carpet boots – some lovely, some garish. The Beatles wore brocade kurthas, snooty trend-setters persuaded the most English of debutantes to shed twin sets and don kaftans. Biba turned an old London department store into a golden temple of excess and fantasy. Kensington market, Portobello Road, Carnaby Street were infused with incense (hashish, too) and oriental escapism. These trends affirmed the East, affirmed us of the East, ecstatically augured a new dawn.[56] The entrepreneur Peter Simon brought over and sold garments sourced in Afghanistan, India and the Far East in his stall on Portobello Road.[57] Soon afterwards he came up with the concept of East-West fusion fashion, opened Monsoon and made millions. The chain is still going – though now it is more sober and mainstream, middle-aged. In the 1970s Laura Ashley revived chintzy Regency and Victorian clothes for young women – I bought two gowns after I arrived in England. I felt good in them, as if they were part of my story, part of my ancestral recall.

The latest designer to revive chintz is Cath Kidston. Her household items, wallpaper and linen are patterned with those old designs appropriated from the subcontinent. Consumers tired of trendy modernism have retreated into Kidston's comforting Indian-Englishness.

You can't take England out of the Orient nor the Orient out of England. Millions of English girls and young women today wear a blend of South Asian and modern styles with practised insouciance, without making a statement. It really is no big deal. It's normal.

England is the place for designers of complex sensibilities, for whom there is no definable West or East. Hussein Chalayan is a designer of clothes that are art, politics, geometry, games and psychology; fashion-writer Susannah Frankel describes him as a constant crosser of borders.[58] He is a young Turk, born in Cyprus, who found his eyes and soul in London, the place he calls home with much passion. He had his DNA analysed and discovered his Y chromosome is Viking. It must, he thinks, have come from explorers and traders in the Ottoman Empire. 'That made me wonder about who we think we are.'[59] You could say that his blood-line and his work epitomize encounters and mergings between the English and Turkish civilizations. One of his most famous pieces is a dress covered entirely in hand-made roses in the delicate pink of an English rose, that emblem of English womanhood. It is both a claim on and a challenge to England.

CLOTHES AS SIGNIFIERS

Clothes carry meanings. From the sixteenth to the eighteenth centuries, large numbers of Englishmen living in India dressed like Indian men, in long *banyan* shirts, flappy, thin trousers and small Hindu or Muslim caps. It was during the Victorian age when stiff, tight, uncomfortably warm English suits became oblig-atory, much to the dismay of one doctor: 'The necessity which tyrant custom – perhaps policy, has imposed on us of continuing to appear in European dress . . . on all public occasions, and all formal parties, under a burning sky is not one of the least miseries of tropical life!' However, informally, the colonials donned cool, loose kurthas and trousers.[60]

After the Indian Uprising of 1857, it was seen as perfidious to wear such garments. Colonizers were obliged to wear 'proper' clothes – shirts, suits and corsets and gowns – to show whose side they were on. There were, though, always moments of surrender. For Edward VII's coronation, his wife Alexandra wore a gown of silk embroidered in India. She succumbed to the seductive power of ornate Indian style.

As a young man Gandhi wore formal English garb, as befitted a London-trained lawyer. When he became a freedom fighter, he gave up the suits and donned a simple, thin white loin-cloth, made by himself, not by Manchester producers. There are more modern, striking examples of clothes used as political messages. In 1987, black MP Bernie Grant arrived in parliament on his first day in full, dazzling, multicoloured African regalia, much to the consternation of security guards and some fellow MPs. David Cameron appointed Baroness Sayeeda Warsi, all too briefly, as deputy chair of the Conservatives, an extraordinary choice for a traditionally white party. The Muslim lawyer sometimes attended cabinet meetings in Downing Street in Pakistani outfits. For some, such clothes were unsuitable and un-English. The truth is that they were entirely suitable and English.

You only have to look at the increasing number of defiantly veiled women in England to understand the significance and power of clothes. Feeling that they don't belong – don't want to belong or are not allowed to – they physically separate themselves from their compatriots using cloth as a wall.

The rise of British Asians into the middle and even upper classes, the fast-growing Indian economy and the global success of Bollywood movies have made pricey Indian clothes modish and desirable. Stars and celebs, women wielding political power and serious influence, wear saris or salwar kameez for official or formal occasions. Cherie Blair, Tessa Jowell, the Duchess of Cornwall, Princess Diana, of course, have all done so, perfectly naturally. You cannot find their equivalents elsewhere in Britain or Europe. Messages are transmitted by the clothes. Diana flagged up self-exclusion from the mores of the England she was born into; Cherie Blair's Indian outfits were serious politicking; while others, through clothes, try to curry favour with the leading politicians and business people of the

East. In contrast, the modest gowns and headscarves worn by British politicians, journalists and royals in conservative Arab lands are considered gestures of respect and courtesy but can also represent supplication and compulsion.

Human behaviour is baffling. As Eastern styles become de rigueur in the West, in the East, the aspiring are increasingly anxious about wearing them. Culture analysts Carla Jones and Anne Marie Leshkowich have studied the trends: 'As Asian economies flourished, then crashed and began to recover, Asians of different classes, ethnicities, and genders faced the decision whether they should wear Western or Asian clothing. The former offered a neutrality of appearance and the hope that one might become an unmarked member of a modern international community in which Western suits, pants, shirts, skirts and dresses are standard fare . . . but at the possible price of a loss of individual or ethnic identity. The latter seemed to celebrate that identity, while at the same time marking the wearer as Other, as not fully at home in the centers of power and normative Western fashion, even as those norms appeared to embrace Asian aesthetics.'[61]

The Spicing of England

I lured my English husband not with my body or eyes or words but with hot lentils, spicy prawns and hand-rolled chapattis. He watched as I cooked. At the end of the meal, he says, he knew he would marry me. Like him, most of his countrymen and women cannot resist a good (or even not so good) curry, fluffy rice, stir-fried this and that, mezes and kebabs.

In 2012 Shelina Permalloo won *MasterChef*, the hugely successful TV cookery competition. Her Mauritian-Indian parents migrated to Southampton in the 1970s and she was born there. Greg Wallace, one of the two judges, was blissed out by her dishes: 'She put sunshine on a plate.'[62] For a *Daily Telegraph* journalist: 'Her food was enticingly exotic and reassuringly familiar.'[63] That combination was quintessentially English. Denied strong tastes, English tongues might simply shrivel up.

No other European nation has surrendered so heartily to Asian, African and Arabian food and, in time, incorporated it wholeheartedly into the national identity. In Scotland, Northern Ireland and Wales people are enthusiasts too, but, thus far, the foods are seen as 'ethnic', different, a parallel cuisine.

TASTING THE EAST

When merchants were hanging around Emperor Jahangir's court in the early seventeenth century waiting for contracts, they were fed 'fowl stewed in butter with spices, almonds and raisins',[64] while the East India Company men who built factories in Masulipatam and Surat between 1608 and 1615 soon developed a taste for pungent food.[65] In China, English merchants discovered soy sauce and soy-based condiments called 'catsups' and took to adding those to their repasts. One John Ovington, eating pillau and chicken in Surat in 1689, noted that 'Bamboe and Mangoe Achar and Souy, the choicest of Sawces are always ready to whet the appetite'.[66]

Indians soon sensed and used the English weakness for Indian nosh. When the East India Company besieged the capital of Tipu Sultan's Mysore kingdom in 1792, he proved more resilient than the company men had calculated. And more calculatedly generous. Two hundred of his men were dispatched to the enemy carrying kebabs and platters of fragrant rice. Lord Cornwallis, leading this war against the sultan, didn't care for foreign fare but his men sure did. The kebabs didn't save Tipu, but India claimed Lord Cornwallis. He is buried in Ghazipur in Uttar Pradesh, a conurbation full of spicy fragrances and strongly scented flowers.[67]

After the Indian Uprising, Indian food was shunned and maligned by English loyalists. Spices, so they said, inflamed natives, made them lose self-control; Westerners would be similarly corrupted unless they gave up piquant tastes and returned to European diets. So, for a while, the middle and upper classes tried hard to do just that. In her researches Madhur Jaffrey found that authentic Indian food was banished from tables: 'During most of the latter half of the nineteenth century most curry sauces were really French white sauces flavoured with curry powder and sometimes with apples and onions. Every now and again mango or coconut or chutney were added as well.' Think of Coronation chicken and you know what she means. Queen Victoria loved her curries and served them at her palace banquets, but under French names.[68]

The Victorian explorer Richard Burton ate a whole array of global foods on his journeys. He became something of an expert. In Zanzibar, for example, he noted: 'The mango, originally imported from India, is of many varieties . . . Arabs spoil its taste by using steel knives: with the unripe fruit they make, however, excellent jams and pickles.' And, 'the sweet limes of Zanzibar are considered inferior to none by those who enjoy the sickly "mawkish" flavour; the acid limes are cheap, plentiful and aromatic; they are second only to those grown about Muscat, the ne plus ultra of perfume and flavour.'[69] Burton had learnt these fine distinctions and discernments from natives. He ate with them, using his hands as they did, while conversing fluently in their own languages. In that moment he was one of them.

In 1819, Sir Thomas Stamford Raffles founded Singapore city, and it became a thoroughfare for Indians, Malays, Chinese and Europeans. The food, inevitably, was a mix of firm British and outlandish Eastern. In 1887, two Armenian brothers and an Arab backer opened the stylish Raffles Hotel, offering a menu 'where curries had been tacked on to traditional Victorian meals'.[70] Rudyard Kipling, in Singapore in 1889, enjoyed a Raffles curry with six different chutneys! A Chinese academic took me to the hotel when I was in Singapore in 2000. He told me that until the 1950s, it was a white enclave, where people like him would not be allowed, but he then added, 'I have to say, the British and English men mostly really love the Orient. This hotel was a child of that love and we must be grateful.'

Many intrepid Victorian empire builders succumbed to spices in spite of forced self-discipline and denial. The British abroad were often homesick, ill, depressed and felt threatened by the hoards. How hard they tried to stay loyal to Kraft cheese and tinned pilchards, sent from the motherland. Sticky English puds and cakes kept their sweet appeal, but in hot climes, plain pies and roasts tasted like undeserved punishment. English palates craved more excitement. The most bigoted settler in Africa yielded to groundnut sauce and local breads made with banana yeast, and, in India, they made up combo recipes like Mulligatawny soup, to reflect their duality perhaps.

I have an old 1950s cookbook specially written for white housewives in Kenya. It contains faithful, precise instructions for toad-in-the-hole, beef tea, custard, steak and kidney pudding and the like. But every few pages, you get mealie and maize fritters and really very innovative curries, including curried tinned salmon, which I used to make when a student.[71]

In my food memoir, *The Settler's Cookbook*, much of it about growing up under colonialism in Uganda, I include a recipe for 'gora chicken', meaning chicken for whities, which Asian women had made up. It was dark, thick, inhumanely, punishingly hot, and was sold to the colonial masters to make them cry.

They did cry and came back for more.[72] Our mums 'repaired' English food: fishcakes were livened up with coriander, shepherd's pie with chillies and turmeric; lime and saffron were mixed into cakes; cardamom and semolina were added to special shortbread, and so on. After eating the mended varieties, Englanders happily forgot the originals, even those made by their mums back home.

ENGLAND'S WAYWARD TONGUE: A LONG HISTORY

During the Roman occupation of Britain, their soldiers and governors feasted on walnuts, chestnuts, fish sauces, herbs and vinegar, peacocks, pheasants, guinea fowl and various spices from their empire. Englanders saw and smelt the Roman fare and some may have eaten it.[73] They must have been blown away by the strange and wonderful tastes.

In 2011 archaeologists came across ancient organic remains in Covent Garden, London. They found coriander seeds, dried meats, leather and wood. The find dated from the fifth to the ninth centuries. Newspapers raved about 'kebabs' relished by Londoners that far back.[74] Ali Khan, only twenty-three and a refugee from Afghanistan, manages a popular local kebab shop in west London. Business is very good. He has framed one of the kebab articles and proclaims his English heritage with great pride.

Strong flavourings, 'all but absent from Britain since the departure of the Romans – returned overland from the Middle East . . . re-entered the British kitchen, inspiring new and vivacious culinary wizardry'.[75] English crusaders hated Islam but loved Muslim food. Edward I spent £1,600 on spices in one year alone and allowed aniseed to be used instead of money to pay taxes.[76] Palace cooks in the thirteenth century perked up meat and fish with imported condiments, and spice platters were passed around at meals so diners could make their mouths burn with extra hot pleasure.[77]

Cooks in big houses were soon adding pepper, cinnamon, mace, cardamom, nutmeg, anise, saffron, caraway and mustard to meat, fowl and fish. Spices 'achieved mythical status, with some people convinced that they were harvested from the gardens of Paradise or found floating on the Nile.'[78] Nuts, dried fruit and sugar were added to pies and stews. Rabbits were stewed in almond sauce, 'gynger' went into cakes, and rice puddings arrived, bursting with vanilla and almonds. In time it became a definitive 'English' desert.

Ever more thrilling, opulent feasts were prepared in the houses of noblemen. In the 1550s, one William Petre of Ingatestone Hall was known for his grand winter parties. His home accounts show purchases of mace, cloves, saffron, currants, dates, ginger, cinnamon, caraway, almonds and rice.[79]

During Tudor times the rich started to consume sugary delights: 'under Elizabeth I tables glittered with sugar creations and courtiers outdid themselves to satiate their queen bee, whose teeth, by her sixty-fifth birthday were black'.[80] Marzipan and Christmas cake hail back to then. Saffron was very popular, though it was staggeringly expensive, and still is. Onions, garlic and spices were used to make salted meats more palatable.[81]

Over the centuries foreign foodstuffs were naturalized: 'This is a country . . . with a 500-year-old history of food piracy, borrowing ideas from other shores, importing their raw materials and learning to cultivate them on our soils'.[82] Traditionalists struggled against these profligate tendencies and trends. Coffee, for example, arrived from the Ottoman region around 1598 and was both taken up eagerly and feared for a long time: 'The Excessive Use of that Newfangled, Abominable, Heathenish liquor called COFFEE has . . . Eunucht our husbands

and Crippled our more kind Gallants that they are become as Impotent as Age.'[83]
Warnings were issued about intemperate desires, tracts were published to re-
establish simple fare. 'Plain English people, the sort the French call rosbif' were
disturbed about and suspicious of 'alien' foods.[84] In 1735 the English caricaturist
William Hogarth set up the Sublime Society of Beef Steaks – the meat to him was
a symbol of his nation at its best and strongest. As one old patriotic ballad goes:

> *When mighty Roast Beef was the Englishman's food*
> *It ennobled our Hearts and enriched our blood;*
> *Our Soldiers were brave and our Courtiers were good*
> *Oh, the Roast Beef of Old England!*

What neither Hogarth nor the balladeer understood is that 'foreign' flavours and
concoctions are essentially English too. In the seventeenth century the English
diarist Samuel Pepys thought a ship's hold full of spices was 'as noble a sight as I
ever saw in my life'.[85] Warren Hastings, as Governor-General of Bengal, grew his
own chillies in a hothouse and mailed them to other addicts. The first cookbook
to include Indian recipes was by Hannah Glasse, published in 1747. Her recipe for
pillau had three or four small onions, thirty peppercorns, rice, some coriander
seeds (heated and beaten to a powder), cloves, mace, rice, fowls, veal or pork.[86]
The pillau I make is not that different. Spices became magic cures too. In 1783,
Sorlie's Perfumery Warehouse in Piccadilly, London, advertised the benefits of its
curry powders – good to eat and for digestion and increased libido.[87]

Sarah Shade, a working-class woman with a crazy sense of adventure, went to
India in 1796. She claimed to have fought off a tiger – and had marks to prove it –
was wounded in an Anglo-French war in southern India, and held captive in

Mysore, where she learnt Indian cooking and the local language. Her curiosity and openness impressed powerful Mysorians and enabled her to negotiate her release. She returned to London and set up a small take-away business: 'making vegetable curries and other Indian dishes. She would cook these meals to order for "East India families", who – like her – had returned to what was nominally their home country, yet found themselves homesick for the vast subcontinent they had left behind.'[88]

In 1773, the Norris Street Coffee House in Haymarket started serving curries to their regulars, with some success. The first Indian eatery in England, the Hindostanee Coffee House, was opened in 1809 by Sake Dean Mahomed (more on this extraordinary man in Chapter 7). A newspaper advert announced its arrival: 'Mahomed, East Indian, informs the Nobility and Gentry, he has fitted up the above house, neatly and elegantly . . . [where gentlemen] may enjoy the Hoakah . . . and Indian dishes, in the highest perfection', with choice wines too.[89] Mahomed's venture failed. The time wasn't right. Now, however, the UK has more Indian restaurants than India. The pioneer must be chuckling and cheering.

In the early nineteenth century, Mrs Turnbull of Hyde Park set up a new service. She would send by post to paying correspondents a hundred curry recipes; she had an arrangement with Beeces Medical Hall in Piccadilly, who would grind spices to her specifications and supply her clients.[90] Around this time Indian herb and spice peddlers were seen on the streets of London and some came to know their buyers intimately.[91] In 1831, the Oriental Translation Committee published a pamphlet with recipes for kormas and kebabs, pickles and pillau, for returnees who 'from a long residence in the East, acquired a strong predilection for Indian modes of life'.[92] In the 1840s Edmund White, the maker of Selim's Curry products, made and sold curry powder as a health food, claiming it stimulated circulation and a sluggish mind.[93]

Yellow-green piccalilli was an English version of Indian pickles, and Lea and Perrins' Worcestershire Sauce would never have been made were it not for a nobleman who returned to Worcester after a spell in India. In 1830, he delivered a recipe to his local shop, run by two clever chemists, Messrs Lea and Perrins. They produced a fiery, pungent infusion, bottles of which the customer happily took away. The leftover brew was stored and forgotten. After some time, they opened the barrels and found the sauce had mellowed, turned aromatic and delicious. So they bottled it, named it after the shop and never looked back. It still sells well.[94] My mum always added splashes of LP sauce to her beef curries just before serving, said it added some extra lift.

In 1846, William Makepeace Thackeray dashed off the first known English ode to curry:

> *Three pounds of veal my darling girl prepares*
> *And chops it nicely into little squares*
> *Five onions next procures the minx*
> *(The biggest are the best, her Samiwel thinks)*
> *And Epping butter nearly half a pound*
> *And stews them in a pan until browned.*
> *What next my dextrous little girl will do*
> *She pops the meat into the savoury stew,*
> *With curry powder tablespoons three*
> *. . .*
> *PS – Beef, mutton, rabbit, if you wish*

Lobsters or prawns or any kind of fish
Are fit to make a CURRY. 'Tis, when done,
A dish for emperors to feed upon.[95]

In 1850, a book was published with recipes for curried lobster, oysters, mutton and rice. The named author was Lady Maria Clutterbuck, but many then believed it was really the work of Catherine, the long-suffering wife of Charles Dickens.[96] Eliza Acton recommended tamarind and bulls' testicles or a calf's head to add flavour to curries; Mrs Beeton added bacon to hers.[97] They must have they felt completely comfortable with Indian food to experiment as they did. Kedgeree came out of that confidence. *Khitchri*, an Indian dish of rice, lentils and turmeric boiled together, was appropriated and, with the addition of smoked fish and boiled eggs, turned into kedgeree, a fine breakfast for the upper classes. Genius.

THE WORLD ON THE TABLE

Volumes have been penned on British food habits in the twentieth century. Here I touch briefly on how the Orient has pepped up the national diet and national identity of England.

During the First World War, spices helped to make food palatable: 'curries have "thrift" written all over them. Recipes appear to tell housewives how to dress up leftover meats with curry sauces using curry powder, milk, sour apples and lemon juice.'[98] After the terrible losses and devastation of the war, people turned to small luxuries. In 1918, the Savoy put two curries on its menu and others followed. Sprightly curries vanquished the most cautious or unwilling in England. This happened with the Scots, Welsh and Northern Irish too, but the English, without doubt, were the first to truly love and know the food.

Small restaurants cropped up in east and west London between 1905 and 1920; cafes near the docks served lascars, and in some small Indian eateries pro-independence students met to discuss their cause. Some were spied upon by the British state. The Shafi in Gerrard Street was opened in 1920 by Mohammed Rahim and Mohammed Wayseem, and in 1926, Veeraswamy came to Piccadilly and is still there today. At the time, its diners were Indian students, travellers and sometimes ex-colonials. Now, its designer dishes draw a more exclusive clientele – wealthy Britons and Indian visitors with deep pockets, big handbags and particular wants. One of them, a model from Delhi, unabashedly told me: 'We don't go to the cheaper end in London, too low class, full of cheap people. But food here is Indian luxurious, you know, it makes you feel you are something. I mean I would never eat in just an ordinary a tandoori restaurant.'

Many English curry houses appeared in the 1930s and by the late 1950s Bangladeshis in east London had opened simple eating places serving modestly priced, flaming hot, orange (or dark brown) dishes to the masses, a habit that has passed through the generations. For the *Daily Mirror*, a working-class paper, 'the tingling of the taste buds, the watering of the eyes – it's almost like being in love'.[99]

The same might be said of Turkish food, the many and different African national dishes, Afghani, Malaysian, Indonesian and other cuisines. Cosmopolitan food crept into the motherland, subverted the imperial order and its absurd pretentions. As my uncle Karim used to say, 'They say they are better than us, then why do they not eat their own grey food? Why do they run to ours? Who is better, then?'

Chinese food really only came to England in the twentieth century. The earliest Chinese arrivals were sailors who, like Indian lascars, had either been sacked or had jumped ship and ended up in London, Liverpool and Cardiff. In 1911, there were around 1,500 such settlers in Britain, many suffering poverty and experiencing overt racism. But, as always, some were sharp entrepreneurs who didn't bow to misfortune, determined to beat the odds and find success. Chung Koon, previously a ship's chef, and his English wife opened Maxim's in Soho in 1908 and, soon after, the Cathay, near Piccadilly Circus. Both quickly became favourite haunts for metropolitan foodies always looking for the next thrill.

In 1930, a few more restaurants opened in the same areas to cater for theatre crowds. In the 1940s, Pathé News warmly welcomed Ley's Chop Suey House and others, each opening presented as proof of England's huge appetites and cosmopolitanism. Two cookbooks were written – M. P. Lee's *Chinese Cookery* (1943) and Buwei Yang Chao's *How to Cook and Eat Chinese* (1946). They didn't fly because their time hadn't come.[100]

Chinese immigration rose after the Second World War and new small cafes opened to cater for these migrants, while a few restaurants for non-Chinese diners were also appearing. Chung Koon's son John started the Lotus House in Queensway in 1958 and it became hugely popular. Customers who couldn't get tables asked for food to be boxed to carry home – the take-away had arrived. John Koon also persuaded Billy Butlin to open a Chinese kitchen in his Butlin's holiday camps, offering chop suey and chips. Punters were ecstatic.[101]

In the late 1950s, Soho food suppliers opened up in the West End, and Chinatown was born. Ken Lo, suave son of a diplomat, published the first of many cookbooks in the early 1950s. In the 1980s, his restaurant, Memories of China, became the talk of the town as the trendy, sophisticated place to eat.[102] Meanwhile less salubrious Chinese grub was becoming ever more popular. Small, cheap, takeaways gradually established themselves across the whole of the UK. The population then would guzzle any dish claiming to be 'Chinese', even if, especially if, it was flavoured with additives such as monosodium glutamate.

Middle Eastern food was first mentioned in 1925 by herbalist Hilda Leyel, co-author of a cookery book with a section entitled 'Dishes from the Arabian Nights': 'their stories are full of expiations of the luscious things they had to eat. Food is treated as a fit subject for poetic ecstasy . . .'[103] Fifteen years later the food began to be seen, smelt and eaten as Egyptians, Yemenis, later Lebanese, Iraqis and others, migrated to London and a few other English towns and cities. In the 1960s and 1970s refugees fled to England from dictatorships in the Middle East and Africa. Food kept their memories of home alive, but at the time it was almost a guilty secret; it did not reach the English. It would, though, as the years rolled on.

The 1970s and 1980s saw two brilliant Indian women, Lalita Ahmed and Madhur Jaffrey, presenting cookery shows on TV. Both were natural communicators, attractive and charming Easterners. They rescued Indian food and educated and enthused eager British viewers. In her time Jaffrey was as popular as Nigella Lawson. She remembers that the day after she cooked a lemony coriander chicken on television, Manchester ran out of fresh coriander.[104] The Californian Chinese chef Ken Hom presented a series on good Chinese cooking and, again, was watched by millions of keen viewers. After Ahmed, Jaffrey and Hom came the wise, erudite and wonderful Claudia Roden, who opened the doors to Levantine cooking and invited audiences in. With her, the English relearnt the story of that region and discovered the foods eaten centuries earlier by their ancestors.

Though the country has always been crazy about foreign food, that didn't stop many English people resenting the migrants who brought the world to them on their tables, and often what they used against incomers was, ironically, food. Until the late 1980s, South and East Asian families were accused of cooking 'smelly food'; many were refused tenancies and had their doors and windows kicked in. My mother was nearly thrown off a bus by a conductor who said she reeked of curry – which she did, because she had forgotten to take off her cooking cardi. That was in 1975.[105] Asian children were teased and taunted that they were stinky, my son included. Some of them gave up eating Asian food and insisted on fish fingers, so they could belong.

In Our Times

The star modernist chef Heston Blumenthal, an avid Englishman, makes 'Rice and Flesh', a dish from *The Forme of Cury* by the master cooks of Richard II, printed in 1390. It is a creamy, saffron risotto served with veal. Blumenthal has also resurrected a cake dating back to 1810, infused with cinnamon and topped with spit-roasted pineapple. These historical dishes are served in one of his most prestigious restaurants. The English historian Tristram Hunt dined there, loved it, and found the food very cosmopolitan: 'its implicit embrace of global influences tells a non-parochial story of British culture. Our diet – like our literature, landscape and art – is mongrel.'[106]

A. A. Gill points out that 'You cannot remotely be interested in food and remain a little Englander,'[107] yet in Buckingham, a place of 'palely loitering xenophobia', he describes meeting voluble purists who say they don't hate immigrants but don't want them spoiling their England. He had to listen: 'It's one of those familiar and wanly fearful moans where I just slip on the bland face and bite my Indian, French, Mauritian, Scottish, Yorkshire tongue.' But then Gill encountered Zakima, a Nigerian who owns a small restaurant. She fed him gbegiri soup from Nigeria, made with beans and dried fish and chilli, and chicken jollof, a West African rice dish. This shire town is both closed and open to the outside. The council publishes a list of food suppliers – halal Indian, oriental, Italian, Kosher, Mexican, South African and South American.

West Ealing in London is packed with Persian restaurants. They are always full – with Middle Eastern customers and white Londoners of every ethnicity. Saharah, an Iranian student at Thames Valley University, is dragged there every week by her fiancé Michael, a computer repairer from Yorkshire. She finds his eating obsession tiresome: 'I say, let's go to an English restaurant sometimes, but he says there is no such thing. He says our food is the best. For me it's OK, but there is no experimentation. Michael has become like my father, he only wants Iranian. It makes me a bit angry sometimes, like he thinks he can just take our culture and eat it.' She was laughing when she said this. A part of her, I think, was really quite flattered.

In July 2005 Islamicist killers blew themselves up and killed and maimed many in central London. Edgware Road was one of the chosen sites of carnage. About 600,000 Arabs now live in Britain and are here to stay. Edgware Road is 'Little Beirut'.[108] The bombers knew they were blowing up a bit of Arabia, the happiest bit, famous for its aromas, fresh-fruit smoothies, falafel and other delights. I filmed there the day after the blasts and a tearful cafe owner mourned: 'This is our home, our kitchen, our heart. These bombers know nothing. Here in England, we are happier than in our countries – the food we make is saying "thank you, England".' Prestigious restaurants such as Momo are finally taking Arab food away from the streets to vast and palatial rooms, recreating the Arabian Nights fantasies of yore. The rise and rise of Persian and Arabian cooking is just another episode in the timeless, endless story of exploratory England.

In the last ten years Thai food has spread around England and the rest of Britain. Pubs, bastions of old ways, have enthusiastically welcomed Thai cooks.

In one Oxfordshire pub, a new manager changed the food from Thai to 'proper English' and lost most of his customers. A bright young Thai woman, Nicky Santichatsak, persuaded an English cafe owner to let her rent the place in the evening after it closed. She served a few Thai dishes and was soon doing so well she took over the premises with financial help from the owner and local customers. She called it Fat Boy's, after the truck drivers who came in for full English breakfasts in the old cafe.[109] Now there is a chain of Fat Boy's in west and south London.

Famous British chefs, such as Gary Rhodes, the late Keith Floyd, Rick Stein, routinely to go off on discovery trips – to India, the Middle East and the Far East. We immigrants have mixed feelings about the way chefs appropriate the local food and sell it back to us, sprinkled with white approval. Such petulance, however, is outweighed by gratification. Jamie Oliver understands that 'one of the lovely things about British cooking is that we adopt great food from all the lovely people who come from overseas to live in our country. We are a magpie nation, take the best bits of other cuisines and embrace them as our own.'[110] This point is echoed by Andrew Marr in a perceptive cultural essay: 'England is mixed and mongrel, and the most internationalist of the European countries.'[111]

French, Spanish and Italian chefs tend not to be exploratory or internationalist, and instead stay within the traditional repertoire. Some fanatically shave off 'outside' influences and get back to basics, remembrances of times past. France, a nation with millions of migrants from its old colonies, is a cultural fortress. Its foodies and cooks cling to the local, the soil – *le terroir de la France profonde* – the ancient and enduring. Admittedly the young do now consume Chinese and Vietnamese dishes, but the custodians of national cuisine disapprove. The Spanish appear to have resolutely erased their Islamic heritage by eating as much pork and ham as they can stomach. Some signs remain – saffron in paella is the most obvious, and milky puddings too – but no mention is made of their origins. Forty per cent of Italians have never tasted non-indigenous food and have no wish to. Some northern Italian towns have been banning 'ethnic' restaurants since 2009, supposedly to safeguard their culture. Milan is among them, so too Forte dei Marmi, a beachside retreat for arty types, writers and cool politicians.[112] There is also a major panic in the country about truffles imported from China. Meanwhile Italian food springs up everywhere, including in India.

Such loony protectionism would simply never happen in England, where the alternative football anthem is, after all, called 'Vindaloo', written by Keith Allen, music by Alex James, bassist of Blur. Andrew Marr observes that 'Bangladeshi citizens have given all England a new national dish, chicken tikka masala, invented in London, a staple of our curry obsession'; he suggests that if Hogarth were alive today, he might well have 'attacked the EU with an installation of giant silver takeaway boxes and an amplified recording of a curry-house belch'.[113]

The Indian food industries have enormous economic and political significance in the UK. More people work in the sector than in coal mining, shipbuilding and steel combined,[114] and billions of pounds are generated by Indian restaurants and supermarkets selling frozen Indian meals. A number of Asians in this industry have joined the rich list and the House of Lords, while the Cinnamon Club in Westminster is now an expensive dive for plotting ministers, whose masala breath afterwards must fill the airless corridors of power.

As Marr writes, 'where the stomach goes, politics and identity must follow'.[115] The English, more than any other Westerners, consumed the East and its food. The food got into the body of their nation, changed its colour, and what it means to be English.

5 Buildings, Spaces and Design

'That the Grecian Architecture comprizes all that is excellent in art, I cannot help considering as a doctrine, which is itself erroneous and servile . . . why should we admire it in an exclusive manner; or, blind to the majesty, boldness, and magnificence of the Egyptian, Hindoo, Moorish, and Gothic, as admirable wonders of architecture, unmercifully blame them, because they are more various in their forms, and not reducible to the precise rules of the Greek hut, prototype or column? or because . . . their proportions are different from those to which we are become familiar by habit?'[1]

William Hodges, painter (1744–97)

Sт Paul's Cathedral in London reminds me of the commanding, exquisite old mosques of Isfahan, Istanbul and Cairo. Muslim ambassadors in London apparently saw the double-layered dome being constructed and threw money at the builders.[2] The story is well within the bounds of credibility: Ottoman and Arab noblemen visiting London would have noticed the rising edifice. Christopher Wren saw similarities between Islamic and Gothic visions: 'He was of the opinion,' stated his son, that 'what we now vulgarly call Gothik ought properly to be named Saracenick architecture refined by

Christians.'³ So, the elegance and splendour of the Palace of Westminster, the centre of power and pomp, is Islamic design, transported and remodelled.

That may be why classicists distrusted the Gothic. The critic John Evelyn was a stout upholder of the classical form. In 1664, he wrote: '[Moors and Arabs] wherever they fixed themselves, began to debauch this noble and useful Art [architecture]; when instead of those beautiful Orders, so majestical and proper for their Stations, becoming Variety, and other ornamental Accessories, they set up those slender and misquine Pillars or rather Bundles of Staves and other incongruous Props to support incumbent Weights and ponderous arched Roofs . . .'⁴ Traditionalists such as Evelyn could not control the migrations of ideas and tastes into England; it was a struggle they could not win. He himself wasn't immune to the pull of the exotic. After beholding a visiting Moroccan emissary in London he wrote in his diary: '[He] was clad in the Moorish habite of coloured cloth or silk . . . a string of pearls oddly woven into his turban . . . a handsome person, well featured, and of a wise looke, subtile, and extremely civile.'⁵

By the late eighteenth century the Orientalist Sir William Jones was of the view that that Indian and Arabic art and poetry had infused English aesthetics with 'new ideas of beauty and sublimity'.⁶ This transfusion is far less evident elsewhere in Europe.⁷

A painting by William Hodges of the Jami mosque in Jaunpur, India, apparently influenced the radical architect George Dance the younger (1741–1825) when he was asked to redesign the south front of the venerated Guildhall in London: 'The original medieval porch was retained, but . . . the projecting turrets, the decoration above the central arch and the scalloped arches of the window have an Indian flavour. It is quite possible that the City aldermen did not recognize the design as oriental and that Dance, prudently, did not enlighten them.'⁸ But if the aldermen were hoodwinked, others were not, and there was murmured disapproval of these men smuggling 'Hindoo-Gothick' into English buildings.[9]

Domestic homes were easternized too. 'Banglas' are traditional, single-storey dwellings found across the Indian subcontinent. In the 1650s the East India Company built similar 'bungalows' for staff and merchants close to factory complexes. Some were small, others luxurious, with long verandas where top chaps gathered for gin and sherry at sundown. Bearers waved fans around their heads and kept out insects. Vast rooms were finely furnished with carved and inlaid coffee tables, lacquered furniture, deep sofas, carved beds. What a life. Bungalows then began to be built in quiet, coastal areas of Britain. They appealed to the cautious English middle classes. The symbol of imperial hubris came to symbolize bourgeois life.[10] Today, the bungalow is as adventitious and commonplace as curry. Home décor, too, was orientalized after the East India Company started trading. Those who 'had not been further than Margate' stuffed their homes with mass-produced exotica.[11] The three flying ducks shared space with prints of India and Arabian deserts.

England's vistas and interiors would be very different without these fixations and passions.

Grand Designs

Cotswold towns and villages are pretty and pristine. Unquiet metropolitan arrivistes escape to these countryside sanctuaries, and rumour has it that some Russian oligarchs have been sniffing around properties. They are all searching for 'real' Englishness – an illusion.

Just ten minutes away from twee Chipping Campden stands Sezincote House, completed in 1810, the 'only Indian Country House ever built in England or Europe'.[12] It is a memento of the lost Empire, with Rajasthani peacock-tail arches, carved lotuses, Mughal pavilions, a Persian garden, Islamic canals playing watery music, a shrine to a Hindu goddess. John Betjeman caught the spirit and idiom of the place in 'Summoned by Bells':

> *Down the Drive*
> *Under the early yellow leaves of oaks;*
> *One lodge is Tudor, the other in the Indian style*
> *The bridge, the waterfall, the temple pool*
> *And there they burst upon us, the onion domes*
> *Chajjahs and Chattris made of amber stone*
> *'Home of the Oaks' exotic Sezincote.*

Today petitions of protest would circulate and council planners would throw out such inappropriate, unsuitable building plans. It may seem counter-intuitive, but people were more broadminded then, even in the shires: 'This is quintessential England, where towns and villages answer to names like Moreton-in-Marsh, Bourton-on-the-Water, Upper Slaughter and Stow-on-Wold. By that measure Sezincote ought to be rechristened Taj-in-the-Vale.'[13] One of these days someone will use it as a setting for a Bollywood movie.

How did such a place come to be made? In 1795, Colonel John Cockerell, grandson of the nephew of diarist Samuel Pepys, bought the estate. The colonel died only three years later and the property passed to his youngest brother Charles, who had been with the East India Company. Charles commissioned another brother, architect Samuel Pepys Cockerell, to build a residence similar to the mansion he had designed for Warren Hastings, the erstwhile Governor-General of Bengal, at Daylesford, a few miles away.[14] These East India men may conceitedly have considered India to be an annexe of Britain, but that bewitching civilization had altered them, and their notions of grace, beauty and opulence, for ever.

SAD ENGLISHMEN

Daylesford, Hastings' grand house of 1790, hints of secrets and pain, love and sedition. Hastings had been through a harsh parliamentary impeachment trial, accused of being 'a spider of hell' and 'a ravenous vulture' who stole from India.[15] In 1788, Edmund Burke had, with others, summoned Hastings to a parliamentary hearing and charged him with misconduct, mismanagement and personal corruption. The hearing, the longest ever in history, went on for seven years, over which time public opinion slowly shifted from revulsion to sympathy. In 1794, Lord Cornwallis, who had replaced Governor-General Hastings in India, took on the inquisitors. They were wrong to malign a leader who 'was universally popular with the inhabitants'. In 1795, Hastings was acquitted of all charges.

Though exonerated, he must have been shattered and, we can guess, very bitter. From being a chieftain in charge of vast areas and millions of people, Hastings had become a pariah, controlling nothing, not even his own reputation. How many sleights did he endure? How many friends melted away? In India the natives had eventually grown to trust this white nabob, who respected their history and culture. For Hastings to feel at home, home had to have visible echoes of India. However, Cockerell 'was not ready to brave public condemnation or laughter so early in his career as to add to a design otherwise completely English a shape so foreign in the Cotswolds.'[16] Nor, I imagine, was Hastings.

Inside they could dash convention, run riot, make sunbursts in gold and red. 'The sculptor Thomas Banks designed great chimney pieces to fire the imagination every bit as effectively as their hearths warmed the toes. Here were maidens in saris carrying water jugs on their heads as they sashayed through the palm trees bearing platters groaning with Bengali fruit. In one, cavorting elephants herald Lakshmi, the goddess of wealth . . . He furnished his rooms with Indian ivory, stacked his library with oriental manuscripts and planted Bengali peaches and mangoes in his beloved garden.'[17] Indian miniatures and landscapes were given prime positions, while great European masters like Rembrandt and Correggio were moved into lonely side rooms. Unlike Robert Clive, who flaunted stolen Eastern treasures and styles as trophies of conquest and supremacy, Hastings furnished his house to express his dual, conflicted self, adversarial civilizations, each loved and hard to love.

Many returnees were, like Hastings, divided souls. After twenty-five years in India, James Forbes settled in safe and orderly Great Stanmore in Middlesex in 1784. Probably unable to adjust to a life so ordinary, he set about building a temple in his garden in which he kept Hindu sculptures presented to him by Brahmins, 'as a grateful acknowledgement of benevolent attention to their happiness during a long residence among them'.[18] The temple, alas, was dismantled in the early twentieth century.

Thomas Daniell, the famous painter of Indian landscapes and monuments, designed a small, perfectly proportioned temple in Melchet Park, Hampshire, in 1800 for Major Sir John Osborne, who had served in India. It was pulled down in 1850, but in the etchings which survive, holy bulls guard the entrance and statues of various Hindu gods are displayed without reticence. Daniell's creation was a facsimile of an old temple in Bihar, India, except for one quirky addition: the

Melchet version had a carved bust of Hastings rising out of the sacred lotus flower, to become an incarnation of a Hindu deity. It didn't end there. Hastings wrote an ode to the temple and his friend Osborne. It was all very mystical, almost cultish.

William Beckford was another compulsive Orientalist. Slave plantations in the Caribbean had made his family staggeringly rich. He spent, spent, spent, was a dilettante and a culture vulture, but also an Englander in whom multilayered psychodramas were played out. Here he is writing to a friend after a walk in his vast grounds: 'One instant I imagined viewing the marble palaces of Ethiopian princes seated on the green woody margin of lakes studded in sands and wilder-nesses . . . I found myself standing before a thick wood listening to impetuous waterfalls and screened from the ardour of the Sun by its foliage. I was wondering at the Scene when a tall, comely Negro wound around the slopes of the Hills and without moving his lips made me comprehend I was in Africa, on the brink of the Nile.'[19] Beckford was bisexual and, like Lord Byron, unable to find peace. He invited friends to 'enjoy India . . . in Fonthill',[20] to sit with him in the Turkish chambers and other dream rooms. The painter Matisse was shown Japanese décor and an Egyptian labyrinth. They named Beckford the 'Caliph of Fonthill'. Another of his houses in Bath, in Lansdown Crescent, was called 'Baghdad'.[21]

A summerhouse was built in the garden of that residence, 'a somewhat touching memorial to his orientalizing past, the more impressive for being so understated'.[22] Small and square, with an arched doorway, studded door, and a domed roof, it nestles shyly in foliage in a corner. My sister lived in a flat near Lansdown Crescent in the 1980s. Her descent into mental illness started there. She used to go on and on, obsessively at times, about the 'Moorish fairy shed', and I thought she was in one of her unreal reveries. It turns out she was not.

Beckford, the rich misfit, left behind his words, possessions and buildings, but remains elusive.

Elizabeth Barrett Browning's father, Edward Moulton-Barrett (1785–1857), is similarly undecipherable. His family wealth also came from slave plantations. In 1809, he purchased an estate near Ledbury in Herefordshire. Having spent his younger days in Jamaica, this domineering, discombobulated, hard man never fitted into conventional England. Some say Moulton-Barrett commissioned William Wyatt, the architect of Fonthill, to design the mansion, named Hope End.[23] The house is no more, but can be seen in watercolours and engravings by a largely unknown painter, Philip Ballard.

Elizabeth described the 'Turkish house' to her husband, the poet Robert Browning: 'crowded with minarets and domes, and crowned with metal spires and crescents, to the provocation (as people used to observe) to every lightening in heaven'.[24] The main structure, reminiscent of a fortified castle, made the Islamic flourishes appear confrontational, bellicose. Inside there were Chinese and Turkish bedrooms, and the hall reminded Elizabeth's mother of the Arabian Nights.[25] Defying Victorian England can't have been easy, but Moulton-Barrett was not a man who sought or felt ease; he was slightly demented.

AND MAD ROYALS

Some English monarchs, such as Frederick Prince of Wales, the eldest son of George II, were also crazy about the exotic. He died before he got to be king and was succeeded by his son, George III (who was actually certified mad). In 1731, Frederick, feeling purposeless and probably useless, leased Kew Gardens and decided to turn it into a wonderland. He built up a collection of weird, imported plants and, after he died in 1751, his wife Augusta commissioned the architect

William Chambers – a Scotsman born and raised in Sweden – to add oriental built features to the garden. Chambers, well travelled and himself a great admirer of Chinese designs, created a mini-Alhambra, an octagonal mosque and a tall pagoda. 'A View of the Wilderness' (1763), a painting by William Marlow, shows all three in situ. The pagoda still stands, but the Muslim edifices did not survive, not even in the historical imagination.[26] (Spookily, a hundred years later, it was another William Chambers, an Englishman, who designed the mosque in Woking, described in the Introduction.)

Frederick went on to buy Carlton House in central London. In 1783 it passed to his grandson, the Prince Regent, later George IV, an unrestrained Bacchanalian. The designer Walsh Porter was hired to make the house into a temple of ornamentalism. Some commentators, such as the Irish poet Thomas Moore, were deeply unimpressed with the result:

> *That same long Masquerade of rooms,*
> *All trick'd up in such odd costumes*
> *(These, Porter, are thy glorious works!)*
> *You'd swear Egyptians, Moors and Turks,*
> *Bearing Good-taste some deadly malice,*
> *Had clubbed to raise a Pic-Nic palace.*[27]

In 1786, when parliament expressed concern about the money spent on Carlton House, the prince skulked off to Brighton and bought an old farmhouse. The downsizing didn't last. He wanted his own Sezincote, but bigger and bolder. In 1815, John Nash created Brighton Pavilion. Its domes, minarets, filigree insets and scalloped arches, its patterns as delicate as embroidery, are gorgeous. You can almost hear muezzins calling out to Brighton's all-night revellers. Inside you can whizz through China, India, meet Buddha's many avatars, and marvel at the carpets, statues and vases, the most expensive chinoiserie ever seen. It is eccentric, decadent, a 'stylistic phantasmagoria'.[28] The palace was both a projection of and an insurrection against the norms of the British Empire. A friend from Mumbai wondered if the excess, the abandonment of integrating principles, reflected England's inchoate feelings about the East? Maybe.

Let's pass to Elveden Hall, and its poignant story. Five miles from Thetford, on the borders of Suffolk and Norfolk, it is surrounded by thousands of acres of land. We don't know when, exactly, it was built, only that Henry VIII handed it to the Duke of Norfolk and it passed through several proprietors. In the 1860s, MP and sporting squire William Newton sold it to Prince Duleep Singh, born Prince of Punjab, who took a loan from the India Office to buy it.[29]

Singh inherited the throne of the Punjab and the wider Sikh empire as a boy. In 1849, his dominion was swallowed up by expansionist East India Company brigands. The thirteen-year-old heir was separated from his mother and exiled to England. He was held in a prison with invisible walls. In what must have been an agonizing ceremony, Lord Dalhousie and other establishment figures made him hand over his family's Koh-i-Noor diamond to Queen Victoria as a 'gift'.[30] With no regard for his feelings, Duleep was vigorously Anglicized and Christianized. The boy, and later the man, obliged until he could no more. Queen Victoria was fond of her 'favourite Maharajah', with his beautiful eyes and teeth.[31] She embodied the anomalies and contradictions of her nation's relationship with India.

At Elveden Singh appointed an English architect 'to make the main rooms reminiscent of an Indian palace . . . The Shish Mahal (Glass Palace) was the inspiration for the drawing room, with convex slivers of mercurized glass that sparkled in the light embedded in the plasterwork. The main rooms were embellished with elaborate pilasters and arches in the Mughal style; the grand marble staircase was built at a cost of £23 a tread, set with splendid cast-iron banisters painted in sealing-wax red.'[32] The interiors were filled with cashmere wall hangings, silk-covered ottomans and also chesterfields and whatnots.[33]

Neighbouring aristos complained the fine old house had been turned into a blot on their landscape. The 'Black Prince', as Singh was known, tried hard to please them and be true to himself. Normally he dressed as an English gentleman, but for special occasions he dressed up in Punjabi finery and jewels, as in the portrait painted in 1852 by the English artist George Beechey. Till the end, his indigenous self fought the Anglo-Saxon overlay. Though he was banned from reconverting to Sikhism, Singh was defiant: 'We love the English and especially their monarch but we must remain Sikh. I am not English.'[34]

The mansion turned into a graveyard of irrecoverable glory. Singh died in Paris in 1893 and was buried in Elveden's churchyard. Lord Iveagh, inheritor of the Guinness brewery, then bought the house and added a new wing and a magnificent Indian hall.[35] A replica of the Taj Mahal was also made and displayed.[36] Thetford displays a splendid statue of Singh on a horse and has acquired his mother's grave-stone, which was found in the catacombs of Kensal Green Dissenter's Chapel in London, both sincere acts of contrition and maybe deliverance from a shameful historical affair.[37]

CONSTRUCTIONS OF DARING AND LOVE

In Sunderland, in north-east England, stands the Elephant Tea House, paid for by grocer Ronald Grimshaw, and built in 1873 by Frank Caws, a man of strong views and preferences.[38] Elected president of the Northern Architectural Association,

Caws' inaugural speech must have made some bottoms shift uncomfortably: 'Though it is best for every architect to work in the style which is most congenial to him, and in which he is most at home, yet, consciously or not, we are all deeply influenced by one another . . . Thus those associations of men which we distinguish as nations . . . the Egyptian, Assyrian, Greek, Roman, Hindoo, Moorish, Gothic, Chinese, and others, have developed distinctive types of architecture, each possessing strong individuality, as though the product of one mind . . .' In sum, he argued that it was foolish and impossible to preserve 'insularity of thought and feeling'.[39]

The ebullient tea house is a mixture of 'Hindoo-Gothic' and 'Venetian-Gothic', with bits of China and Buddhism dropped in. Made of brick, terracotta and faience, it sports spires, turrets and arches, variously shaped windows, and in some niches, beneath the ogee arches, elephants carrying tea chests look out on the street with their trunks raised in good cheer. It was hugely popular with usually cautious Northerners. Such buildings were not eccentricities, but deep imprints on England, its sons and daughters.

Mr Marshall[40] is a practising Christian. He worked in Syria and then Pakistan, signed the Official Secrets Act. I was invited to his home. The floors were covered with Kashmiri and Persian rugs; the living room had Egyptian lanterns, carved and inlaid furniture from Damascus, wonderful calligraphic paintings. An open Koran stood on a bookstand. Outside, hidden under some trees, he was building a 'mosque-like place for reflection', with a small fountain and Moorish tiles. I asked him why. Because he wants to call his God in their way, to learn Islamic radiance and intensity.

Brigid Keenan (aka Brigid Wadham, who appears earlier in the book) is married to an Englishman, a retired diplomat. Their home, too, is full of lovely things picked up during postings in Arabia and Asia. When they were sent to Damascus, she felt lost and alienated in their grand diplomatic residence. 'So I went around the old city and found this house, in a terrible state but I had to have it. My Syrian architect friend Naim and I restored it. That is where I was meant to be. Every morning we would be woken up by the haunting chorus of the dawn call to prayer from the Great Mosque. Later I would walk a few yards up the road from my front door, carrying our own plates to be filled with hummus and *fuls* (pickles) for breakfast and on the way back I'd buy bread, still untouchably hot from the oven.'[41] Syria lives on in her English head and heart, the Syria that is now devastated by civil war. As I left she said, 'There are many such stories of happy integration. I wish people knew them.'

Internal Extravagances

DREAM ROOMS

Badminton House in Chipping Sodbury, Gloucestershire, has been the seat and stately pile of successive Dukes of Beaufort since the late seventeenth century. It smells of old money, tradition and unbroken privilege. But back in the eighteenth century, it was infamous for a weirdly wonderful Chinese bedroom. The bed was beech, japanned in red, yellow, blue and gold, overhung by a pagoda canopy. Chinoiserie, silks and Chinese patterns added authenticity. The mirror frame above the bed was alive with flurrying, flying golden creatures, and a Chinaman sat at the top looking down, watching couples in congress or slumbering. It was all too, too much for some who stayed there. A visitor named Mrs Elizabeth Montague, a society hostess of severely conservative taste, was aghast. She penned a note in 1749: 'Thus it is happened . . . we must all seek the barbarous, gaudy goût of the Chinese; and fat headed Pagods and shaking Mandarins . . . Apollo and Venus must give way to the fat idol with a sconce on his head.'[42] Others felt the same way.

Extraordinarily – or perhaps not – many of the finest items were made by John and William Linnell, craftsmen of good English stock. As was the famous Thomas Chippendale, who used Chinese and Japanese techniques to make elaborately fashioned furniture known as 'Chinese Chippendale'. Oriental furniture made by these supreme craftsmen has pride of place in the palaces and stately homes of England.

Indian and Islamic elegance too insinuated itself into unusual places. There was a vogue for Arab billiard and smoking chambers in the 1880s; one of the most stunning examples was in staid St Albans, Hertfordshire. It had a carved and inlaid table, a magnificent ceiling, cushioned sofas in alcoves, and the light filtered softly through filigreed windows. A similar decorative billiard room was made in the home of the Duke of Connaught, Queen Victoria's son. Such decadent, faux-Ottoman pleasure dens must have been filled with smoke, deals, plots and, probably, sexual banter – an extension of old English clubs and smoking rooms.

Lockwood Kipling, the father of Rudyard, epitomized how East and West did meet, often. Born in 1837 in Pickering, Yorkshire, he was a craftsman and artist[43] who was appointed Professor of Architectural Sculpture at an art college in India in 1865. Five years later, he became principal of the prestigious Mayo School of Arts in Lahore, now in Pakistan.[44]

Bhai Ram Singh, a talented young carver, turned up at the Mayo School and was soon appointed head of carpentry and cabinet work. In 1883, the Duke of Connaught asked Kipling and the young Indian to add interest to Bagshot Park, his manor house in Surrey.[45] Fireplaces, cornices, even skirting boards were carved with Indian patterns, the place was zinged up. Upon seeing Ram Singh's work, Queen Victoria decided she wanted an Indian room of her own, a durbar hall, in Osborne House on the Isle of Wight. The queen often escaped to Osborne, away from state duties. With her went Albert and, in widowhood, her lover John Brown, and later Abdul Karim, her Muslim servant turned 'good friend'. Portraits of Karim and the dispossessed Prince Duleep Singh were hung on the walls. A photograph taken of Ram Singh at work in Osborne house shows a turbaned man with a fertile black beard. He looks confident, centred. The gorgeous hall took three years to complete. Hardly anyone in England or India knows of this designer of genius.

By the late nineteenth century South Asian and also Turkish and Arabian carvers and artists were regularly brought in to add splendour to big houses. Two Indian Muslims, Mohammed Baksh and Mohammed Juma, humble men, attracted high praise from high society and were sought after by big spenders.[46] At times these gifted craftsmen, so praised and in such demand, must have forgotten while they were in England that they were not free men but unwilling subjects of the Empire.

Vainglorious Britons possessed the East then, but were possessed by it too. The Foreign and Commonwealth Office, the epicentre of the Empire, had its own Indian hall of pomp and ceremony, financed by colonial subjects. The Durbar Court is still impressive. The ceiling features Islamic geometric shapes; the arches, scale and élan are intoxicating. Other oriental rooms to marvel at are in India House on Aldwych, now the Indian High Commission. Designed by the architect Sir Herbert Baker, it was inaugurated in 1930 by King George V. Baker had previously worked with Edwin Lutyens, the master designer of imperial Delhi.[47] A critic in the *Observer* thought it was intolerable that such a building was permitted on a prime London site, and intensely disliked the mixing of the occidental with the oriental, 'like oil and water', he said.[48] But it did work: the synthesis was beautifully achieved. The central dome inside was painted by various Indian artists and craftsmen. Hindu myths and tales, erotic figures, Mughal scenes in full colour, as dazzling as any you would find in the palaces of Rajasthan, look down and defy proponents of cultural segregation.

Eastern techniques, proportions and shapes destabilized English belief systems and claims of supremacy and, confusingly, at times reaffirmed those beliefs through appropriation.

BATHS

Moving from the elevated to the intimate, to baths. A cleansed body before prayer is a religious obligation in both Islam and Hinduism, and in Turkey and Arabia baths have, over many centuries, been places to meet, get a deep cleanse and relax. The Romans had brought baths to Britain, but the habit hadn't spread, not even among the wealthier classes. That changed after the sixteenth century, when Englishmen and women began to travel to the East.

The Turkish public bath arrived in England in the middle of the nineteenth century and became popular among all sections of the population. In 1861, Thomas Wakely, the founder and editor of the *Lancet*, noted that the Turkish bath had also 'attracted considerable attention in the medical profession'.[49]

One of the finest Victorian Turkish baths can be seen in Harrogate in Yorkshire. 'The Bath's Moorish design with great vaults and arches soar to a high arabesque ceiling ornately decorated with colourful stencilled design. The walls are expertly rendered, vibrant glazed brickwork, while underfoot the picture is completed with elaborately assembled mosaic and marble terrazzo floors, all adding to historic fantasy qualities. For the interior fittings, Victorian dark wood blends with Islamic design in a beautiful embodiment of Orientalist fusion.'[50]

In 1850, the Scottish diplomat David Urquhart wrote a book on the healing, beautifying and sensual effects of Ottoman baths: 'the body has come forth shining like alabaster, fragrant as cistus, sleek as satin and soft as velvet . . . there is a sense of life and consciousness that spreads through every member . . . you condense the pleasures of many senses, the existence of years.'[51] Reading Urquhart's book changed the life of Charles Bartholomew, an Englishman who suffered from gout. He went for 'bath therapy' and allegedly was cured. In 1859, the convert proceeded to build a string of Ottoman baths in the seven major cities of England, from Bristol to Manchester. By 1861, the trade journal *The Builder* confirmed that Turkish baths 'are now springing up everywhere'.[52]

And that led to a new demand for lovely bath products. Among the most coveted was Hammam Bouquet, a best-selling perfume for men and women created by William Penhaligon in 1872, described as 'animalic and golden . . . redolent of old books, powdered resins, and ancient rooms. At its heart was the dusky Turkish rose, Jasmine wood, musk and powdery orris.' It proved a hit with respectable gentlemen. 'The seductive and musky fragrance intoxicated the senses with fantasies built on the romances of the Empire, of naked sultans in steamy baths, of harems and boudoirs which reeked of sex.'[53] Yes, it was, in part, that salacious Orientalism despised by Edward Said. But it also showed England under the influence of the East, submitting to its cultural power.

The most upmarket and seductive Turkish bath, in Jermyn Street in London, opened at the start of the twentieth century. In the 1950s, the American journalist A. J. Langguth saw with his own eyes 'men who came to sweat poisons from their system and youths who came to strike beguiling poses in Turkish towels . . . they provided a discreet place to inspect a young man before a cup of tea at Lyons.'[54] Some years on, the gay comedian Kenneth Williams confessed he frequented gay Turkish baths and thought they were fabulous.[55]

Dream Gardens

For 200 years there was an extensive park on the south bank of the Thames where crowds went to frolic, eat, drink, pick up whores, meet secret lovers, listen to music, gamble, gambol, dance and watch entertainment. The Vauxhall Pleasure Gardens were opened in 1661, just after the Restoration, and finally closed down in 1859. One of the buildings looked like a Turkish tent; Chinese temples and chinoiserie graced quiet parts, men and women dressed like pashas and Scheherazades after sunset.[56] The grounds were 'splendidly illuminated at night with about 15,000 glass lamps, these being tastefully hung among the trees which line the walks, which produce an impression similar to that which is called up on reading some of the stories of the *Arabian Nights' Entertainments*'.[57]

From the mid-seventeenth century Englanders (like other Europeans and Americans) were curious about tranquil, spiritual Japanese gardens, which they had heard of but never seen. Japan was closed off from the world – mysterious and inaccessible. When the country finally opened its borders in 1845, there was a plant rush, as frenzied as the gold rushes. Intrepid nursery owners brought over trees, seeds, cuttings, instructions. Without such people we would not have the gorgeous Japanese maple or wisteria, common in China, Korea and Japan.[58]

And we would have no Kew gardens, with its glass-houses of orchids and palm trees, and unabashed arboreal internationalism, initiated by Frederick Prince of Wales. The engraver George Vertue (1684–1756), when in Kew in 1750, recorded that Frederick 'was directing the plantations of trees [and] exotics with the workmen – advising and assisting . . . for three or four hours'.[59]

The eccentric Victorian lawyer Sir Frank Crisp (1843–1919) owned Friar Park, a neo-Gothic manor near Henley-on-Thames. In the grounds a medley of plants from around the world were cultivated, including a delicate Japanese garden. A Japanese visitor humbly complimented the owner: 'How beautiful – we have nothing like this in Japan.'[60] George Harrison, of the Beatles, bought Friar Park and lived there till he died. Harrison's friend Ravi Shankar, the virtuoso Indian sitar-player, loved the Eastern gardens of paradise cultivated and rooted in English soil.

In 1910, for a major bilateral British–Japanese exhibition, an authentic Japanese garden was created in White City, a fairly soulless area of London. 'The British public came, gazed, marvelled, and all round the country a flurry of azaleas, maples, bamboos and even tea houses appeared in suburban gardens.'[61] In the same year, Gunnersbury Park in West London opened a Japanese garden which the *Journal of Horticulture* declared 'the most strictly true and magnificent garden of Japanese design and composition to be found anywhere in the kingdom'.[62] It eventually died but in 2002 was restored after a touching ceremony of prayers and revival led by a Japanese priest. A similar garden, complete with a Shinto shrine, was made in Cheshire between 1910 and 1913 by invited Japanese gardeners.[63] It, too, was restored in 2002, with advice from the Osaka University of Art.

By the end of the eighteenth century, possibly earlier, homes and parks started to install glass-houses, conservatories and pavilions. The horticulturalist John Claudius Loudon published blueprints for glass-houses with ogee domes copying Mughal designs. By 1864 they had become 'an integral part of living'.[64]

Love of oriental plants, shapes and designs remains strong in England. Towards the end of the 1990s, in multiracial Leeds, the council funded an 'Alhambra garden', which replicated the most beautiful aspects of the original in Granada in Spain.

In the same decade, Prince Charles backed a new school for Islamic arts. Since 2005, the Prince's School of Traditional Arts has been run by a respected Arab architect, Dr Khaled Omar Azzam. The students are trained to produce old Islamic visual formations, sounds and colours, most of all gardens and courtyards. Now, similar schools are being set up in Egypt and the United Arab Emirates. With a charming rotation of history, England sells Arab beauty back to Arabia.

In May 2001, the prince won a medal at the Chelsea Flower Show for what was called his 'Carpet Garden'. The garden specialist Mike Miller assiduously followed the patterns of old Turkish carpets and recreated the secluded courtyards one glimpses in Marrakesh and Damascus. The garden is now established at the prince's residence, Highgrove, settled in.

Exhibitions and Exhibitionists; Design and Designers

The India House Museum in Leadenhall Street, London, was once the place to go. It was established in 1647 and by 1729, vast amounts of money were spent to turn what was a nondescript building into a grand mansion. This was further extended as the years went by. Huge crowds visited this cave of treasures, badly set up and claustrophobic though it was. The Victorians were particularly fascinated by the building and the objects it displayed, a visual reminder of British trade and territorial annexations. Warren Hastings, one of the founders, hoped it would expand British minds. However, as one acerbic modern writer notes: 'The story of the British Empire is a story of shrinking minds.'[65] After the Indian Uprising of 1857, that shrinking quickened. Thereafter, for most Britons India was a savage place which needed taming, though there were, as always, exceptions, individuals whose imaginations could not be tightened or restrained.

Insiders and outsiders with heads full of fancies seem to find themselves in England. Thomas Hope was born into an old Scots family of merchant bankers based in the Netherlands. In 1794, he migrated to England and bought a mansion in Duchess Street, London. Feeling liberated, Hope commissioned Thomas Daniell to paint him a picture of a mosque in 'Hindustan'. From that grew an obsession – his home was to be turned into a dazzling oriental fantasy.

One ceiling, in Hope's own words, 'imitated from those prevailing in Turkish palaces, consists of a canopy of trellice-work . . . [it displays] foliage, flowers, peacock feathers and other ornaments of rich hue and of a delicate texture'.[66] The journalist James Fenton conveys the scale and ambitions of Hope's make-over: 'One has to imagine something on the scale of the Wallace Collection in Manchester Square in London, a house built around a courtyard and incorporating a palatial display of rooms . . . in addition to the Egyptian and Indian rooms, an Aurora room and a "Lararium" (a shrine for the household gods).'[67] Opened to the public in 1804, Hope House provided a virtual Grand Tour for aspirational middle classes. In his country retreat in Deepdene, Surrey, the irrepressible Hope carried on his love affair with Eastern ideas and imports.[68]

In 1815, enthused by Hope, William Bullock, another multimillionaire, decided he too wanted a notable establishment for his collection of curiosities, brought by Captain Cook from the South Seas. He had a museum built in Piccadilly with an extravagant Egyptian façade. Londoners must have looked up at it – with its Pharonic pillars and two replica statues it was as unreal as a film set – and wondered about Bullock's sanity. Over the years, the Egyptian Hall diversified, introduced magic shows, spiritualist evenings and more bizarre events, and became known as England's Home of Mystery. It was enormously popular and successful throughout the nineteenth century, but by 1910, the building was seen as an architectural disfigurement and was demolished.[69]

Orientalist ventures seemed to succeed initially and then fade into obscurity. On one antiques website I found an engraved print of a Turkish dinner party in Hyde Park: a group of wise-looking, hirsute, gowned and turbaned men of a certain age sit on a crumpled carpet around a low table, eating with their hands.[70] Another print was of a much-used four-poster bed, with cheerful harem women hovering around it.[71] These images capture what the public saw at the Turkish and Oriental Museum, which opened on Hyde Park Corner in 1854, to fabulous reviews: Ottoman-style rooms, real Turks in silk and satin, baths, coffee shops, life-sized wax figures of concubines, sultans and janissaries, weapons, shishas and other objects of desire brought Turkey to life as never before. The *Daily News* found the exhibition 'as instructive as it is interesting'.[72] *Lloyd's Weekly* was ecstatic (and tactless): 'Knightsbridge could not go to Mohamet, so Mohamet has obligingly come to Knightsbridge; and what's a thousand times better, he has brought Mrs Mohamet and all the little Mohamets with them.'[73] However, interest in the Ottoman theme park waned after a few years and the whole enterprise was wiped from national memory.

In 1854, a Royal Panopticon was built and opened in Leicester Square, with the aim of promoting discoveries and interest in science, manufacturing and arts. The man who pushed through this plan was Edward Marmaduke Clarke, an unorthodox Irishman. A council was appointed to oversee the project. The members, most of them Englishmen, were persuaded by Clarke to choose a

Saracenic exterior and interior. The architect, Thomas Hayter Lewis, after some hesitation, agreed to the idea. In later life he became an aficionado of Islamic style.[74] Sketches were published in the *Illustrated London News* and *The Builder*. Reactions were mixed. Sophisticated experts thought the building would be 'more out of tune with its sober Georgian neighbours than the Egyptian Hall in Piccadilly', yet would be 'an enchanting palace in a city of sternest realities'.[75] It was built with a giant rotunda, two flanking minarets, crested ironwork and cusped arches. The inside was stupendous. Modelled on Cairo mosques, it shone with shimmering glass mosaics, was painted in deep, rich colours, lit with lanterns and skylights, and had a softly burbling central fountain.[76]

But though the aspirations were noble, the centre did not thrive and in 1858, the Panopticon was turned into the Alhambra Theatre for ballet, music-hall entertainment and even circuses. In 1936 the management of Odeon cinemas took it over, and unceremoniously bulldozed it. Another theatre of the same name and style was built in Bradford in 1914 and is still going.

THE GREAT EXHIBITION AND THE V&A

The Great Exhibition of 1851 was hubristic and chauvinistic, yet also visionary, politically charged and interrogative. John Cassell, in his phenomenal guide to the show, had this to say about India: 'the brightest jewel in Victoria's crown; India the fervid, dreamy country of the rising sun . . . We gaze at the myriad objects, rare and beautiful which [India] contributes, and our thoughts wander back to the days when she was free and powerful'.[77] That last sentence must have ruffled feathers and furs.

A lot of white visitors were disdainful of and nosy about foreigners. Turks in goatees and 'dark Bedouins in their bedclothes' caused some consternation and much titillation but there were also countless instances and responses of utter delight and genuine respect. In a modernist move, the Turkish, Egyptian and Tunisian sections were handed to creative artists and curators of those back-grounds, so they could promote their countries and histories with pride and without prejudice. There was something for everyone – the bigot, the egalitarian, the cynic and the infinitely curious.

On the first day, over 25,000 people crowded into the Crystal Palace in Hyde Park. By the time the exhibition closed, six million had been around the sparkling, pulsating palace. The 'gorgeous manufactures of India' produced the greatest sensation – howdahs, hookahs, shawls, carpets, arms and jewels made visitors stop and wonder.[78] Six years later came the Indian Uprising and the British public became disenchanted with their 'jewel'.

One of the legacies of the Great Exhibition was the Victoria and Albert Museum (the V&A) in Kensington, a repository of global decorative arts, relics and artefacts. Since 1857, it has displayed, with intelligence and intimate knowl-edge, beguiling items from Europe and the non-European worlds.

In July 2006, a few years after the al-Qaeda attacks of 9/11 in the US, the Jameel Gallery of Islamic Art was opened at the V&A. Funded by a Saudi multi-millionaire, the gallery was one of the many triumphs of senior curator Tim Stanley. He understood its political as well as its artistic significance: 'It is very important that at the moment people get a balanced view of the great Islamic civi-lizations, which were once self-confident and open to the world.'[79] Enchanted by the Middle East and its stories as a boy, Stanley went on to study the languages, literature and arts of the Islamic empires and nations. Whenever I've met him, I have come away uplifted by his fervour and knowledge. In the Jameel Gallery he showed me oil paintings from Iran, an Iznik tile-work chimney from Turkey, an

Egyptian wood-and-ivory minibar, Saracenic inlaid metalwork, and the wondrous
Persian Ardibil carpet.

This sixteenth-century carpet, measuring 11 by 5.5 metres, is made of wool and
silk and now lies under protective glass in gentle lighting. To William Morris, the
creation was 'of singular perfection; defensible on all points, logically and consis-
tently beautiful'.[80] Morris was a Victorian textile designer, artist, Socialist and
Pre-Raphaelite painter; in his work his different selves were woven together
harmoniously, as were multiple traditions and histories, especially English
medievalism and Orientalism, the former part of his heritage, the latter learnt and
acquired. He once confessed: 'To us pattern designers Persia has become a holy
land . . .'[81] He had only oriental rugs on the floors of his homes and often castigated
his country and its capitalist system for its destructive impact on the inherited
crafts of artisans of the East. Imperialist compatriots must have found Morris's
theories and allegiances objectionable. By this time the East had become, for
many, the barbaric antithesis of unsurpassable and unbeatable England.

LEIGHTON HOUSE

In Leighton House in Holland Park, London, there is no discord between England
and Islamic civilizations and instead, spirits of both light each other. Venetian and
Sicilian flourishes add European splendour. All the elements are harmonized as in
an integrated, visual symphony. The home of the Victorian English painter and
sculptor Lord Frederic Leighton, it is now a museum. Designed by the English
architect George Aitchison, it was built in phases between 1869 and 1881.
Aitchison was a man of soaring ideas. He yearned 'to see London, and all the great
manufacturing towns, changed from dismal cities to those in which every building
is full of colour and artistic composition, made lovely by light and delicate or

deeply coloured harmonies or resplendent with gilt, bronze, polished granite, porphyry and glass mosaic.'[82]

Leighton's vision came from his travels: 'Algiers made a deep impression on me. I have loved "The East" as it is called ever since.'[83] In Egypt he met (and later painted) the notorious polymath and sexual buccaneer Sir Richard Burton. It was a useful contact.

Burton later removed tiles from a Muslim tomb in India and sent them to Leighton to reuse on the house. In Syria, Leighton himself obsessively searched for 'oriental draperies . . . tiles, long necked jars with blue ground and white flowers'.[84] He somehow acquired fifteenth-century tiles and had even earlier samples brought over from Persia. (Such men marvelled at the Orient but freely violated it too.) It was all for his breath-taking Arab Hall, in the centre of which was a fountain made to remind him of the unceasing songs of bubbling fountains in Damascus.

The paintings on the walls depict English landscapes, Arab streets and homes, classical and Biblical subjects, Persian, Arab and European faces. Leighton, like his friend William Morris, looked outward and deep into his English cultural history. Over the entrance, an intricate, 5-metre panel of tiles (also sent by Burton) carries this verse from the Koran in calligraphic script:

> *In the name of the merciful and long-suffering God*
> *The Merciful hath taught the Koran,*
> *He hath created man and taught him speech.*
> *He hath set the sun and the moon in a certain course,*
> *Both the grass and the trees are subject to him.*[85]

Violet Paget, the Victorian author who wrote supernatural fiction and books on the Renaissance under the pseudonym Vernon Lee, thought Leighton House was 'quite the 8th wonder of the world'.[86]

Following Leighton's death in 1896, his plates from Iznik, Turkish and Persian prayer mats and cloths, Anatolian and Persian pottery, Chinese porcelain, oriental costumes, Japanese vases, screens and mandolins, and the rest of his vast collection were valued, sold and scattered. But the house remains. There would never be another such creation, nor a lord like Leighton ever again.

Mosques and Temples

The Woking mosque, inspiration for this book, in Surrey, the first to be built on English soil, means little to the mostly English inhabitants of the town and county. Most modern British Muslims, too, are uninterested in how and why the mosque came to be built, in 1889, at a time of colonial exploitation and racism.

Architect Shahed Saleem explains the significance of this place of worship then: 'The Shah Jahan mosque almost perfectly captures the spirit of late-nineteenth century Orientalism . . . it was a time when, for curious Europeans, there was a mysterious and fantastical place, "the East". It was a place of strange customs, flamboyant dress and exotic women. It sits alongside similar examples such as the Brighton Pavilion, 1825, and Leighton House, 1864, both examples of exotic flamboyance.' Importantly, they also represented 'the very real culture transfer that was taking place . . . between Victorian England and the Middle East and India'.[87] His observations are astute though will not be appreciated by neo-crusaders.

The next purpose-built mosque to grace England was in Southfields, London.

Constructed in 1925, Fazl, as it is known, belongs to the Ahmadiya community, a reformist Islamic sect which seceded from mainstream Islam during the Raj. Its followers are considered blasphemers by conservative Muslims. To escape perse- cution, Ahmadis, many of them highly educated professionals, moved to England in the early part of the twentieth century and felt secure enough to have a striking prayer house built in suburban England. Even today, such a mosque would be razed in Pakistan or Saudi Arabia. Hundreds of Ahmadis are routinely maimed or killed across the Muslim lands, but in England they are free to live and pray in peace.

Thomas H. Mawson, the architect-builder, was again of good, indigenous English stock. Fazl mosque is pristine white, with a discreet dome which seems not to raise its head too high above the parapets. The base is square and suggestive of art deco, though the overall impression is of purity, otherworldliness and spiritu- ality. Pathé News covered the opening with some ebullience, welcoming the mosque on a site where Celts, Romans and Saxons had left their mark. In 2003, using private donations, the Ahmadiya community built another mosque in Morden, outer London, the biggest in Europe.

Though not a mosque or temple, the numinous Chattri memorial near Brighton also represents a profound bi-national connection. The Chattri (meaning umbrella) remembers the 800,000 Indian soldiers who fought in the First World War. E. C. Henriques, a young Indian architect living in London, produced the plans with guidance from Sir Samuel Swinton Jacob, famous for making magnifi- cent palaces and mansions in India. The cream-coloured monument has pillars and a dome, and is mounted on a carved platform. It is a circle of serenity and grav- itas. The inscription to the loyal soldiers reads: 'With grateful admiration and brotherly affection', and Edward, Prince of Wales, gave a stirring speech after the unveiling in 1921. British Asians visit the site to affirm links between British and Indian histories and claim their ancestral place on English soil.[88]

The London Central Mosque in Regent's Park tells, perhaps, the most surprising story. Most Britons think it is a Saudi folly imposed on London, but the designer was a Coventry-born Englishman, Sir Frederick Gibberd (1908–84), and the land was paid for by Winston Churchill and his wartime government. Previous attempts to build a mosque in London had failed, but in 1940, Lord Lloyd took up the cause: 'It was pointed out inter alia, not only that London contains more than any other European capital, but that in an empire which contains more Moslems than Christians it was anomalous and inappropriate that there should be no central place of worship for Mussulmans. The gift, moreover, of a site for a mosque would serve as a tribute to the loyalty of the Moslems of the Empire and would have a good effect on Arab countries of the Middle East.'[89]

After the war, oil-wealthy Arab leaders provided substantial funds for the prestigious project and in 1970, following an open competition, the job went to Gibberd, architect of Heathrow Airport. Gibberd spent many long hours studying Islam and Islamic architecture. There is some unintentional symmetry in the fact that the mosque is close to the Nash terraces – Nash, after all, dreamt up the Brighton Pavilion. The young Muslim men who bombed London in 2005 must have been to this beautiful mosque. I wonder if they knew that it only came to be built because England blessed the plans and gifted the plot to Muslims.

The Aga Khan, leader of my Shia Muslim community, is a connoisseur and funder of Islamic architecture, old and new, around the world. He obtained permission to build a mosque and cultural centre in South Kensington, close to the vast Victorian museums. Top architects and designers were brought in and they produced a tactful and understated edifice with strong lines and definitely no domes. Inside it is all geometric shapes, fountains and filigree lamps. Previously a consortium, named after Shakespeare, had plans to build a national theatre on the land. It was not to be. What is more, Nicholas Soames laid the foundation stone for the mosque in 1979 – the same Tory Lord Soames who is volubly against immigration – and the centre was inaugurated in 1984 by Margaret Thatcher; yes, she who had complained on TV in 1978 that England was 'rather swamped by people with a different culture'.[90] I can't explain why these top English Tories welcomed the Islamic hub in the heart of London, but they did. Up on the roof is a tranquil garden, the sort you might find in Iran, Syria or Iraq. From there you can see the Natural History Museum and the V&A and other symbols of a time when Britain ruled the waves. My mosque joins the skyline and the story.

In 2011, plans to open an Islamic centre in east London were greeted with a furore that bordered on hysteria. Ali Mangera, a young, idealistic architect working on the project, talked to architecture correspondent Jonathan Glancey, who was moved by the drawings and saddened by the hostility: 'To Victorian revellers, artists, diplomats and academics who first encountered Islamic buildings – the Alhambra in Spain, the Taj Mahal, the mighty domed mosques of Istanbul – the architecture and the culture which inspired it seemed little less than divine. Today the relationship between Western and Eastern culture is much more fraught.'[91] On the Muslim side too there is little understanding of why their faith now elicits fear among Englanders rather than respect. As I write this, Mangera's building remains unmade.[92] Maybe it's just as well.

Temples came much later to England than mosques. The Sikh Guru Nanak Gurdwara in Birmingham was originally a chapel, which was purchased in the 1960s. As the number of worshippers grew the chapel could not accommodate them. So on the site a proper, Punjabi gurdwara was constructed, the largest in

Europe. As always, the place of worship became a statement of settlement and commitment. In 2003 another vast gurdwara was built in Southall, west London, an area inhabited by large numbers of Sikh migrants since the 1950s and now their descendants. Both structures are loud, garish and as cheerful as a bhangra dance; they look as if they've have just skipped over from India.

Truth to tell, no mosque or gurdwara has ever matched the arresting Neasden Hindu Temple (BAPS Shri Swaminarayan Mandir) inaugurated in 1995. It transformed a grey suburb into a place fit for the gods. Made of marble and granite by superb skilled artisans brought over from India, the temple is a masterpiece, sublimely beautiful, a bouquet for the world's most diverse and exciting city. The capital and the nation fell in love with it. The Edinburgh Mosque has been similarly embraced, which shows that modern Scots too can be open to the East.

In England these passions go back a long way, but it would be a mistake to assume such inclusive tendencies will continue into the future. Today, when more overt, everyday racism against Muslims swills around, and multiculturalism is fiercely opposed, English acceptance of Eastern iconography is limited to certain individuals and particular political and cultural cliques. Architecture can either affirm or divert the beliefs and stories of a people and a land.

A Suitable Architect for India

This all too brief section considers the English influence on India's landscapes and skylines. Brian Sewell, the brainy, upper-class and emphatically English art critic, doesn't care for architectural migration of any sort and, when I met him, said so with his trademark impatience: 'The landscape peppered with Gothic spires in India seems to me ridiculous. Why don't people learn anything? It is so destructive to have done that . . . We did it first and set the bad example. I mean, it's like peppering the English skyline with minarets.'[93] I can't agree with that, obviously.

Surat, a port city in Gujarat with origins going back to ancient times, has a multilayered history and diverse population. Various Indians fought battles and signed treaties, outsiders showed up for this reason or that. Baghdadi Jews, persecuted Armenians, Mughals, the Portuguese, Dutch and finally the British settled or staked claims. In 1608 the East India Company docked its ships there and within four years had built its first factory and trading post. Surat's graveyards keep their stories and secrets.

I was taken by a local enthusiast to the English cemetery. We walked along a small lane into the overgrown garden and came upon some enormous mausoleums, a number of them nearly 15 metres high. Under the biggest and most overbearing lie the bones of Sir George and Sir Christopher Oxenden (who died in 1659 and 1669 respectively). With domes, peaks, arches and pillars the tomb tries to recreate a little of the sumptuousness of the Taj. Other monuments to the dead copy Hindu and Islamic forms, but not after the 1857 Uprising, from what I observed. An inscription for Mistress Mary Price, wife of William Andrew, the local governor who died in 1774, read: 'A spotted veil of smallpox rendered a pure and unspotted soul to God.'[94] Several memorial stones are now in poor condition, but this burial ground will, one hopes, always be there – elegiac, elaborate, sepulchral remains of times past and lingering links.

Lord Cornwallis, the expansionist English commander who defeated Tipu Sultan in 1792, is buried in Ghazipur, Uttar Pradesh. He died of a fever a few months after being reappointed Governor-General of India in 1805. His tomb overlooks the Ganges and is circular, with pillars holding up a dome – like the

Chattri memorial on the South Downs, only bigger. Candles are lit and placed there by locals and visitors. Tourist brochures proclaim it as a precious heritage site.

Imperial neo-Gothic piles, as overweening and splendacious as St Pancras station in London, can be seen all round the subcontinent, statements of British dominance. The statues of British generals, colonels and viceroys have a message in stone for natives: 'Never forget we were here.' And they don't forget.

New Delhi was the axis of power during the Raj and insignia of hubris. Sunil Khilnani, Professor of Politics at King's College, London, explains why the old Mughal city was not only possessed but remade: '[Delhi] was the summation of British efforts to hoist the imperial pennant on Indian territory. The coastal presidency cities of Calcutta, Bombay and Madras had not been built by a single driving vision: their fitful styles – Classical, Indo-Saracenic, Gothic – reflected wavering ideological and aesthetic intentions. New Delhi was a pristine thing . . . Durbar city could be engraved permanently into the rocky Indian landscape.' It had to acknowledge past empires and surpass them by illustrating a 'rational modernity', the primacy of Western science and art.[95]

The English architects Edwin Lutyens (1869–1944) and the lesser-known Herbert Baker (1862–1946) were called upon to design the grand imperial city. They delivered geometric grids, with homes for officers of the Raj precisely graded by class, brassy gates and monuments, administrative buildings and ostentatious palaces for viceroys and other VIPs. The glories of the old city became backwaters. New Delhi's buildings were handsome and well proportioned, attractive and confident. If Martians took away Lutyens' Delhi, the city and its people would feel bereft, robbed.

William Emerson (1843–1924), son of a silk manufacturer in Whitechapel, designed Calcutta's awe-inspiring Victoria Memorial in a meadow – impressive and lovely, but too big, in my view, too forward. It was opened in 1921. Calcuttans think of it as a magnificent landmark and go there to rest or play cards and cricket, while lovers cavort in the grounds. Emerson's All Saints Cathedral in Allahabad is also invasive and brash. The same architect dreamt up the Gothic Crawford Market in Bombay, which has lost many of its original features but not its charm. The market was made for ordinary Bombayites to use and treasure. Lockwood Kipling made the central fountain, which now looks neglected and tired.

In *Colonial Modernities: Building, Dwelling and Architecture in British India*, a fine collection of essays, the editors agree that: 'Along with the English language, and the colonial legal and administrative institutions . . . the buildings of British India and Ceylon were arguably among the most tangible and enduring legacies of the European colonization of South Asia.'[96]

Raj Kumar, an expert on art and architecture, deprecates the stagnation that followed independence: 'After the British left India in 1947, Indian architecture fell into an abyss . . . perhaps there was an identity crisis whether to bask in the glory of the past or move forward with the times using new ideas, images and techniques . . . the fact remains that contemporary architecture in India has failed to inspire even fifty years after independence. Our cities are still symbolized by pre-independence buildings. For instance, Calcutta is symbolized by the Victoria Memorial, Delhi by the Rashtrapati Bhavan [previously the Viceroy's Palace], Mumbai by the Victoria Terminus and Gateway to India, Chennai by the Victoria Memorial Hall.' Unlike in art or music, Kumar says, Indians produced no 'transformative architecture'.[97] He hopes salvation from mediocrity will come with an emerging generation of architects who brilliantly merge styles – Roman, Gothic, Rajasthani, and Mughal.

In the heyday of Empire, perhaps surprisingly, perhaps not, Indian monarchs sought out English architects. Tastes synthesized and a hybrid style emerged. According to Professor Cannadine, an expert on Empire and opulence: 'in its exuberant asymmetries and its aura of instant antiquity, [it] was very much the spirit and values of the Gothic Revival transported to India. Just as the maharajahs' palaces were orientalized versions of Eaton Hall or Cardiff or Arundel or Windsor Castles, so the Victoria Terminus at Bombay, the High Court at Hyderabad and the University at Madras were extravagant extensions or reworkings of similar buildings in London.'[98]

Class comradeship concealed tensions and the truth that many of the Indian kings and princes were deeply conflicted. Those deemed 'good' by the British received increased incomes from the Raj, while others kept wealth by not making trouble and by flattering emulation.

The British thought Mysore a well-run kingdom, so the royals had plenty of money to spend. Lalitha Mahal, one of their many palaces, strove to imitate St Paul's Cathedral. It is brilliant white, columned and domed (but this time the dome imitating England rather than the other way round), with bits of Italian palazzo style thrown in. Replicas of furniture from English manor houses and palaces were sought out and bought for a magnificent Viceroy Room good enough to receive the king's masters. Anglophile Muslim nawabs in Lucknow similarly filled their palaces with furniture, tableware, decanters (the wine was French) and other paraphernalia they thought was nobly English. Apparently venison and cherry brandy went down very well.[99]

English architects relished having freedom from strict classical principles. In

1890, Major Charles Mant created the Laxmi Vilas Palace in Baroda, four times the size of Buckingham Palace. The exuberant architect died before the palace was completed and the project was taken over by another Englishman, Robert Fellowes Chisholm,[100] while the grounds were landscaped by William Goldring of Kew Gardens, also English. Chisholm fashioned an august Indo-Saracenic Senate House for Madras University and a general post office borrowing freely from Hindu design. The most famous of the cohort was Sir Samuel Swinton Jacob, an English engineer who was consultant for the Chattri memorial near Brighton. In Jaipur, Indians revere Sir Jacob, the master builder, who designed the fabulous Albert Hall Museum in their pink city and, even more importantly, wrote *The Jeypore Portfolio of Architectural Details*, in twelve volumes, setting out 'new' forms and recording old Indian decorative arts and crafts. Like Lockwood Kipling, and William Morris in England, Jacob appreciated and feared for old traditions and wanted them preserved and enhanced.[101] Jacob's palaces are as majestic as all palaces must be. But the colleges he designed in Lucknow, Delhi and Indore are, in some ways, dreamier and more memorable.

Other Colonized Lands

In the Middle East the colonial encounter was long, deep, ambiguous and made as big an impact as in India, but very few architectural footprints remain of that past. Author Mark Crinson observes: 'Only a few buildings are Orientalist in appearance; many, indeed, seem to turn their faces firmly away from any visual affiliation with the Orient, though this in itself may embody their particular position on Orientalism.'[102] That may be true, but there were plenty of Englishmen and women who did turn their faces to the Near East. And some were architects and designers.

James Wild (1814–92), son of water-colourist Charles Wild, was the most conspicuous of them. In 1841 he was the architect of Christ Church in Streatham, London – elegant and composed, heterogeneous, definitely English, but with visibly Byzantine and Islamic elements. For the following six years, Wild was in Egypt, working with Egyptologist Richard Lepsius. And then he was asked to design St Mark's Church in Alexandria. (It could never happen today.) His plans, again, were exuberant and experimental, tri-cultural: Byzantine, Islamic and Romanesque. The site was a gift from Egypt's Pasha Muhammad Ali, who wanted the church to 'harmonize with the neighbouring buildings, and be worthy of the English people'.[103] Leaflets seeking subscriptions promised the building would not be 'repugnant to the feelings of the local population'.[104] It was built in 1854, a little toned down but still extraordinary, intermingling transgression and convergence in a street full of genteel neo-classical hotels and mansions. E. M. Forester apparently thought it vulgar and inappropriate.[105]

Wild's brother-in-law was the Anglo-Welshman Owen Jones (1809–74), a man also enraptured by the homes and mosques of Egypt, Moorish Spain and Turkey. Captivated by the Alhambra, he educated himself about Islamic forms and colours and published books on the themes, among them the magnum opus *The Grammar of Ornament*. With Wild, he designed the Alhambra and Egyptian courts at Crystal Palace after the Great Exhibition closed. And then, in 1861, came a commission from Egypt's Said Pasha to design a pavilion for him in Gazirah. Jones's drawings were visionary and wondrous, but never materialized, sadly for him, and probably for Egypt too.[106]

Throughout the ex-British colonies, public buildings were built by the rulers who never expected the imperial sun to set. In most places they still survive, even if in a state of rack and ruin. The Custom House in Rangoon, the lavishly domed

Sultan Abdul Samad Building in Kuala Lumpur, railway stations and court houses of the early twentieth century elsewhere appear in tourist brochures, some undergoing loving renovation. In Burma, 180 colonial buildings have been saved because the public wouldn't let them die.[107] Growing up in Kampala, I was in awe of the High Court in the centre, the bandstand facing it, and the 1950s elegance of Drapers Department Store. I do hope they are still standing, not because of history but because they are so clean, cool, graceful and well made.

I end with thoughts shared with me by an English-Iranian architect who now lives in London: 'What I learned from my father is culture kept in a freeze box, cold, preserved, not alive, and really meaningless because it never changed. My mother, she taught me culture is a warm, moving river, turning, picking up things, leaving things, alive. I am an architect because of her. I am so happy my mother was English.'

6 Ways of Seeing, Thinking, Feeling

'Tis in worldly accidents
As in the world itselfe, where things most distant
Meet one another: thus the East, and West,
Upon this Globe, a Mathematick point
Onely divides; Thus happinesse, and miserie,
And all extreames are still contiguous.'

Sir John Denham, *The Sophy*, 1641[1]

T HE INTELLECTUAL AND CULTURAL flows between the Orient
and England gathered pace in the sixteenth century, when England was hungry
for information, fresh ideas and alternative views of the cosmos. Each new find
instigated further interest, in a feverish quest that goes on to this day. This chapter
looks at a few of the figures who contributed to that fruitful exchange in key areas
of the arts and sciences.[2]

Philosophy and Science

The earliest scientific knowledge comes from the East. In China, medical knowledge and practices such as acupuncture go back some 8,000 years but were

largely unknown elsewhere. The Chinese method of making paper did get to India and Arabia and thereafter the written word became the mode of pursuing and disseminating new knowledge. Anatomical and medical developments in India were recorded in Sanskrit as early as 600 BC. In mathematics, too, India led the way. Between AD 400 and 1200, Indians had figured out a basic decimal system, sine and cosine, the zero and other mathematical building blocks.[3] Their findings and formulations travelled along the trade routes from India to Arabia. Between AD 750 and 1250, Arab intellectuals translated and incorporated into their own knowledge Sanskrit medical texts as well as philosophical material from Ancient Greece, Persia and other older civilizations. When Europe was in its dark age, Arabia burnt the flames of enlightenment. (Now it is the other way round.)

Arab philosophies and inventions were studied and praised by Europeans even as they mounted brutal crusades against Islam after 1096. The following story illustrates that central contradiction. In 1143, Peter the Venerable, a French abbot, commissioned an Englishman, Robert of Ketton, to translate the Koran into Latin so that Christians could properly repudiate the Muslim religion. The paymaster must have been highly vexed when Robert eschewed his commission and instead became engrossed in Islamic scientific, mathematical and philosophical disciplines, even translating Arabic texts on algebra, alchemy and the astrolabe.[4]

Arab intellectuals laid down the foundations for modern science and philosophy. Of all those who criss-crossed borders to better comprehend the rules of nature, planetary formations, the universe and God, I give just a few examples.

Ibn al-Haytham, or Alhazan (965–c.1040), authored over a hundred books, experimented with optics and light and astrophysics, and was a radical freethinker: 'the seeker after the truth is not one who studies the writings of the ancients and, following his natural disposition, puts his trust in them, but rather the one who suspects his faith in them and questions what he gathers from them, the one who submits to argument and demonstration, and not to the sayings of a human being whose nature is fraught with all kinds of imperfection and deficiency ... He should also suspect himself as he performs his critical examination of [texts], so that he may avoid falling into either prejudice or leniency.'[5]

Ibn Sina, or Avicenna (980–1037), was a legendary physician, scholar of the natural sciences and 'arguably the most influential philosopher of the pre-modern era'.[6] His *Canon of Medicine (al Quanun fil-Tibb)* was a comprehensive textbook, translated into Latin and taught all across Europe. The young Thomas Aquinas was influenced by Avicenna's metaphysical discourses.[7] The polymath was absolutely committed to critical enquiry.

There were many more in this pantheon of phenomenal Arab scholars, men such as Al-Kindi (d. 866), who wrote over two hundred books on mathematics, physics, geography and studies of the Greek philosophers; Ibn Rushd (d. 1198), a scientist, linguist and philosopher; and Ibn Khaldun (d. 1406), one of the earliest sociologists and historicists. Muslim chemists such as Jabir ibn Hayyan, or Geber (d. 815), were evidence-based investigators: 'The first essential in chemistry is that thou shouldest perform practical work and conduct experiments, for he who performs not practical work nor makes experiments will never attain to the least degree of mastery.'[8] Many centuries later, Robert Boyle, the founder of modern chemistry, practised and advocated these principles.[9]

Scholars across Europe were tantalized by Eastern erudition, but although English scientists, mathematicians, alchemists and astronomers learnt from innovative Indians and were interested in what was going on in China, for a long time Arabs were considered the most advanced thinkers in the world. For example, the astronomer Roger Long (1680–1770) acknowledged: 'From the year 800, almost to the beginning of the fourteenth-century, Europe was plunged in darkness, and the most profound ignorance; but during this period several able men arose among the Arabians, and chiefly at Bagdad, which is very near the ancient Babylon; and some useful works were performed by them.'[10]

By the early seventeenth century, the English were as greedy for the riches of the mind as they were for material wealth. King Charles I ordered key documents to be brought from the Levant, and had detailed questionnaires sent out to assess the quality of Arab and Persian information. William Laud, his formidable Archbishop of Canterbury, backed expeditions to find manuscripts, which were deposited in the Bodleian Library, Oxford. In 1630, Laud had become Chancellor of the University and, 'horrified by the somnolent complacency of the place', sought to shake up the establishment, internationalize its vision and introduce oriental languages into the curriculum.[11]

Dr Rim Turkmani, physicist and fellow of the Royal Society, curated an exhibition in 2011 about this information gathering: 'This was about genuine curiosity mixed with respect, a lust for knowledge, not domination. There was a glut of information in the Arabic world, a scarcity in England.'[12]

This intellectual curiosity was fuelled by trade. In the seventeenth century, the English had a large caravanserai in Aleppo and elsewhere. The chaplaincy in Aleppo 'served as a studentship in Arabic and Oriental studies', and its chaplains were men of distinction.[13] Edward Pococke, whom Laud appointed to the first Chair of Arabic at Oxford, was one of them. Although Pococke set out to discredit the Koran and other Islamic texts, his pernickety attention to truth and detail came in the way of religious propaganda. In 1671, he translated a twelfth-century philosophical fable by Ibn Tufayl about a boy raised by a gazelle who discovers for himself the guiding principles of the universe and the hand of God.[14] This moral and religious novella possibly inspired Daniel Defoe's *Robinson Crusoe* and 'may also have had a role in shaping English empirical philosophy as it was developed by John Locke and others'.[15] Pococke turned out to be one of those who saw truths and beauty in places, people, customs and civilizations he was perhaps meant to recoil from.

In contrast William Bedwell, appointed to the first Chair of Arabic at Cambridge in 1632, was a simplistic bigot committed to the propagation of the one true religion – Christianity. His proudest publication was *Mahomet Unmasked, Or a Discoverie of the Manifold Forgeries, Falshoods, and Horrible Impieties of the Blasphemous Seducer Mohamet: With a Demonstration of the Insufficiencie of His Law, Contained in the Cursed Alcoran.*[16] After such a title what need is there to read the book? There were several more in this band of fervid Islam haters, as the critic Ziauddin Sardar points out: 'from Edward Pococke (1604–91) . . . to Simon Ockley (1678–1720), author of *History of Saracens*, to George Sale, who translated the Qur'an, the dominant theme was hatred and abuse.'[17]

I think that judgement is unjustifiably harsh, despite the base intent of some of the men. Individuals like Robert of Ketton were too intelligent to become Christian propagandists, while in the seventeenth century Henry Stubbe, born in Lincolnshire, a physician and scholar, published *An Account of the Rise and Progress of Mahometanism: With the Life of Mahomet and a Vindication of Him and His Religion from the Calumnies of the Christians.*[18] He was pilloried but remained unbowed.[19]

As the scientific revolution in Europe broke from the old traditions, the Royal Society was founded in London in 1660. Most of the Royal Society trailblazers were English – Robert Boyle was born in Ireland to the very English Earl of Cork and Catherine Fenton; Edward Bernard, mathematician and astronomer, was a Northamptonshire man; John Wallis, who had an asteroid named after him, was the son of a clergyman in Kent; the astronomer Edmond Halley was from Shoreditch, East London – but they also included the German theologian Henry Oldenburg and the Polish astronomer Johannes Hevelius. These natural philosophers were keen to know more about Arabic empiricism. Emeritus Professor Salim Al-Hassani notes that they were well aware of 'the many scientific resources written in Arabic and Persian . . . [and] were not in the least bit shy of crediting their Arab scientific predecessors.'[20]

Boyle learnt Arabic and Persian fluently, as did his peers, because Latin translations of Arabian material were thought to be unreliable by this time. Bernard, for example, read the original text of Ibn al-Haytham's *Book of Optics* because he was dissatisfied with the medieval Latin version: 'the proxility of the book proceeds from the ignorance of the interpreter rather than the inelegance of the Arab'.[21]

By the end of the seventeenth century, chairs of Arabic were established in Oxford and Cambridge and large collections of Arabic and Persian manuscripts were being collected by the Royal Society and Oxbridge libraries. Edmund Castell (1606–85) spent eighteen years compiling an elaborate dictionary of Hebrew, Arabic, Ethiopian, Persian and Syriac. He was financially ruined and personally depleted at the end of this obsession. Luckily his talents were noted and he was made Professor of Arabic at Oxford; he later arranged for his gravestone inscription to be carved in Arabic. It read: 'With hope of a better life after this one.'

During the seventeenth and eighteenth centuries, nearly forty Royal Society fellows were involved in the 'Arabick interest' in one way or another.[22] The society even elected three Arab fellows, all learned ambassadors – Muhammad Ibn Haddu in 1682, Mohammed Ben Ali Abgali in 1726 and Cassem Aga in 1728 – and their portraits were painted by enthusiastic English artists.[23] On the frontispieces of many of their books are magnificent tributes to their Middle Eastern antecedents.

English travellers to Muslim territories also brought back scientific and medical wisdom. Several, for example, had witnessed children being vaccinated against diseases. Lady Mary Wortley Montagu,[24] scarred by smallpox, observed babies being immunized in Turkey in 1719. Old women brought pus from smallpox sores in nutshells, and smeared it into scratches made by needles. The children got ill for a couple of days but recovered fast.[25] She had her own children 'treated', and persuaded her upper-class friends to do the same.

By the early eighteenth century stories about Eastern treatments and procedures – including rudimentary plastic surgery – were reaching England, but white physicians remained sceptical.[26] In 1792, two British doctors in Mysore saw a man whose nose had been reconstructed after it had been chopped off during a ferocious battle. They found the Indian 'surgeon' and watched him do it again. In 1794, the operation was described in *The Gentleman's Magazine* and in 1815, English doctors started to perform similar operations in London.[27]

Most of these connections have vanished into the mists of time. In Europe the problem is partiality and expurgation, while England simply neglects those pre-imperial associations. Professor Al-Hassani wants to reverse the amnesia: 'Unfortunately, much of the respect and understanding the founders of the Royal Society had for their forebears has been lost and the celebration of scientists in our school books is often confined to those from the West.'[28]

The current membership of the Royal Society includes prominent Asian and Arab names. Physicists like Turkmani and Dr Jim al-Khalili, and top physicians such as leading IVF doctor Mohammed Taranissi carry on the work of their

Arabian antecedents but in England, a fact that is both tragic and heartening. Al-Khalili, the son of an English mother and Iraqi father, makes obscure scientific information comprehensible in the most poetic way. Language is his paintbrush. The next section explores the infinite colours and textures, the inestimable capacities, of the English tongue.

Language

The metaphor of England's cultural promiscuity is its language, the lingua franca of the world long before the American century. Though languages are connected to power, the appeal of English comes from its porosity, adaptability and liveliness.

No other language is as wanton or as responsive to the world's diverse streams and currents. In London and Manchester around 140 different languages and dialects are spoken or written. Foreign words are happily absorbed into the lexicon. Mainland Europeans are more purist and protective of their national tongues, the French most of all. They are rigid and watchful and disapprove of any linguistic infiltration. It is scandalous that the vast majority of white Britons are monolingual. But on the plus side they are happy enough to let their language grow, be appropriated, changed daily, infused with music, lilts and sounds, including those from places once subdued and occupied by imperial masters.

In *The Story of English*, the authors acknowledge that 'above all, the great quality of English is its teeming vocabulary, 80 per cent of which is foreign-born. Precisely because its roots are so varied . . . it has words in common with virtually every language in Europe: German, Yiddish, Dutch, Flemish, Danish, Swedish, French, Italian, Portuguese and Spanish. In addition, almost any page of the

Oxford English Dictionary and *Webster's Third* will turn up borrowings from Hebrew, and Arabic, Hindi-Urdu, Bengali, Malay, Chinese, the languages of Java, Australia, Tahiti, Polynesia, West Africa and even the Aboriginal languages of Brazil'.[29]

Here is a sample list of older words that hail from India but are now naturalized: avatar, chutney, pukka, guru, catamaran, dungarees, cummerbund, bungalow, cheetah, shawl. And from Arabia: assassin, alchemy, alcohol (!), safari, coffee, candy, loofah, kismet, sofa, gazelle. The migration of such words into the English language is a gift and perhaps sweet retribution for colonialism. In return England hands over English to the nations of the world, to use, play with, nativize and eventually own.

The Caribbean impact is the strongest on modern urban English. You hear it in schools and on the streets. Dominic, seventeen, son of two posh English barristers, told me: 'I don't want to speak like my parents. I don't want to be like them. My heroes are black. They're cool and sexy. The school doesn't like it, but they can't make me talk like Boris Johnson.' Bollywood is now the biggest film industry in the world, its stars more famous worldwide than Hollywood idols. That explains why filmy Hindi is also picked up and added to street slang. In 2013, linguistic researchers at York University found a completely new English spoken in London: 'Multicultural London English (MLE) is a dialect combining elements of West Indian, South Asian, Cockney and estuary English.'[30]

THE LANGUAGE OF COLONIALISM AND FREEDOM

Back in the imperial age, potent anti-colonial speeches against foreign occupation were made in English by liberationists such as Jawaharlal Nehru and Gandhi in India, Jomo Kenyatta of Kenya, Nkrumah of Ghana. The same is true of Nelson

Mandela and the anti-apartheid movement. Words, lifted from their masters, proved stronger than weapons.

The linguist David Crystal is a renowned expert on English and its many avatars: 'Whenever English arrives in a country and people adopt it as their lingua franca, they quickly adapt it to suit their circumstances. Within a few generations, a regional vocabulary can grow to tens of thousands of words and grammar, pronunciation and patterns of discourse can be affected . . . Virtually any part of the English-speaking world can be used to illustrate the growth of a new kind of literature in which language has been adapted to express local cultural identities.'[31]

In 1919, Sol Plaatje wrote the first black novel in English in South Africa. Decades later, as African countries struggled to become independent, talented novelists and polemicists would stun and at times scare the old European rulers. Wole Soyinka, Peter Abrahams, Chinua Achebe, among others, wrote provocatively and beautifully, their African identities finding true expression in the white man's language.

In 1965, Achebe pondered this conundrum: 'Those of us who have inherited the English language may not be in a position to appreciate the value of the inheritance. Or we may go on resenting it because it came as part of a package deal which included many other items of doubtful value and the positive atrocity of racial arrogance and prejudice, which may yet set the world on fire. But let us not in rejecting the evil throw the good out with it.'[32]Achebe is right, for that would be to throw out eloquence and our understanding of the world.

I spoke Gujarati, Hindi, Swahili and my home tongue Kutchi before I learnt English at school, yet I could not express the thoughts in this book in any of my original four languages. Is that a loss or a gain? It is a gain carrying within it terrible loss. My children cannot speak any of those languages and don't even want to try. Their mother's tongues have been supplanted by their mother tongue: English. My consolation is that English receives constant 'transfusions of new blood from other tongues'[33] and my offspring unknowingly use Eastern words that pass themselves off as English.

Some of the most arresting writers in contemporary England are migratory souls, several of them also biracial, bicultural or bilingual. They include Salman Rushdie, Hanif Kureshi, Ahdaf Soueif, Timothy Mo, Bernardine Evaristo, Caryl Phillips, V. S. Naipaul, Andrea Levy, Kazuo Ishiguro, Ben Okri, Abdulrazak Gurnah, Nadeem Aslan, and many others. Timothy Mo describes their collective impact as a 'coup in the sleepy little kingdom of England'.[34] Or perhaps a home-coming.

Mo's father is Chinese and his mother an Englishwoman. They lived in Hong Kong where as a child Mo picked up 'low-class rural Cantonese'. His parents divorced and his mother married an ex-navy Englishman whom Mo describes as 'the great father figure of my life'. When he was ten, they sailed for the UK. By the time the ship docked the little boy had forgotten Cantonese: 'The words wouldn't come. English had replaced it.' At the age of twelve, after reading *The Pickwick Papers* and *Don Quixote*, he decided he would be a writer, in English, the tongue he decided was his to own, love and grow old in.

For Caribbeans, English is a poignant reminder of enslavement. Their previous histories and tongues were cut off and tossed into the seas during transportation. You would expect the descendants of slaves to spit out the language they were made to speak. Instead they make love to and in English, lay eternal claim to it.

In India arguments rage over the primacy of English and the downgrading of indigenous languages. I agree with those who fret that this dominance is killing linguistic diversity, as important as biodiversity is in the natural world. But emerging forms of English resist uniformity and are a sign of creative requisitioning. Fusion English is proliferating in global, urban hubs. Every time I visit India, I hear more people speaking 'Hinglish': 'the hippest slang in the streets and college campuses of India . . . Hinglish is now the fastest-growing language in the country'.[35] There is a co-ownership here, a partnership, openness.

The same is happening in China, where 250 million people speak or are learning to speak English. Soon there will be more English (or 'Chinglish') speakers in China than in the whole of the British Commonwealth. English public schools, bastions of old power and Empire, are now going out to recruit vast numbers of Chinese, Arab and Indian pupils. Chinese writers in English are enthralling readers and winning awards. One of the most original is Chinese-Londoner Xiaolu Guo, born in a fishing village in China. In 2007 she wrote *A Concise Chinese-English Dictionary for Lovers*, which charts the psychological journey of a young Chinese émigré in London as her home language recedes and is supplanted by English.

Painting and Drawing

Like language, art is a product of society and politics. It can glorify the status quo or rise against what is by imagining what could be. From the seventeenth century onwards, a number of English artists were drawn to the Orient. Some were superficially enthralled with the exotic, while others were intentionally or unintentionally subversive.

In the 1760s, the English artist Tilly Kettle was known for his pictures of stage performers in 'elaborate and exotic costumes'.[36] But he craved the real thing. In 1768, he went to India and was immediately commissioned to paint Indian maharajahs and East India Company nabobs, who wanted to be portrayed as the new aristocracy in all their ostentatious grandeur. One Captain Foote, dressed in fabulous Indian clothes, even had himself painted by Joshua Reynolds (in England) in 1761.

Possibly bored with vanity art, Kettle branched out, painting subjects which moved him. His temple women were ascetic yet feminine, his dancing girls animated but never coarse, and even the powerful revealed their inner selves. In the Victoria Memorial in Calcutta, now called Kolkata, hang his picture of the Nawab of Oudh, his princelings and puffed-up British colonials, and a portrait of Sir Elijah Impey, the first Lord Chief Justice of the Indian Supreme Court. Both paintings were clearly commentaries on British power. Indian artists, used to stylized profiles, copied Kettle's realistic portraiture. His work was 'fundamental for the spread of European trends in Indian painting'.[37] Kolkatans, known for their left-wing radicalism, safeguard the artist's memory.

Kettle got rich and took an Indian mistress, who bore him two daughters. Then he returned to London, married an Englishwoman called Mary, and had more children. But money fell away, as did work. Unhappy and depressed, he tried to return to India overland, through Syria. He died somewhere along the way and lies in an unknown grave.

William Hodges, from London, went with Captain Cook on his second voyage in 1772–5 and was overwhelmed by the light in the Pacific. He experienced something close to an epiphany. It seems he felt he had to go abroad again. In India between 1780 and 1784, he painted picture after picture – rivers, temples, palaces, scenes of such beauty the paintbrushes seem lovesick.[38]

In 1784, Thomas Daniell, son of a Surrey innkeeper, and his nephew William followed a similar artistic trajectory. They produced six volumes of painted scenes of India: 'The aquatinting in colour set a new standard, and the views brought to the British at home a sense of acquaintance with a new reality ... They commanded an accuracy of observation, a sharpness of detail, combined with a breadth of tone and shadow and an essential luminosity.'[39] These men seemed possessed by the spirit of that land.

The English traveller-artist George Chinnery (1774–1852) spent half his adult life in India and the rest in China, where he is buried. He is celebrated in Macau and Hong Kong and Delhi, yet his own people barely know the man or his art. Chinnery was flamboyant, but found life trying; he was always in debt and in trouble. Most of his emotions went into his art. A picture of two siblings shows this beautifully. Their father was Scotsman Colonel James Achilles Kirkpatrick and their mother Khair-un-Nissa, a young Mughal noblewoman.[40] Though dressed in extravagant finery, the young children look sad, dismayed, which presages their fate perhaps. Later packed off to England, they never saw either parent again. Chinnery painted Nissa's portrait too, and again her face looks overcast, sombre. His pictures of Chinese merchants and landscapes are similarly empathetic, perhaps suggestive of his disapproval of the way Europeans behaved in Eastern lands.

Other European artists were also mesmerized by the Orient. The most renowned was Johann Zoffany, a German who settled in England, whose compositions include pulsating pictures of Indian life, the Anglo-Indian family of William Palmer, and Dido, daughter of a black slave and English father.[41] The most famous Scottish artist to find success in the East was George Willison, appointed portrait painter to Mohammed Ali Khan Waleja, Nawab of Carnatic.

Today few tread in the footsteps of these old, illustrious, deeply engaged wandering artists. One rare exception is Martin Yeoman, who has painted landscapes in India, Yemen and Arabia. Fellow artist Lutz Becker describes him as: 'The traveller, in search of the Other, [who] found himself entangled in a set of painful realizations: despite the fact that the travelling was a quest for an alternative, for the unusual, for change, the traveller found only himself, and could not be the Other . . . Martin Yeoman is a traveller who is prepared to be changed by his experience, who is ready to take on the risk self-questioning entails'.[42] Yeoman's pictures are dreamy, misty; they admit that the unreachable can only be glimpsed by an outsider's yearning eyes through a glass, lightly.

INDIAN ARTISTS PAINTING COLONISTS

In a number of paintings by Indian artists of the seventeenth and eighteenth centuries one finds irony, fury, conceit, moments of intimacy and equality. A watercolour from 1650 shows humble Europeans in one corner carrying gifts to Emperor Shah Jahan, seated high above them. A panel on a painted box from the late seventeenth century has a 'European Prince' playing a flute in a garden, looking like a Hindu god, making a point about hubris, perhaps, and a picture entitled *Three Grotesque Europeans and a Child* (1760) is a bitter, visual remonstration.[43] A number of miniature paintings depicted erotic, sexual acts between European men and Indian courtesans, again with a hint of disapproval.[44] Between 1760 and 1764, Dip Chand painted William Fullerton of the East India Company, in full English regalia, smoking a hookah; in a second painting his poised Indian mistress does the same.[45] British officials seemed to have loved this style and several of them became avid collectors.

A watercolour of Elijah Impey's wife was painted by an unknown Indian artist.[46] She lounges in an opulent room, flanked by servants, while a supplicant trader hands her a hat. Other hopeful artisans and sellers sit on the carpet. The artist may have been gently mocking her, or cringingly obsequious, or a real admirer. This lady had a reputation for nurturing local talent. She commissioned Mughal-trained artists Ram Das, Bhawani Das and Sheikh Zain-u-Din to paint over two hundred pictures of birds, fish and reptiles.[47]

CHINESE AND JAPANESE ART

Europeans – mostly the Dutch and Portuguese – feature in pictures and objects in Japan and China from around 1600. A lacquered, tiered food box with three Portuguese men in European pantaloons and hats dates from around this time.[48] A detailed and beautifully painted six-panel screen (1630s) shows a Portuguese ship arriving at a Japanese port. There are solemn Jesuit missionaries on board, officials, traders, presents, including live peacocks and tiger skins. There is something innocent about these depictions, interest in the Europeans and no suspicion.[49] Sixty years later, the images were more mixed and less naive, particularly those by Chinese artists. An arrogant European wearing Chinese clothes was painted in 1690; and two ivory figures show Europeans from the eighteenth century bearing gifts, including ivory and a scroll.[50] They look devious. Portraits were painted of Englishmen and women in fancy native clothes and of natives dressed up to look like Samuel Johnson. A particularly absurd example is a Chinese painting on glass of dull Mrs and Miss Revell trying to look exciting in local costume.[51] A porcelain punch bowl, made in China in 1750, is decorated with a carefully painted copy of Hogarth's *A Midnight Conversation*, and a late eighteenth-century Japanese plaque honours philosopher John Locke, in black and gold. Such works provide invaluable insights into history that is often surprising.

English landscape painting was transmogrified by Eastern artists and artisans, signalling respect and affectionate appropriation. For example, the first ever copperplates in Japan were made by Edo artist by Shiba Kokan (1747–1818). Two of these depict the stately homes of Stowe and Cliveden, copied from imported images.[52] Chinese aesthetics, as we know, were beautiful to the English eye. And that love continues to be returned right up to the present day.

In 1933, the Chinese artist Chiang Yee came to England and published travelogues enhanced by lovely drawings and paintings. In one picture a typical Chinese tree is in the foreground and behind it, far away, rises the church tower of Christ Church College, Oxford. It's fresh and a little disorientating. English landscapes were lifted out of familiarity, their charm augmented by a captivated outsider. Chiang Yee's work was seen by many enthusiasts at a major exhibition at the Burlington Gallery in London in 2012.[53]

In the 1940s, an even more curious tale unfolded, involving Stanley Spencer, the eccentric and definitively English artist from Cookham, Berkshire. It is the perfect little English village, yet Spencer, writes culture critic Patrick Wright, was 'intensely interested' in Islam, India and the opium dens of London, in chinoiserie and Chinese painting.[54] In 1946, four Chinese artists were invited to the UK by the British Council. One of them, Chang Chien-ying, joined the Chelsea School of Art, while another, Fei Cheng-wu, went to Camberwell. And they were befriended by Spencer, who had long dreamt of going to China.

In 1950, *Picture Post* printed a profile of Fei with his pastoral 'fusion' landscapes, some of which were exhibited at the Royal Academy, a first for an Asian painter. Chang was also featured in *Picture Post*, which praised her creative series on the English summer as seen by Chinese eyes. These painters found an 'affinity between English mistiness and the behaviour of ink on absorbent Chinese paper'.[55] Chang told one reporter, 'I want to paint Chinese scenery in the Turner style.' Collectors and art lovers bought some of these Sino-English pictures.[56]

Fei and Chang visited Spencer at his home and they got on splendidly. The Englishman made drawings of Chang. Later he was best man at their wedding in Kensington Registry Office in 1953.[57]

The following year, Spencer went, with a cultural delegation, to China and ruminated loudly: 'Yes, we ought to know New China better and the New China needs to know Cookham better. I feel at home in China because I feel that Cookham is somewhere near, only just round the corner.'[58] Was that just him being batty, or provocative, or had he become aware of the ties between England and the East?

ORIENTALIST PAINTERS

The Orientalists were Europeans who painted Arabian deserts, mosques, homes, scenery and people. In modern times, the genre has been roundly damned by post-colonialists. Here I focus on the work of English Orientalists.

The Muslim feminist writer Fatema Mernissi wonders whether these men were Cartesians recoiling from rationality itself, 'perhaps enchanted precisely with the "dark" or unconscious qualities of Islam that in their own civilization were connected to danger'.[59] Their artistic responses seem to have arisen from the depths of their psyche, from withheld desires, the wildness of dreams, blackness.[60] The Empire may have programmed them to hate idleness and 'moony nights in chaos-inducing realms',[61] but many English gentleman-Orientalists were hypno-tized by those mystical cultures.

John Frederick Lewis (1804–76) spent many years in Egypt, unlike some other Victorian painters who imagined they knew Arab life because they had read anthropological accounts. In *The Carpet Seller*, the merchant is Lewis, though this is not acknowledged. Wearing embroidered pantaloons and top, with a high sash and an untidy turban, he sits on a stool, obviously frustrated, his legs splayed provocatively, feet turned in. He is cradling a sword – it looks as if he could slash the space around him. 'I want this to be my place,' the image says, 'but it can't be, not now, not ever, not really.'

In Lewis's contemplative *A Lady Receiving Visitors*, golden light bathes everything, the intricate patterns of stained-glass windows and delicate female court courtesy tell you this is a room of grace. Pictures of interiors by Arthur Melville and Frank Dillon also show sequestered spaces where light is poetry and dance. The bearded Arab men in these paintings are sagacious and noble and still, not ugly, excitable terrorists; homes and mosques are tranquil, not full of plots. Emily Weeks, curator of the Yale Center for British Art, is surely right to interrogate received wisdom: 'these paintings have in fact much left to tell . . . perhaps most importantly, genuine moments of cross-cultural understanding and respect and commemoration have yet to be restored to the historical record'.[62]

It is true, however, that the harem paintings represent a gross intrusion and are indeed voyeuristic, because they urge us to look upon those not meant for our prying eyes. But what if some of the women, weary of a controlled, invisible existence, welcomed the attention of strangers? Like Leila, a woman gorgeous in red and gold, painted by Frank Dicksee – sensuous, sated, lips hot, the eyes wide open? Veiled and sequestered, she would be nothing. Here she dominates our senses and we smell her and her lilies.

So is this, then, a clean bill of health for all the Orientalist painters? No. Some British paintings, including those by pre-Raphaelites, though technically impressive, show minds misshapen by alienation, perhaps opiates, certainly colonial scorn. In Holman Hunt's *The Lantern Maker's Courtship*, the suitor pushes his hand into the veiled face of a compliant, yet nervous woman, as if all that passes between Arab lovers is unrefined and grubby. Nothing feels normal – even the sleeping dog is curled up as if wanting to die. In William Allan's *The Slave Market, Constantinople* (1838), captured white women give off the glow of translucent divinity while his swarthy Arabs are beasts. We are meant to imagine what happens next as white skin is mounted and tainted by blackness. Prejudiced though they were, British Orientalists did not sink to the coarse pictorial xenophobia of the French Orientalists such as Jean-Léon Gérôme (*For Sale: Slaves at Cairo*) and Ingres (*The Turkish Bath*).

The critic Brian Sewell agrees there were fundamental differences between 'Central European and English responses to the Arab world. The English response, literary and also artistic, was so deep and prolonged – nothing in the German response corresponds to that. With France, how interested and excited they were by the horror of the East. That never comes through in English painting or English writing. You don't see anything frightening.'[63]

England's artistic elite are no longer lured to the East. We have no soulful Lewis or sensual Dicksee. That is a loss and a shame. A hundred years from now, there will be hardly any visual narratives which transcend the chasms splitting the Middle East and the West. There will be plenty of war art instead, from Iraq and Afghanistan.

EXOTIC ART MADE IN ENGLAND

Meanwhile exceptional artists from or of the East flourish in twenty-first-century England. Many are Muslims who could not produce their art in Islamic countries. Their work is a benign composite of the Occident and Orient, sometimes fearful,

sometimes hopeful, mostly searching. The highly regarded London artist Saleem
Arif Quadri, a Muslim Sufi from India, moved to England in 1966 – first stop
Nuneaton in Warwickshire. He intuitively understands the relationship between
India and England: 'There is conflict and affinity like that between mother/child,
teacher/pupil, love/hate. And then there is a bond, respect and admiration,
between two civilizations which cannot be broken.'[64] His paintings have birds,
birds of migration, images of movement, an imagined God who loves beauty. They
are displayed in public spaces in Birmingham, Winchester, Nottingham and
Oldham, which commissioned him to make a piece marking 150 years since the
city got its charter.[65] Good old England.

Other British Muslim artists contemplate their duality, or paint invocations to
Allah, or spiral out of confining spaces. Like Quadri, the best of them live in
English conurbations, tough places which seem to unlock and free their art.

Suad Al-Attar, winner of multiple awards, was born and raised in Baghdad in
the 1960s, when that city was ultra modern and chic. During Saddam Hussein's
brutal reign she fled to London with her husband and daughters. England rescued
her talent from terror.[66] During the illegal war on Iraq, she was afraid again and felt
betrayed, expressing her fury in her paintings. Inner peace is slowly returning.
Since 2010, her canvases are full of old Babylonian folklore, trees of life, white
horses, imagined paradises. Leighton House has shown her work several times in
solo exhibitions, a perfect tribute to Lord Leighton, whose home was a homage to
the Orient.

The photographer Peter Sanders converted to Islam following some vivid
dreams. The author Michael Sugich describes Sanders as: 'deeply spiritual, deeply
intuitive, deeply mystical, deeply Muslim, deeply English . . . He is as comfortable
in Chesham, Piccadilly or Harrogate as in Makkah, Lamu or Timbuktu. He is

Mohammedan in his approach to life, Blakean in his mystical love of traditional England and ability to see beyond difference and into the essence of things.'[67]

Sanders' photographs are works of art. One has a British Muslim woman serenely painting calligraphy, in another Salma Yaqoob, erstwhile vice-chair of the Respect Party, sits bathed in soft sunlight in a very English room with old furniture. The artist Mohammed Ali is shown making murals with aerosol cans, and the academic Timothy Winter, a convert, leads his Muslim male choir, singing 'songs for the British Isles', in the grounds of a Cambridge college.[68]

Across England, non-Western artists of merit are growing in number and audacity. The following stand for all those who are challenging and changing art and their nation.

Yinka Shonibare, MBE, is not oriental, but he is exotic, knowingly so, and is finely tuned in to the English temperament. Born in England, raised in Nigeria, he returned to his birthplace to follow his dream of becoming an artist who would do more than make beautiful art. He was soon noticed. For one tableau he sculpted headless life-sized statues of white people dressed in eighteenth- and nineteenth-century fashions but made with bright African fabrics – visual annotations on slavery and Empire. His enormous model of Nelson's ship in a bottle, with sails again made of African prints, was placed on the fourth plinth in Trafalgar Square, another evocation of entwined, buried histories. The model faced Nelson's column, with its carvings of black men on his ship, now forgotten by England.

Then there's Chila Burman, born in Liverpool in the 1960s. Her parents, traditional and hard-working, were from the Punjab. They must have been disconcerted when she decided to go to the Slade School of Art instead of becoming a lawyer or doctor – every Asian parent's dream. Her multimedia, insubordinate, dazzling work is mostly in bright, primary colours, inspired by Bollywood, Liverpool, surrealism, and her dad's ice-cream van. Her themes are big: memory, migration, female rights and sexuality. One set of pictures has big, brown, luscious bosoms in bras of every variety. Poster-sized copies were put up around London tube stations. This is real, warm, multicoloured London, they said: snuggle up, welcome. England's approval brings her admiration from her own. Such is the way of the world. A millionaire in Delhi told me he was keen on buying Burman's work because Richard Branson liked it and had bought one. Does one laugh or cry?

England on Stage

The political upheavals, world exploration and international exchange that rapidly transformed England in the sixteenth century were reflected in the golden age of English drama. New, bold theatre companies and writers came forth and dramatized the tumultuous, seemingly borderless world and their nation's domestic fears and dreams. In our times, waves of globalization are leading to mass disenchantment with politicians, unanticipated conflicts, mergings, cultural and identity predicaments. Once again, British dramatists, many of them English, are creatively aroused by the turmoil.[69] (Arguably, in relatively untroubled periods – the late Victorian age, for example, when theatre was increasingly popular – English drama was more pedestrian.[70]) In this section I look at the similarities between Elizabethan and Jacobean drama and contemporary theatre, which uses and updates those early English plays to interpret and dramatize our thrilling, dangerous, borderless world.

STAGING PROTEAN ENGLAND

Until the sixteenth century, most dramatic enactments were of Biblical stories or Christian morality. The mystery or miracle plays of the twelfth and thirteenth centuries were performed by small bands of players who found rooms in inns, courtyards and open spaces to tell these otherworldly and salutary stories. *The Harrowing of Hell*,[71] for example, in which Jesus faces down Satan, was performed during Easter. By the fourteenth century, morality plays about vice and virtue had supplanted the fervently religious dramas. The oldest extant play from that period is *The Castle of Perseverance* (1450), which has Man embattled by many temptations and influences. This genre carried on into the sixteenth century. One of the best known was *Lusty Juventus* (c. 1547–53) by Richard Wever, in which a young man with a fortune is led astray by debauchery and hedonism.[72]

Once Henry VIII (1491–1547) separated the English church from papal authority and established the Protestant Church of England, the old order broke down, fixed notions dissolved, leaving England with dilemmas, sliding and fluctuating identifications. From the 1530s to the death of Elizabeth in 1603, national identity was shaped by the Reformation.[73]

The first playhouses were built in the 1570s by actor-manager James Burbage and other enthusiasts, including rich funders. They were regarded as dubious and dangerous by the religious and ruling authorities. The mayor of London and courtiers often shut them down and at times banished the troupes, who, undeterred, constructed theatres beyond the capital, and thus expanded the appeal of what was previously thought to be a symbol of London's degeneracy.[74]

Plays served to reinforce the break with Catholicism, explains the theatre director Michael Boyd. Catholics were stereotyped as the monstrous 'Other', while the English Protestants were cast as humane and liberal. The rise of the mercantile over the religious experience was played out in drama as well as in life: 'There is the thrill of destruction of the barrier, of escape from claustrophobia, of finding the new and unknown, of notoriety and freedom.'[75]

There was another strand too. Plays set in strange lands were a device for appraising post-Reformation English monarchs, plots, power struggles and the long periods of conflict which made the people feel unsafe and nervous.

This was a golden age of drama. A number of talented and daring playwrights emerged out of the new religious and political settlement, and tried to define and stage the new Englishness, with all its problems and contradictions. Shakespeare, of course, became the voice of this new creativity and liberty. I write on his impact in greater detail in the next part of this chapter. The most famous of the rest were Ben Jonson (1572–1637), John Fletcher (1579–1625), Thomas Kyd (1558–94), Christopher Marlowe (1564–93) and John Webster (1580–1634). Many of their plays – including those about monarchs – were set outside England and featured foreigners. Audiences would get their fill of swarthy baddies but they would also warm to exemplary Eastern rulers and probably go home thinking about those who held power in England. The writers used allegory and devices to protect themselves. The times they lived in were feverish, mistrustful and unpredictable. It was an exciting time to be a writer, but perilous too. Some died too young.

Instability increased in the second half of the seventeenth century, as the country went through oppression, the Civil War, regicide, Cromwell's Commonwealth, further oppression and the restoration of the monarchy. Playwrights once again had to disguise dramatizations of these upheavals by setting their plays in Persia, Istanbul and other Eastern locations.[76] 'English fascination with the orient [was linked to] religious and political anxieties at home . . . As religious anxiety mounted in England, so did the rhetorical appropriation of Ottoman history and religion by proponents of all factions.'[77] Audiences, by this time, understood multiple meanings, were sophisticated and wanted more than worthy messages dressed up and put on stage.

Sixteenth- and seventeenth-century theatre-goers wanted to be amazed, explains Greg Doran, the artistic director of the Royal Shakespeare Company: 'There is an element of wanting excitement, novelty, to see on stage something that will transport them to another world, of which they knew little but were becoming more aware. They wanted the theatre to take them places, leave what they knew, meet strangers, and through those stories think about what was happening in their own kingdom.'[78]

On stage, the foreigner could be Spanish, Italian or French, portrayed as menacing or backward Catholics to be scorned, derided, laughed at or feared. Jews and non-white peoples were also part of the canon of inferiors.

Crude brown, black and Semitic nasties were omnipresent in Elizabethan and Jacobean theatre. They feature in Marlowe's *Tamburlaine* (1587/8), George Peele's *The Battle of Alcazar* (1588), Thomas Kyd's *Soliman and Perseda* (1590), Thomas Dekker's *Lust's Dominion* (c. 1600), Thomas Heywood's *The Fair Maid of the West* (1602), Robert Daborne's *A Christian Turn'd Turk* (1612), Thomas Goffe's *The Raging Turke* (1618), John Fletcher and Philip Massinger's *The Knight of Malta* (1618) and Thomas Middleton and William Rowley's *All's Lost by Lust* (1620).[79] The list is long.

In his book on race and sex in early English drama, social anthropologist Fernando Henriques concludes that 'The Moor from Africa is depicted as a savage, lustful creature . . . and is contrasted with the valorous, noble-hearted, white-skinned European.'[80] Black or mixed-race devil-women led white men astray.

Other popular themes – as you might imagine – were conversion, circumcision, castration; submissive, ravished Christian beauties; enslavement, sexual intemperance and violence. In a closely argued essay, Professor Emily Bartels observes: 'In Renaissance England, the rise of cross cultural interest and exchange was accompanied by an intensified production and reproduction of their vision of "other" worlds, some handed down from classical descriptions, others generated by actual encounters and recorded as travel narratives, others shaped by the dramatic and literary conventions already in place.' A racialist ideology emerged alongside 'the nation's nascent imperialism'. Non-white characters were demonized for being 'incontestably different or too appealingly the same'.[81]

However, the best writers were nuanced, and, to reiterate, were critiquing their own societies and polity through the words and behaviours of the outsiders in their plays. Sometimes the object of satire is the uncouth Englishman and the outsider is the antithesis.[82] '[Playwrights] enter into a debate on native and foreign values . . . the dramatists' preoccupation with native error overrides traditional patriotic and antiforeigner sentiments. In this process the satire inherent in the foreign type is directed away from the foreigner and aimed at the Englishman.'[83]

Art imitated life. Englanders by then had seen high-born and self-assured Easterners and Africans in London or knew people who had. When Moroccan ambassadors rode into town from Dover, curious crowds came to gaze at them. Peele's *The Battle of Alcazar* was written after one such celebrated visit. Peele was a friend of Shakespeare. Did Shakespeare witness such a parade himself? Did he see the faces of radiant young Englishwomen as they looked upon the oriental gentlemen, some very handsome indeed? In drama, as in so much else, England responded to the Other in a variety of ways.

The crusader narrative was disrupted: 'The boundaries between East and West were permeable and constantly shifting . . . By Elizabeth's reign, in nuanced ways, both Ottomans and Persians had begun to occupy a rather more ambivalent position in relation to the Protestant English.'[84]

Take John Fletcher's *The Island Princess* (1647), the first English play set in the Far East – in the Molucca Islands. It is an action-packed story of Portuguese occupiers, native resisters, and Islam totally misrepresented as polytheism. The heroine, Quisara, in the end sees the light and converts to Christianity. The biggest baddie is, of course, a 'native'. Yet, as with Shakespeare's Caliban, the most potent speeches against European domination are given to the villains; as Doran points out, 'They knew what audiences would accept and also added the counterarguments.'

The outlander's passions and motivations were examined and the tone was often searching; there was metaphysical awe. The most determined post-colonial hawks will not find racial debasement in Denham's *The Sophy* (1641). Set at the court of Persia's King Abbas, it explores the existential fear suffered by the powerless and the most powerful, the tragedy of murderous succession.

John Dryden's *Aureng-Zebe* (1675), set in Agra in 1660, is very similar. Its main dramatic axis is also the conflict between a king and his sons. Dryden deftly delineates noble yet flawed characters, and includes profound reflections on life and death, as in the lines: 'Death in itself is nothing; But we fear/ To be we know not what, we know not where.' Aureng-Zebe, in the play, is a man of honour. In reality he was fanatically Islamicist, the most ruthless of the Mughal emperors, and has few admirers in India. That an English playwright should ameliorate the reputation of an appalling oriental despot would not happen today. Would, say, David Hare, try to do the same with the life and times of Egypt's Hosni Mubarak? I don't think so.

The play's most dramatic moments 'address domestic political crises through their quasi-transparent coded allegories [and] . . . explore the anxieties and fantasies associated with England's growing economic and cultural imperialism'.[85]

Eighteenth-century Englanders were as fascinated and often horrified by the Orient as were their forebears, though by this time, stories from beyond the shores of Europe were familiar to most. Children sometimes performed Dryden's Indian play. A picture by Hogarth of 1731 shows one such performance at the house of John Conduitt, Master of the Mint, in Hanover Square in London.[86]

The *Arabian Nights* were read and some of the tales were put on stage, most often as displays of the bizarre. The first, *Aladdin and the Enchanted Lamp*, was performed in Drury Lane in 1782; in 1797, Richard Hole, a remarkably perceptive critic for his times, excoriated fellow Europeans and their pathological inability to understand the context and meaning of the tales: 'The sedate and philosophical turn from them with contempt: the gay and volatile laugh at their seeming absurd-ities: those of an elegant and correct taste are disgusted with their grotesque figures and fantastic imagery . . . How are we to reconcile these circumstances? Does human nature vary in different parts of the globe? or are we to consider the Arabians, notwithstanding what we have heard of them, as children in intellect and ourselves arrived at the maturity of knowledge? . . . [W]e attend with equal delight to the incantations of the witches in Macbeth, and to Puck's whimsical frolics . . . Let us be cautious therefore of condemning the Arabs for a ridiculous attachment to the marvellous, since we ourselves are no less affected by it'.[87]

SHAKESPEARE

Shakespeare is and always will be the most resonant voice, the spry and bustling mind and expansive soul of England. The Bard apparently never left these shores, but his imagination swept off to Rome, Egypt, Venice, unknown isles with magic and mystery. To the insightful Michael Boyd, 'The sense of the Other is constantly present in Shakespeare. His central grammatical DNA is antithesis, to oppose one thought against another. It is a permanent habit of his, reflected socially, politically, emotionally and religiously. Caliban and Shylock are the Other, but there is always fascination with the unknown world, unseen humanity in this age of exploration.'

Shakespeare gives us both moral clarity and moral conundrum. Those forces play out strikingly in his plays of transgressive love, with rebellious couples crossing thorny borders, the colour line, the culture line, the faith line, old enemy lines. Upon them falls the rage of bitterly divided clans and nations and other hoarders of hostilities. The lovers are possessed, yet have choices.

Illicit, uncontainable desires don't always get their way and humour contains warnings. In *A Midsummer Night's Dream*, Bottom's infatuation with Titania, the otherworldly temptress, is more than a big laugh. It's a drug, a loss of memory, of selfhood, which he must recover. She too must be reconciled with Oberon. Each to their own to restore order, that central Shakespearean imperative.

In *Titus Andronicus* both Romans and Goths are bloodthirsty and callous. Far worse than them, however, is the devilish Aaron, the manipulative outsider, secret lover of Tamora, Queen of the Goths. Bassianus, the Roman, scorns her for loving him:

> *Believe me, queen, your swart Cimmerian*
> *Doth make your honour of his body's hue*
> *Spotted, detested and abominable.*

A child is born, a child the mother wants slaughtered to cover her sin. Aaron snatches the baby and proclaims his blackness:

What, what, ye sanguine, shallow-hearted boys!
Ye white-limed walls! ye alehouse painted signs!
Coal-black is better than another hue,
In that it scorns to bear another hue.[88]

I can hear these words tumbling out of a black rapper's mouth, see it as graffiti on urban walls. Shakespeare avoided the easy judgement. The most powerful and arrogant – like Tamora – are weakened by stormy desires. I imagine Queen Bess in the audience, elderly, maybe a little prickly to be reminded of her own weakness for courtly and comely Muslim ambassadors. What rumours must have swirled around them in those plot-ridden, gossipy times.

Othello was first staged in 1604, a decade after *Titus*. Since then, life has not only reflected the play but overwhelmed it. Ira Aldridge, the first black thespian seen on stage in England, was an American 'negro' who had fled savagely racist America. In October 1825 he appeared at the Old Vic in Waterloo in a play adapted in 1696 by Thomas Southerne from Aphra Behn's novel *Oroonoko* (1688). The central story was about slaves who fall in love and rebel, and was the first such sympathetic portrayal of those who were forced into slavery. The audience was enraptured but London critics were hostile. Aldridge carried on. At long last, he got his big break. He was invited to play *Othello* in Covent Garden. Actresses and theatre-goers warmed to him but the racist press hated him touching Desdemona, played by Ellen Terry. The director and producer capitulated and sacked the actor. Aldridge chose to marry Margaret Gill, 'an English lady of respectability and superior achievements', thus provoking further outrage.[89] (Art and life knotted together and could not be disentangled.) Embittered, the couple left England and migrated to friendlier climes.[90]

In 1930, another black American actor, Paul Robeson, came to England and was again reviled by the London press. Robeson played *Othello* at the Savoy Theatre with Peggy Ashcroft as Desdemona. When they touched, *The Times* critic walked out and his peers booed. Later Robeson proclaimed: 'I am killing two birds with one stone. I am acting and I am talking for the negro as only Shakespeare can.'[91] As only Shakespeare can. There was electricity between the two stars. Many years later, Ashcroft confessed (unabashedly) that they were having an affair: 'How can you not fall in love, in such a situation, with such a man?'[92]

When Othello is on stage before his fall, the air is suffused with eroticism. In 1904 the authoritative scholar A. C. Bradley considered the black man's allure: 'There is something mysterious about his descent from royal siege; in his wanderings in vast deserts among marvellous peoples; in his tales of magic handkerchiefs and prophetic Sibyls . . . his sojourn in Aleppo.' The tough war hero watched, with a poet's eye, 'Arabian trees dropping their medic'nable gum and the Indian throwing away his chance-found pearl'.[93] But, for all his charms, Othello is 'very simple. He is not observant. His nature tends outward. He is quite free from introspection, and is not given to reflection. Emotion excites his imagination, but confuses and dulls his intellect.'[94]

One modern reviewer agrees: 'The problem in every modern performance is that Othello is so unreflective . . . Although [he] has been assigned nobility and great poetry, he is one of Shakespeare's most unreflective characters. Unlike Shylock, who reflects on his status as a Jew, and is bitterly aware of his degraded position as such, Othello never questions his Blackness or reflects on his precarious position in a world of white men.'[95]

To the anti-Orientalist writer Rana Kabbani, Shakespeare's black characters are all animations of various bigotries: 'Othello . . . still remains a savage, although a somewhat noble one. His excitable nature and passionate instincts flaw him . . . The play ultimately condemns the idea of interracial sex . . . The black man cannot be allowed to "tup" the "white ewe".' *Antony and Cleopatra* expounds crude and irredeemably partisan values: 'the West is social stability; the East pleasure . . . Octavia modesty and wisdom, [Cleopatra] the sexual urge, unappeasable, intransigent'.[96]

It is never wise to fit Shakespeare into a tight, interpretive frame. Othello is not a lewd black gangster, but a soldier who can woo with fine words. We do not cheer when he falls on his sword. I don't expect the first audiences to see the play did so either. We are left with several undertows of feeling – he has been lulled into false complacency by his white peers, deracinated by their acceptance, and lost all instincts of survival, to become easy prey for Iago. We hate the way Othello murders his sweet wife, but feel for him, and with him, as he realizes how gullible he has been.

In *Antony and Cleopatra*, assimilation is not a demand but an irresistible force. Antony marries Octavia, tries to be true to her and his nation. His Roman identity is overcome and he is rendered helpless, becomes a victim of disorder. That theme again. Cleopatra pulled Julius Caesar too, in earlier times. He came out of the trance, just in time. Mark Antony, colossus of the Roman Imperium, yields to louche Egypt. Caught as he is in tempests of passion, he does not heed calls to duty. The pull is not just that of a sensual siren. It's a culture war and the Orient wins.

SHAKESPEARE'S EXOTIC CREATIONS AND MODERNITY

Britain now has the highest numbers of mixed-race couplings, and children, in the Western world. Their compulsions and fears, joys and sorrows were so consummately showcased by Shakespeare 400 years ago there seems little more left to say.

Princess Diana had two infidel lovers, extravagant strangers, dangerous men, 'from here and everywhere'.[97] One was the son of the Arab merchant of Cairo Mohamed Al-Fayed, hated by the establishment. After her death in a car crash in Paris, rumours flew that she was pregnant. What if, like Tamora in *Titus*, she had given birth to a dark baby with frizzy hair? Imagine what might have been the reactions across England.

Throughout the centuries of colonialism to now, Shakespeare, England's noblest son, has inspired, awoken, aroused and spoken for the peoples of the world, even those who remain resentful about England's previous dominance.

I interviewed an Arab settler in London whom I shall call Dr F., born in Cairo in 1943, when the country was governed by the British. (The Ottomans and Napoleon also once ruled this mighty land.) In 1952, a revolution by the army led by Gamal Abdel Nasser overthrew the king and, after further battles and resistance, ended British occupation. What Dr F. told me was revealing and fascinating. He still can't forgive European colonialism but he has lived in Europe for nearly fifty years. In 1963, he joined the RSC in Stratford as a 'guest trainee'. He has translated around thirty English plays into Arabic – including those by Ben Jonson, Christopher Marlowe and Shakespeare, his hero: 'His morals are morals we can follow. He is always relevant, relevant everywhere. Who else can write about love, hate, power? I directed some of his plays in big theatres in Cairo. I am a classically trained actor – I can do Shakespeare in Arabic and in English.'

One of the first successful Merchant Ivory films was *Shakespeare Wallah* (1965), based on the true story of the actress Felicity Kendal's family. Her father Geoffrey, mother Laura and other actors were roving players in India, taking the Bard's greatest tragedies and comedies to small towns and villages, creating new enthusiasts in their wake. I have met Indians who still remember this troupe. Jennifer Kendal, also an actress, married Shashi Kapoor, from the most famous Bollywood acting dynasty. Indo-English artistic bonds have deep roots.

Shakespeare was entrenched in British East Africa, too, and was regarded as an essential part of citizenship training and human development. When independence was approaching, Tanzania's first president, Julius Nyerere, translated *Julius Cesar* and *Macbeth* into the national language, Swahili, and sent actors to perform the plays in villages so people would think about the responsibilities and temptations of power. His country has been among the most stable in Africa. Tanzanians tell me that what Nyerere planted in the national psyche can never be uprooted or forgotten. Anthony, thirty-three, a black Tanzanian priest, can still recite speeches by Mark Antony and Brutus in Kiswahili. He was taught them by his grandfather, a Marxist secondary-school teacher.

So long after the imperial sun set, are those Shakespearean connections really that strong? Yes, absolutely – not as lingering vestiges of historical British control, but in their own right, as tales of here and now and the future, as enactments of modern tragedies and comedies in all the conflict zones of the globe. Elizabethan playwrights used Eastern stories to reflect on their own society. Today dramatists on the subcontinent and in Arabia employ the same trick, staging British and European plays to cast light on their own political predicaments and chaos, finding clever theatrical ways to fool censors and echo what audiences think but can't say. And the works of Shakespeare are the most popular and potent.

Sulayman Al-Bassam, a Kuwaiti playwright and director, explains: 'If you are an Arab theatre-maker looking to take a pop at authority in today's Arab world, Shakespeare is your perfect bedmate, co-conspirator and alibi.'[98] 'Shaikh Al-Zubair', as Shakespeare is known, enables artists to communicate 'illicit meanings, transgressive actions and contentious critiques'.[99]

Religious authority and theological differences, turbulent wars, gender inequality, oppression, tyrants, contested kingships – these are 'daily fare in today's Arab world', says Al-Bassam, who is adept at avoiding censors but never letting the relevance of his productions slip into mere entertainment. His adaptations of *Hamlet* (2001) and *Richard III*[100] (2007) had meanings within meanings and reflected Iraq better than any journalistic work: '[It] is not a mercantile desire to cash in on the Shakespearean corporate tag . . . nor, as some Shakespeareans might have it, to ape our former colonial masters. It is rather the belief that with "Shaikh Al-Zubair" as our partner, we can inquire deeper into the pressing concerns of our people, and of the world outside.'[101]

I have always said that for white Europeans around the world, Shakespeare is a genius, music to their ears, consummate and wise, but not really relevant to the way they live now, at least not in the way it undeniably is for people of colour the world over. We live the dramas and dilemmas in his plays, from forced marriages to politics; they are real, happening right now.

The Globe and the Royal Shakespeare Company have turned Shakespeare into a playwright of the world, not just of Stratford-upon-Avon and little England. As recently as the 1990s critics were still fretting about the casting of 'coloured' actors in 'white' roles. They even objected to a naturally dark-skinned Othello. In the twenty-first century all that seems so passé, really rather backward. We saw how much had changed when, in 2001, David Oyelowo, of Nigerian heritage, born in Oxford, raised in Tooting, London, was chosen to play Henry VI for an RSC production. The most conservative reviewers suspended disbelief and were gripped by the performance. Not since Aldridge played Richard III in the mid-nineteenth century had a black man been cast as an English king in a Shakespearean historical drama.

In 2006–7, Michael Boyd, then artistic director of the RSC, set out to stage every one of Shakespeare's plays in a year-long festival, some following established traditions, others innovative and surprising; some by British companies, the rest from far and wide. Al-Bassam's *Richard III* was part of that extraordinary festival, as was a Japanese *Titus Andronicus* directed by Yukio Ninagawa. And the most astonishing was *A Midsummer Night's Dream* by director Tim Supple, who scouted around India to pick his cast and created a version which had several Indian languages woven into the original text. It was the most exotic of exotic productions and a triumph, still remembered. English audiences didn't mind the pandemonium of languages intruding into one of Shakespeare's most popular plays.

BLACK AND BROWN ON THE ENGLISH STAGE

This last section – all too brief – is about playwrights and directors of Eastern or Southern heritage whose work has history, some history.

The play *East is East* was first staged in 1996, a collaboration between Birmingham Rep, the Royal Court in London and Tamasha, an innovative troupe showcasing new writing and reclaimed stories from the British theatrical canon.

Written by the actor and writer Ayub Khan Din, the play was based on his own life, growing up as one of the many children of an immigrant Pakistani father and a white, working-class mother from Salford. In the play, the compromises made by the husband and wife seem to crack as they all get older. The father gets more tyrannical because of guilt and fear that the family is not properly Pakistani and Muslim. Things fall apart. It was poignant, funny, authentic – the other, barely known story of England. British Asian audiences reacted as Londoners must have done when they first saw plays at the first theatres that sprang up in the capital in the sixteenth century. They were gripped by the story and the energy of live performance, had seen nothing like it ever before: a Pakistani/white family in a deprived northern city, linked by class and love, separated by religion and race. White audiences were surprised and enraptured for other reasons. Britons know little about working-class white women who made lives with Asian men in the 1950s and 1960s, and faced down the bigotry that must have assailed them on all sides. The play was ground-breaking in every way.

Sudha Bhuchar and Kristine Landon-Smith, the co-founders of Tamasha, and Jatinder Verma, the director and founder of Tara Arts, are consummate cross-cultural theatre professionals who find Asian talent and revive tales from, and of, the East. More daringly, they take European classics and relocate them in unexpected milieus. Verma directed *The Tempest* in 2008, and made Prospero a wise yet vengeful Muslim and Miranda a veiled innocent. It was immensely powerful and evocative of present-day realities. Bhuchar and Landon-Smith co-wrote a script based on *Wuthering Heights* but set in Rajasthan, a perfect fit. There are lesser-known playwrights, English and of Eastern heritage, whose plays are also about creative syntheses, but there are not nearly enough to reflect the nation today.

In 2012, the year of the London Olympics, Boyd dreamt up another extrava-
ganza – a World Shakespeare Festival.[102] An all-Asian ensemble production of
Much Ado About Nothing was staged in Stratford-upon-Avon and in London, to
rollicking reviews. The director was Iqbal Khan, a British-Pakistani and the first
Asian ever to direct a play in the West End. Khan grew up in inner-city
Birmingham, one of five brothers, raised by a widowed mother. As a young boy
he'd spent his afternoons listening to Shakespeare's plays recorded on cassette.
He never saw himself as an outsider: 'People who were suffering [racism] then
were clearly identifying themselves as "the Other" and attracting that attention.
Intellectually I was more interested in Shakespeare, Dickens, classical music and
cricket.'[103] He admits to feeling 'that tension between who I am and who I am
expected to be'.[104] I suspect that if Khan had grown up in a middle-class Asian
family in England or Pakistan, he would feel no such tension. English education
and culture makes them who they think they are. And if he had grown up during
the heady days when subjugated folk were fighting for freedom, he wouldn't feel
it either. Gandhi or Nehru and millions of others accepted and valued their cultural
duality. Khan is a product of post-modernism and identity struggles, internal
and external.

Though the director disowns ethnic identification, he has chosen to direct
plays about the British Asian experience, with the panache and intimacy of a true
insider. In 2008, Khan revived Din's *East is East*, which was acclaimed by critics
and audiences of all backgrounds.

Khan, the willing assimilator, effectively exploits the English infatuation
with the East. He located his RSC production of *Much Ado* in Delhi, and cast
Meera Syal as Beatrice and Paul Bhattacharjee as Benedick, older lovers giving
it their all. It felt plausible because India still has joint families, arranged

marriages, uncompromising ideas about 'honour' and obedience to elders.

As part of the same World Shakespeare Festival, *Julius Caesar* was directed by Doran, with all black actors and set in Africa. The production was incomparably vibrant and forceful; it brought alive and gave shape to failed African politics over the past sixty years. The portents, soothsayers and extra-worldly influences swilling around in Rome felt real because they *are* real in today's Africa. Mandela often quoted lines from the play in prison, and discussed it with his young son Thembi when the boy was allowed a visit. Thembi died before his father was released – a tragedy worthy of a Shakespeare play.[105]

THE MAGICAL EAST TODAY

In recent years, two London directors, two of the best, have worked hard to rescue the *Arabian Nights* from previous distortions, prudery and superciliousness. The first was Dominic Cooke, who selected a range of stories – 'adventure, quest, romance, and fabliau-style capers . . . [and] rediscovered the early roots of the *Nights* in exemplary literature and turned it into a kind, moral fable'. Most radically of all, Cooke used the weird and fantastical to make audiences question their own unshakeable beliefs.[106] When I saw the performances, I was struck by how the show, with all its exotica, felt as if it belonged on the London stage, was an intricate part of its canon.

In 2011, Tim Supple produced his own *One Thousand and One Nights*, the most authentic version ever. He commissioned Lebanese novelist Hanan Al-Shaykh to write the script and then spent months in the Middle East setting up workshops for actors and musicians, just as the Arab uprisings were breaking out. The book, which had been corrupted by Europeans in the eighteenth century, and then suppressed by Islamic societies, was rehabilitated by Supple, a brave act of love. Over six mesmerizing hours, the epic explored the ups and down of marriage, love, fidelity, fate, women, men, the most outrageous sex, destiny, family and rulers. I interviewed Supple while the show was on in Edinburgh and he explained why he took on such an impossibly big project: 'When it comes to Arabian cultures, we swing from romantic notions to fearful ones. We have to hear people as they really are.'[107] I sensed that he was referring to the post 9/11 Western view of Arabs and the Middle East.

The Royal Court, until recently headed by Dominic Cooke, has punched above its weight and always, always reached out to the world, not merely in its choice of themes, plays and actors, but also through outreach partnerships, so that the excellence of British theatre is shared and new dramatists – from India to South America – emerge to make theatrical pieces which are grounded in their cultures but also universal and of artistic merit. In 2012, I spent a fortnight in Mumbai, India, watching works by young writers as part of the Writer's Bloc festival. The plays were in English, Hindi and Marathi. Five experts from the Royal Court, with a Mumbai threesome who run the Rage Theatre Company, created this festival. The alchemy produced blazing creativity.

One evening while there, I spoke to the youngish people who were ardent supporters of the festival and what they called 'new Indian theatre'. Shobha, a dancer and aspiring playwright, is a 'huge fan' of Shakespeare and other early English playwrights, also David Hare and Caryl Churchill: 'Without the English men who started the first theatres, there would be no modern theatre. I think India, and the freed Arab countries, are like England was in the 1500s. It is chaotic, everything is changing, no one knows what is coming, even in India, because too much is changing too fast. So I see our lives reflected in English plays. Culturally that county seems to understand us better than we do ourselves.

And the opposite too – if they hadn't travelled, they could not have written these plays.'

Or indeed painted the pictures, or built up scientific knowledge or given the most versatile and expressive language in the world to the world.

7 People

'The efforts all these years to live in the dress of Arabs and imitate their mental foundations quitted me of my English self and let me look at the west and its conventions with new eyes: they destroyed it all for me . . . sometimes these selves would converse in the void; and then madness was very near, as it would be for any man who could see through the veils at once of two customs, two educations, two environments.'

T. E. Lawrence, *Seven Pillars of Wisdom*[1]

'T. E. Lawrence, some say, loved Arabs, and others that he was a British spy. The truth is somewhere in between. He represents the unstable, love-hate relationship between East and West, England and us.'

Dr Kamel Abu Jaber,
Director of the Royal Institute for
Inter-Faith Studies, Jordan[2]

THE ENGLISH, AS THIS book attests, are drawn to mesmeric and sometimes discombobulating people and places. They try valiantly to put on 'the moral equivalent of a frock coat, button themselves right up.'[3] But the urge to break out is strong within roving and also homebound Englanders, with the world on their streets, in dancehalls, eateries, parks and shops. These cultural free spirits are found not only in wanton London, but all over the land, from north to south.

Philip Marsden is a travel writer who takes readers on secular pilgrimages, outside their margins of understanding. In 2011, he wrote *The Levelling Sea*, about the seaport of Falmouth, which, between the sixteenth and nineteenth centuries, was a boisterous intersection, a boom town and hot spot for pirates.

Peter Mundy, a local man, sailed away around 1628, drank 'cha' (tea) in China, joined the East India Company, and watched the Taj Mahal go up. Two hundred years later, the anti-slavery and anti-imperialist writer James Silk Buckingham took off from Falmouth and traversed the Ottoman Empire, Persia and India, spreading his moral messages.[4] He published vivid narratives on Arabia and, in 1818, established the *Calcutta Journal*, which boldly criticised the East India Company. For that 'disloyalty' he was expelled from India and the periodical was banned.

As in other port towns, strangers disembarked in Falmouth and some never left. One of them was freed slave Joseph Emidy, who arrived in the early 1800s, became a celebrated musician and composer, and was admired by colleagues of Haydn and Beethoven.[5] Falmouth is a microcosm of outgoing, intrepid England.

This final chapter is about some of the most remarkable men and women who unbuttoned their tight coats and released their audacious, intrepid selves. It is a small selection from a vast number of national extroverts, several of whom left records.[6] I have grouped them under various headings, though some individuals clearly belong to more than one category.

Travellers, Adventurers and Anthropologists

The historian Richard Knolles (c. 1545–1610) did not leave cosy England, but passed the travel bug to many of his kinsmen. In his modest schoolmaster's study in Sandwich, Kent, using existing printed chronicles and testimonies, he penned his *Generall Historie of the Turkes*. Published in 1603, it 'offered a panorama of colourful, vivid and lasting images of an otherwise unutterably strange part of the world'.[7] The book became a bestseller and may have influenced Shakespeare.[8] Samuel Johnson later opined that Knolles, despite his genius as a scholar, had sunk into obscurity because of 'the barbarity and remoteness of the story he relates',[9] which shows that even the great Dr Johnson didn't quite understand the wanderlust of his people.

The Sherley brothers were among the first wave of Englishmen who sailed off to unknown, mysterious parts of the globe.[10] Sir Thomas Sherley, born in 1542 in the small Sussex parish of Wiston, was an MP, a privateer, and a convicted serial fraudster. His eldest son, Sir Thomas the second (1564–1634), like his father also an MP and brigand, was taken captive in Constantinople and thereafter turned into a fanatical Christian, filled with hatred for the Ottomans and Islam. He spent years futilely trying to muster support for a European war against the Turks and ended up a bitter man.

Sir Thomas's two younger brothers, Sir Anthony (1565–1635) and Sir Robert (1581–1628), didn't share his chauvinism and were rather more successful. They were smart tacticians and fearless mercenaries who presented themselves at the Safavid court in Persia and won over the ruler, Shah Abbass. Here is Anthony in full flight: 'And now that I am in Persia . . . since he [the king] is both one of the mightiest Princes that are, and one of the excellentest . . . besides, the fashion of his gouerment differing so much from that which we call barbarousnesse, that it may serve for as great an Idea for a Principality as Platoes Common-wealth did for a Gouerment of that fort'.[11] Flattery got him to high places. Anthony was made a *mirza* (a prince) and Robert a top courtier. The brothers soon became fabled characters and their tales were recounted with awe throughout the seventeenth century.

Shah Abbass gave them 5,000 horses and paid them handsomely to train his army to fight like the English militia. Later the two brothers became his emissaries. Robert arrived in Rome dressed in Persian garb, but with a crucifix fixed to his turban. For portraits, he donned splendiferous Persian cloaks and turbans, looking every bit the Eastern potentate.[12] His Circassian wife, Teresia, was painted wearing golden, gossamer gowns, a pale and lovely Scheherazade. Sir Thomas must have been horrified by the 'betrayal' of his younger brothers, so too other hidebound gentlemen.[13] Little England deplores those who break codes of loyalty and acceptable conduct, but has never been able to stop them.

Sir Henry Blount (1602–82) must surely have read Knolles and known about the brothers before he toured the Ottoman Empire and recorded his impressions.[14] A traveller, he believed, should, 'be weyning his minde from all former habite of opinion', to be not 'an old man' but 'fresh and sincere' and make his own judgements.[15] Though appalled by the sight of enslaved Christians, Blount retained his objectivity. Turks, he decided, were ruthless but also contemplative and profound, more loyal too than the 'superficial' and flighty English. Never dry and cerebral, Blount evidently took pleasure in enchanting courtyards, birds, fountains and orchards, and handsome Arabian horses. He represented a type:

the Englishman who was centred and sturdy, who sought new experiences and knowledge and did not instinctively belittle other civilizations.

A number of Englishwomen too freed themselves from conventional expectations and bias when they went east. One of the best known is the feisty, unafraid and clever Lady Mary Wortley Montagu (1698–1762), mentioned in the previous chapter. Her landowning family had a comprehensive library, so our lively heroine got hooked on books when young. By the age of fourteen she was writing poems, epistolary novellas and flowery letters. When she was old enough, her father decided to marry her to an Irish nobleman, but she eloped with Edward Wortley Montagu MP. Her glittering soirees were attended by intellectuals, artists, politicians and groupies. Sadly, in 1715, she contracted smallpox, was dropped by fashionable society, satirized even. Edward was posted to Turkey as ambassador and she went with him. Turkey welcomed her wholeheartedly.

Lady Mary was reputedly the first white woman ever to be allowed into the inner sanctums of Ottoman homes, baths and palaces. She studied and experienced the culture without the shadow of prejudice, often exploding received ideas. Turkish women were less restricted than was she. They couldn't understand how European women could wear corsets and dresses like boxes and prisons.[16] In the baths in Adrianople, local women lolled about naked, drinking coffee or fruit juice, embroidering, doing each other's hair. She found them beautiful and easy, particularly admired the freedom from 'surprize' or 'impertinent Curiosity', 'disdainful smiles or satyric whispers'.[17] That, obviously, was a reference to the way she was mocked and scorned in England after she was scarred by smallpox.

She 'escaped from her confining society and [experienced] a new world without the prejudices into which she was born'.[18] Lady Montagu saw what few of her compatriots could see, without ever losing her critical sense.

After the eighteenth century more Englishwomen went overseas to get away from their proscribed lives, to accompany their husbands or to serve their churches and nation. They could be harsher, more rule-bound and racist than men, but a good number were happy to go beyond their cultural borders and seemed to find their true selves in alien societies. The boldest and most fiercely independent of them seemed not to have the herd instinct.[19]

The irrepressible Lady Hester Stanhope was born in 1776. Her father, an earl, tried to keep her within the confines of female domesticity and when she refused to comply, disowned her. William Pitt the younger, her uncle, unmarried, relatively relaxed about female behaviour and clearly fond of Hester, invited her to live with him. When he died, Pitt's state pension went to his niece. In 1810, Hester set out for the Middle East via Turkey. She rode on horseback at breakneck speed, sometimes in sober English dresses, sometimes in Turkish clothes, resisting categorization. Her 'life was packed with more drama, adventure, romance and exoticism than experienced by most mortals'.[20] Stanhope had a wild love and sex life, though not, ultimately, a happy one. To Arabs she became known as Queen Hester,[21] and to Bedouins she was ul-Huzza, 'star of the morning'.[22] It all went to her head and she began to believe she was chosen to do wondrous things as foretold by a fortune teller.[23]

In Egypt, she draped herself 'in purple velvet and gold brocade, with a cashmere shawl as a turban and another as a sash.'[24] The pasha liked the costume but was more turned on by her 'profound diplomatic insights and practical economic and military advice'. She was smarter than any man he'd come across.[25] He gifted her a magnificent stallion. Eventually she settled in a beautiful spot in the Lebanon; from there she wielded significant influence through informal alliances and some mystical tricks. Detested by many in her homeland, Stanhope not only bloomed but learnt to see, feel and think differently in the Orient. As did other resilient and audacious Englishwomen. Some even ventured to censure their own kinsfolk, which can't have been easy or cost free.

Fanny Parks (1794–1875) arrived in India in 1822 and spent twenty-four years on what she described as her 'pilgrimage' wandering around the subcontinent – to her, a 'bright, beautiful' land. She was dismayed by the way some Europeans carried on at the Taj Mahal and wrote down these thoughts: 'Can you imagine anything so detestable? . . . [they] have the band to play on the marble terrace, and dance quadrilles in front of the tomb! . . . I cannot enter the Taj without a feeling of deep devotion . . . the deep devotion with which the natives prostrate themselves when they make their offerings of money and flowers at the tomb.'[26]

Emily Eden (1797–1869), sister of George, Governor-General of India (1836–42), saw the Mughal Qutub Minar tower in Delhi and, like Parks, was ecstatic and also discomfited: 'Of all the things I ever saw, this is the finest. Did we know about it in England? I mean did you and I in our ancient Briton state know? Don't feel ashamed, there is no harm in not knowing only I do say it is rather a pity we were so ill taught.'[27] Julia Charlotte Maitland (1808–64) found it painful to witness the 'rudeness and contempt' with which the English treated their servants, while Constance Gordon-Cumming (1837–1924) 'scoffed at their feeling of racial superiority'. Several English daughters of the Empire broke ranks and attacked their government and the East India Company for impoverishing India.[28]

Between 1837 and 1910 over a thousand British women, many of them English, wrote travelogues.[29] Their gaze and understanding was different to those of men and they defy the stereotypes of sexless, spinster missionaries and snooty memsahibs. The Indian scholar Manoj Mishra writes that 'They like things Indian, ranging from architecture to festivals, rulers to servants, art and culture to the honesty and integrity of Indians. They are neither slow in praising the traits of Indians that move them . . . nor slow in condemning the behaviour of their countrymen they find nauseating.'[30]

The same was true of women travelling through Arab lands. Jane Digby (1807–81) was perhaps the most spectacular example of such female insubordination and autonomy. Beautiful and upper class, her first husband was Edward Law, who was appointed Governor-General of India in 1824. Young Jane divorced him a few years later. There followed three more husbands and many beaus, including European aristocrats and an Albanian outlaw. For years she seemed to be on an interminable, exhausting quest for fulfilment.

At the age of forty-six she travelled to Syria and within a month found herself an Arab 'of surpassing attractions . . . a splendid creature, very possessive, who swept her off her feet and into the black Bedouin tents of his encampment out in the desert'.[31] The affair burnt out. Then one day, while haggling over the price of a camel, Digby met a cultured and sensual Bedouin nobleman, Sheikh Abdul Medjuel el Mezrab, twenty years her junior. She was entranced. They married and were parted only by her death.[32]

They lived half the year in goatskin tents wandering with tribal nomads, the other half in a splendid palace Digby had had built in Damascus.[33] The relationship was torrid, explosive and special: 'Jane was quick to adopt Arab ways. She smoked narghilye and liked to go barefoot, wearing the traditional blue robe and yashmak. She learnt to outline her eyes with the smudge-line of kohl that is an essential part of an Arab woman's maquillage, and flung herself into the life and habits of the tribe. Both outwardly and inwardly, she was one of them.'[34] An aristocrat threw it all away and became a wild desert flower. It is both a remarkable and unremarkable story.

Take another example. Mrs Hervey,[35] a Victorian gentlewoman, was an 'exceptionally bold and attractive adventuress who had flung herself into travelling as a consolation and escape from an unhappy marriage. Her travels were unbelievably daring, especially for a sheltered lady of those times. They took her to the remotest parts of Asia – through Tartary, Tibet, China and Kashmir.'[36] Army wives, claimed Hervey, were 'galley slaves',[37] trapped and bullied. She knew that from bitter personal experience. Such candour and gutsiness is rarely found among army wives, even today, when duty trumps everything.

Hervey felt she had to go and find life, find the person she really was. En route she ran into Sir Henry Lawrence, top chap, President of the British Board of Administration in the Punjab. The encounter proved testing. He thoroughly disapproved of a married woman gadding about. Mr Hodson, Sir Henry's assistant, was awed by Hervey: 'A very pretty creature, gifted and with indomitable energy and endurance . . . she has been pony-riding through country few men would care to traverse, over formidable passes and across the wildest deserts in Asia. For twenty days she was in Tibet without seeing a human habitation; often without food or bedding'. They met the nomadic lady on a dark, stormy night. Hodson gave her his tent, cot, warm stockings, towels and brushes, and declared he had never spent a pleasanter evening.[38] Imagine the consternation!

In the chronicles of the nation, one finds many such embodiments of the irrepressible heart and probing mind of England. Edward William Lane (1801–76) was a great savant. His *Description of Egypt*, a comprehensive social study, completed in 1828, was only published in full in 2000. He also penned an Arab–English dictionary and translated *One Thousand and One Nights*. Inexplicably, though post-colonial sages accept Lane was assiduous and intellectually honest, they still besmirch him for his labours.[39]

A trained engraver, Lane arrived in Egypt in his early twenties: 'As I approached the shore . . . I felt like an Eastern bridegroom, about to lift up the veil of his bride, and to see, for the first time, the features which were to charm, or disappoint, or disgust him.'[40] I find Lane's anticipation not insolent but touching, candid. He lived among Egyptians, dressed in local clothes, adopted an Arab persona, calling himself Mansur Effendi, a name engraved on the signet ring he wore till he died.

Sometimes his Victorian eyes disapproved of what he saw: 'dancing in private entertainment to the sounds of various instruments . . . licentious, with one or two of the performers generally depicted in a state of perfect nudity'.[41] And at other times he was profoundly affected: 'The temperance and moderation of the Egyptians with regard to diet are very exemplary. I have scarcely seen a native of this country in a state of intoxication unless it was a musician at an entertainment or low prostitute'.[42] The texts were illustrated with precise, delicate etchings. He knew he was trespassing and trod gently, with integrity.

In her biography of Lane, the Egyptian-American professor Leila Ahmed examines her subject's psychological attachments: '[He] loved Egypt, unreservedly . . . his entire life and the work he undertook would be an act of devotion and service to that country and culture he so much loved and in which he felt, almost from the start, more at home than he did in his own land.'[43]

Lane's sister, Sophia Poole, after separating from her husband, joined him in Egypt and made herself useful by researching the lives of women, with whom Lane could have no contact. In England, Sophia's lively, non-judgemental jottings, published in the 1840s, 'caused a mild sensation. It might be permissible for a learned chap like Lane to immerse himself in the exotic culture of the East – but an Englishwoman? A Christian wife and mother dressing herself up in Turkish "trousers" and visiting the city's harems? Living in what she insisted is a haunted house, and witnessing barbarous murders almost on her own doorstep? And, worst of all, taking Turkish baths with natives?'[44] Yes, and loving every minute of it!

Young Egyptians I've met thank the Lanes for leaving such a lucid record of old Cairean life. Hamid, a landscape painter, is one enthusiast: 'My English teacher told me to read Lane. I understand so much about that time. It is a joke, isn't it, that I know about my own people from an Englishman who was a colonialist?' Hamid admires maligned Orientalist painters too, in particular the way they painted light and shade indoors.

In Harriet Martineau (1802–76) we find a Victorian sensibility with modern tendencies. She was the first female English social scientist, a feminist before the word was articulated, and a proponent of human equality. Out in Egypt, she couldn't stand the vanity and stupidity of supremacist Europeans she met there: '[I was] shaped and determined by what I saw and thought during those all-important months I spent in the East.'[45] She found beauty everywhere, in the bright skies of Alexandria, in Arab men and women, 'the brown complexion . . . the beautiful eyes, soft, clear and intelligent; and the exquisite grace of carriage and gesture.'[46]

She found much that dismayed her too: older wives discarded in polygamous households, slaves used and abused, Christians maltreated by Muslims. Sometimes she herself was spat at and insulted, yet she maintained her objectivity and moral understanding: 'I wish that, in return for our missions to the heathen, the heathens would send missionaries to us, to train us to a graceful use of our noble natural endowments – of our powers of sense and limb, and the functions which are involved in their activity . . . There is no saying how much vicious propensity would be checked, and intellectual activity equalized in us by such a reciprocity with those whose gifts are at the other extreme from our own.'[47] Like Lane, Martineau engaged with the East within the colonial framework, but frequently breached that paradigm, to record observations which, even today, seem extraordinarily tolerant and fair.

Florence Nightingale (1820–1910), frozen in history as the lady with the lamp, had a tremendous back story, again illustrating the stubborn strength and wide-ranging interests of plucky Englishwomen. In her late twenties she was miserable, mainly because she was under family pressure to marry. In 1849, friends took her to Egypt. The trip was transformative: 'She had wondered for many years why she was not satisfied with the comfort, privilege and love in which she had been nurtured. By the time she left the Nile she understood why this was.'[48] In a letter sent from Luxor she wondered how 'people come back from Egypt and live lives as they did before'.[49] She attended mosque in full burkha. Some men and women were praying, others were gossiping or weaving baskets, a few were asleep breathing in the holy air. 'She loved the sense of ease in the mosque, and recognized something honest and also noble in the worshippers.'[50]

These women weren't moral relativists. Nightingale could not reconcile herself to the position of women in Egypt and had other misgivings. But Cairo made her spirit soar: 'a forest of minarets, domes and towers. The Nile flows his solemn course beyond, the waters being still out (it is now high Nile) and the three pyramids stand sharp against the sky. Here Osiris and his worshippers lived; here Abraham and Moses walked; here Aristotle came; here, later, Mohamet learnt the best of his religion and studied Christianity; here, perhaps, our Saviour's mother brought her son to the light.'[51] What a prayer, what an evocation. Certainly, she was also irritated by Eastern fatalism and lassitude. But she did find enlightenment and meaning in Egypt, land of alien gods.

So did Sir Wilfred Patrick Thesiger (1910–2003), though today some are slightly repelled by his disposition and approach. He was a maverick: an explorer, anthropologist, photographer, an efficient circumciser of boys, idealizer of the pre-Industrial world. In one photograph, his bearded face is gaunt, his eyes angry, around his head is a carelessly wound cotton turban and he holds a gun; he looks a bit like Osama Bin Laden.

The Thesigers were barons and viscounts, and Wilfred was of course educated at Eton and Oxford. Born in Addis Ababa, his young head was filled with stories of tribes and vast deserts by his father, a British diplomat. He never forgot them and all his life craved 'barbaric splendour, for savagery and colour and the throb of drums'.[52] Today such language and sentiments are rightly abhorred, but something inestimable has also gone.

When you look at the photographs Thesiger took of desert life, they are works of art, acts of love. And the books written by this self-taught anthropologist, botanist, ethnologist, geologist and zoologist are out of this world, in every sense. *Arabian Sands* and *The Marsh Arabs* when read by future generations will seem to them magical realism, not works of non-fiction.

According to his biographer Alexander Maitland, Thesiger was 'most at ease among tribal peoples, to whom family dignity and loyalty were essentials of everyday existence; whose traditions had not been subverted by Western materialism'.[53] He wanted to find different ways of living and being.[54] But his views were inconsistent and confusing. To Middle Easterners and Africans, he was a hero, divinely blessed; he gave away thousands of pounds to tribesmen. Yet he never refused medals and honours, wore tailored suits, played convoluted diplomatic games. He was in and of the establishment, but stood outside it too.

In our times, illustrious travellers of all backgrounds carry on evocatively recording disappearing worlds.[55] Notable Englishmen include Eric Newby, who wrote the masterpiece *A Short Walk in the Hindu Kush*, and the photojournalist Nick Danziger, whose empathy enables him to catch the light and sounds and soul of the East. Danziger adopted three orphaned Afghani children and made them his own. Colin Thubron, an English Etonian, takes us to Damascus, whispering its beauty into our ears, to elusive Lebanon, where we hear the noise and its thumping heart, off to teeming China, where unfathomable numbers become names, memorable characters. In her eventful life, Brigid Keenan, for years the wife of a British diplomat, has written wonderfully about her travel and times in Islamic countries. She has the empathy of Martineau, Nightingale and others who went before. Like them, she assimilated into local life and allowed herself to change: 'I liked to go and sit in the Great Mosque of Damascus at the end of the day, during the evening prayer; we went so often, in fact, that I had my own little chador made . . . We found the mosque such a calm and spiritual place.'[56]

It's lazy and unfair to question, as some do,[57] the motives of such wanderers and writers. They 'tend, by their very natures, to be rebels and outcasts and misfits: far from being an act of cultural imperialism, setting out and vulnerable on the road is often a rejection of home and embrace of the other'.[58]

Imperial Shapeshifters, Cultural Exiles and Nomads

That sense of being out of place, discernible in many English itinerants and often articulated by self-exiled Englanders today, is a very English malaise. Most other humans migrate for economic, political or family reasons.

Lord Byron's alienation from his homeland was palpable and often expressed in letters: 'I shall leave England forever. Everything in my affairs tends to this, and my inclinations and health do not discourage it. Neither my habits nor constitution are improved by your customs and climate. I shall find employment in making myself a good Oriental scholar.'[59] The missives are a mixture of desolation and dreamy, lifelong imaginings of the East.

Just before he died, the poet told a Greek prince: '*The Turkish History* by Rycault and Knolles was one of the first books that gave me pleasure when I was a child; and I believe it had much influence on my subsequent wishes to visit the Levant, and gave, perhaps, the oriental colouring which is observed in my poetry.'[60] Those empathies and longings are evident in the famous portrait of Byron by Thomas Phillips (1813). On his head is a silk turban, with one end hanging down, a raffish touch. His velvet Albanian jacket and cloak are effete, excessive. His eyes seem far, far away. Three years later, Byron seems to have finally decided to leave England. His sexploits were causing national disquiet and in Eastern countries, up to a point, a white man could play free and loose. However, it would be trite to assume he went off simply to find sexual excitement. Byron was a complicated man, with tortuous desires and unpredictable affinities. Politically he was pro-Hellenic and against Ottoman power; culturally he felt an affinity with Mohammedans, Sufism and the Koran, which, he thought, contained 'the most poetical passages far surpassing European Poetry'.[61] He was a nowhere man, looking for erotic rapture, spiritual ecstasy and cosmic answers.

Like Byron, many famous, upper-class English misfits were escapists and fantasists. Some of those featured here were also suspected of colluding with devious imperial machinations. Were they despicable, two-timing bounders or divided souls? I can't decide.

Take Sir Richard Burton (1820–90), the Anglo-Irish explorer, diplomat, undercover agent, linguist and sexual 'deviant'. He translated the *Kama Sutra*, recorded racist and graphic observations about black phalluses, artful African and Eastern women and young boys happy to be buggered.[62] None of that shocked England nearly as much as the ease with which Burton cheerfully went native, in Africa, India and Arabia.

In India, Burton learnt Sindhi, Urdu, Punjabi and the Dravidian languages, was made a Sufi master and an honorary Sikh. He fell madly in love with a Persian noblewoman in India, but she sadly and unexpectedly died.[63]

Burton was one of the first white men to go on Hajj to Mecca. Disguised as an Arab, he got circumcised and learnt all the rituals: 'I may truly say that, of all the worshippers who clung weeping to the curtain, or who pressed their beating hearts to the stone, none felt for the moment a deeper emotion than did the Hajj from the far-north . . . But, to confess a humbling truth, theirs was the high feeling of religious enthusiasm, mine was the ecstasy of gratified pride.'[64] His countrymen thought Burton's pilgrimage was odious.[65] He retorted: 'what is there, I would ask, in the Moslem Pilgrimage so offensive to Christians – what makes it a subject of "inward ridicule"? Do they not also venerate Abraham, the Father of the Faithful?'[66]

I don't mean to glorify all the idiosyncratic Englishmen and women in the East. Some were no more than fortune or pleasure seekers. But they all sought out and negotiated unfamiliar terrains and societies in ways that intrigue and at times impress me.

Burton's wife Isabel was from an upper-class, English Catholic family. When still a young girl in the 1830s, 'she first began groping towards her lodestar East'.[67] In the woods, she found gypsy encampments and spent time among Romany people. She devoured books on the East and was enraptured.[68] Then, on a school trip to France, wide-eyed Isabel met Burton (aged thirty) and fell madly, fervently in love. A few years later, defying her parents, she married him and remained steadfastly committed to him in spite of his many betrayals, capriciousness, variable moods and loyalties.

Isabel was patient when Burton went off on his excursions, but she missed him terribly. When he got a government posting in Syria and could take his wife, she wrote: 'My destination was Damascus, the dream of my childhood. I should follow the footsteps of Lady Mary Wortley Montagu, Lady Hester Stanhope . . . women who lived of their own choice a thoroughly Eastern life . . . I am to live among Bedouin Arab chiefs: I shall smell the desert air; I shall have tents, horses, weapons and be free . . .'[69]

Their house in Syria had a courtyard, menagerie and a fountain. The muezzin's calls to prayer drifted from the mosque next door. Isabel went to public baths and harems to watch and gossip, was invited to circumcision and wedding ceremonies. She remained a devoutly Catholic Englishwoman, but one with an open heart and mind.

The Burtons were summarily dismissed by the Foreign Office in August 1871 – for being too close to Syrians, it is thought. 'When the news spread, the house was surrounded by Arabs, who walked up from the city, or Bedouins who galloped in from the desert, to protest and grieve . . . Their laments rose from the black tents they pitched on the hill-slopes all around.'[70]

They are buried together in a Roman Catholic churchyard in Mortlake, a middle-class suburb of London. Isabel chose the design of the mausoleum, shaped like a Bedouin tent, festooned with crucifixes and Islamic symbols. The memorial affirms her Catholic faith and their love of the Orient.

Wilfred Scawen Blunt (1840–1922) was a poet, writer and diplomat, whose mother had converted to Catholicism. That may explain why he never fitted into the British establishment, why he questioned colonialism and was attracted to oriental peoples. In 1895, he warned the British occupiers of Egypt: 'the Egyptian question, though now quiescent, will reassert itself unexpectedly in some urgent form hereafter, requiring of Englishmen a new examination of their position there, political and moral'.[71] Arabia for him was a 'sacred land' which had taught him much, most of all the virtue of humility.[72] He respected the tenets of Islam, supported Arab calls for independence and knew how to make a worthy nuisance of himself. His wife Annie, the granddaughter of Lord Byron, had inherited similar sympathies. It is a crying shame that these imperial code breakers have been misrepresented or written out of the histories of England and the endlessly troubled Arab lands.

Blunt was among those governed by morality and wisdom; other non-conformists relished political trickery.[73] Then there were sensitive Englanders abroad who did good, yet never found peace or a way to sew their different parts into a coherent whole.

One such was Gertrude Bell (1868–1926), who succeeded in changing the course of history. As Christopher Hitchins puts it, she 'midwifed Iraq'.[74] From a privileged background, she graduated from Oxford after just two years with a first-class degree. In 1892, while in Persia visiting her uncle, the British ambassador, Bell met the diplomat Henry Cadogan, a gambler with a fast-dwindling fortune. They rode together, read verses by the Persian poet Hafez, and fell in love. Her parents were apoplectic and she duly dropped Cadogan, who tragically died a year later. 'His death reinforced Bell's personal impressions of the East as the domain of the emotional and it became for her a constant refuge from hard-hearted, sometimes unfulfilling, personal relations in the West.'[75] Sadly, her romantic and sensual hopes were never to be realized.

Bell learnt Arabic and Persian and six other languages, studied archaeology, cherished the region and its peoples. From Persia she rhapsodized: 'I never knew what a desert was till I came here; it is a very wonderful thing to see; and suddenly in the middle of it all, out of nothing, out of a little cold water, springs a garden. Such a garden! Trees, fountains, tanks, roses and a house in it, the houses which we heard of in fairy tales when we were little: inlaid with tiny slabs of looking-glass in lovely patterns, blue tiled, carpeted, echoing with the sound of running water and fountains. Here sits the enchanted prince, solemn, dignified, clothed in long robes. He comes down to meet you as you enter.' And in another letter to her father: 'you know, Father, it's shocking how the East has wound itself around my heart till I don't know which is me and which is it. I never lose the sense of it . . . I'm more a citizen of Baghdad than many a Bagdadi [sic] born, and I'll wager that no Bagdadi cares more, or half as much, for the beauty of the river or the palm gardens, or clings more closely to the rights of citizenship which I have acquired.'[76]

Between 1898 and 1912, Bell – who was also a self-taught cartographer – undertook ambitious archaeological excursions and later opened a museum in Baghdad to display some of the finds. Through that work she acquired deep knowledge about the lifestyles and beliefs of tribal peoples and settled Arabs. This information would prove vital for her government in the shifting political topography as Arabs rebelled against Ottoman rule and were backed by Britain and France, which both had their own plans for domination of the region.[77] Bell, a sinuous power broker and operative, would use it to further her own ambitions and those of her state.

Bell played divide and rule, manipulative games. However, as her biographer Janet Wallach recognizes, she also united local tribes, ethnicities and faiths,[78] pushed for a bordered, shared, political entity. With the support of Winston

Churchill, a new nation was born. Iraq was a 'monument to her genius, to the versatility of her knowledge and influence, and to the practical idealism tempered with honest opportunism which were the outstanding characteristics of a remarkable Englishwoman.'[79]

Sir Mark Sykes, a Conservative politician who pushed British interests in the Middle East and thought Arabs were 'animals', reviled Bell: 'Confound the silly chattering windbag of conceited, gushing, flat-chested, man-woman, globe-trotting, rump-wagging, blethering ass.'[80] Arab men, on the other hand, were in awe of her. She moved as an equal among them and was given the name 'al-Khatun', a trusted lady of the royal court.

In 1925, she went back to England and was miserable and ill; she fled back to Iraq, where she developed pleurisy. By this time her influence had diminished. She was found dead after taking an overdose of sleeping pills. In 2011, a bronze bust of Bell was found in her beloved Baghdad museum and is now given pride of place. Iraqis used to say: 'There is only one al-Khatun, for a hundred years they will talk of Khatun riding by.'[81] They were right, believes the Middle East correspondent James Buchan: '[The] historical waters have closed over T. E. Lawrence . . . But "Miss Bell" is still a name in Baghdad. Even in the conversations with the vicious and cornered cadres of Saddam Hussein's regime, her name will come to evoke, for a moment, an innocent Baghdad of picnics in the palm gardens and bathing parties in the Tigris.'[82] England, though, barely remembers this ambitious, powerful and imaginative woman.

For me the most extraordinary of all these insider-outsiders was Harry St John Bridger Philby (1885–1965),[83] father of Cold War spy Kim Philby. A charismatic maverick, he defied all the norms of society yet inveigled himself into top positions. He was, at various times, a colonial officer, intelligence operator, masterful Arab negotiator, oil intermediary and major geopolitical player.

Born in 1885, in Ceylon, he was the son of Harry Montagu Philby, a coffee planter, and Queenie, the daughter of a colonel. When he was six, his mother moved to England with her children. He won a scholarship to Westminster, went on to Cambridge, where he studied oriental languages. One classmate was Jawaharlal Nehru, who was to become the first prime minister of independent India. In 1908, Philby joined the Indian civil service, became proficient in Urdu, Punjabi, Persian and Balochi. He married Dora Johnston, as patient as an angel's statue. Their son Kim, named after Kipling's boy hero, was born in Ambala, a province near Punjab.

In 1917, Philby was sent by the British government to Arabia. He was expected to instigate and spur on the Arab insurgency against the Ottomans and was indeed a well-paid member of the British Secret service. Unfortunately for his masters, his instincts were not wholly patriotic and he soon identified with the Arabs. In time he went on to oppose the creation of a Jewish state in Palestine (and so was branded an anti-Semite) and became particularly close to Arab leaders, most of all Ibn Saud. The two men admired each other and soon developed a deep bond. Over the time it took to create a new state of Saudi Arabia, Philby metamorphosed into an Arab, willingly surrendering his psyche and previous self to the Middle East. He admitted feeling a 'strange sensation of being at home and being at ease . . . an actual physical feeling of relief after the intensity of organized life of the great European cities'.[84] That relief was emotional, certainly, but sexual too. Stoic Dora put up with his shenanigans from afar and so did most of his British admirers. He was often invited to London by worthy societies to talk about his journeys into unexplored deserts, especially about the flora, fauna and birds that he had seen and assiduously recorded in his notebooks. The lectures were a sell-out.

Like other social renegades, Philby both shocked and thrilled conformist Englanders, until, that is, they decided to drop him: 'I was between two doors . . . my own people having turned me adrift for my uncomfortable opinions on matters Eastern and Arab, while the Arabs [were] ready with a welcome, and a very genuine one.'[85] In 1930, he converted to Islam, renamed himself Sheikh Abdullah, wrote books in praise of Wahhabism, the strict version of Islam imposed in Saudi Arabia. He married Rozy Abdul Aziz, a sixteen-year-old girl given to him by Ibn Saud. Their two sons became Saudi citizens. After his ally and friend Ibn Saud died, Philby was banished to Lebanon in 1955.[86] As he was dying in Beirut, with Kim at his bedside, Philby moaned: 'God I am bored!'[87] He lies in a Muslim cemetery in the Lebanese capital.

Perhaps one key reason why these men and women broke away is that they couldn't bear boredom or to live colourlessly and conventionally.

Mascots, Friends and Allies

Here I pick a small number of illustrative stories of foreigners in England who were courted, befriended, admired and, at times, idolized over the centuries. In some cases the attraction was shallow or whimsical, but there were many instances of intense connectivity and lasting trust. The outsiders included princes and paupers, slaves, servants, radicals and scholars. So what does this tell us? That even during slavery and a period of ruthless English conquest and profiteering, when racist belief systems were embedded in Western societies, there were always non-compliant, free-minded Englanders who reached out to outsiders. It is a compulsion. And a fine compulsion too.

In 1733, the artist William Hoare of Bath painted a black man with contemplative eyes, a chiselled face and Afro hair. He is wearing a khanzu, the traditional male Muslim robe, and a turban, both white and pure. A small orange book on a strap hangs round his neck, resting in the middle of his chest, close to the heart. The man was Ayuba Suleiman Diallo, also known as Job ben Solomon, born in West Africa into a clan of powerful Muslim clerics. In 1730, Diallo, himself in the slavery business, was captured by African agents of white slave-traders. He was no angel but conducted himself with noble dignity, his saving grace. Diallo was transported to a tobacco plantation in Maryland, USA, tried to escape and was recaptured. Thomas Bluett, an English lawyer and evangelical Christian, was moved by the elegant slave's tale, obtained his release and brought him to England. The lawyer recorded Diallo's story, the first slave narrative to be published.[88] Plots were underfoot to trick and recapture Diallo, so his well-heeled English supporters put down a bond to secure his freedom.

The portrait is quietly respectful; it seems to ask how such a poised dignitary could have been subjected to the mortification of slavery. Here was a black man, not subservient and abject but a Muslim patrician.[89] The book he wears as a pendant around his neck contained handwritten verses of the Koran.

Diallo, the Muslim outsider, fraternized with elites and royalty, key intellectuals and social reformers; Sir John Sloane asked him to help translate the Koran into English, and his main backers became embryonic abolitionists. He returned to his homeland and was lost to England. The portrait, too, was lost for several centuries, but is now owned by the Qatar National Museum, and is on loan to the National Portrait Gallery in London.

Captain Cook brought Omai to London in 1774, the first South Sea Islander to set foot in England.[90] He was a royal, beautiful and arrogant. In 1776, Joshua Reynolds painted the Polynesian in oriental robes and a turban, in a portrait that was more than the picture of a gorgeous stranger. Modern art critic Adam Nicolson detects embedded messages. The backdrop is Derbyshire, 'made softly and suggestively exotic by some unreal trees, half-elm, half-palm, tropical fronds sprouting from the temperate trunks . . . Its meaning transcends "here". It was painted by an Englishman, but that Englishman was reaching out beyond the confines of the parochial and the known, not simply to depict the exotic as a specimen of the odd and the unfamiliar – Omai is no weird butterfly pinned to a board – but to make something new and beautiful precisely because currents meet and mix within it. This painting is deeply and centrally internationalist.'[91]

The naturalist Sir Joseph Banks introduced Omai into society and he was, like Diallo, an instant hit, much admired. He dined at the Royal Society, rode and hunted on grand estates. King George III, it seems, granted him an allowance, and Fanny Burney was stunned by his 'understanding, far superior to the common race of us cultivated gentry'.[92] When Omai returned to Polynesia with Captain Cook in 1776, London society was bereft. Lord Sandwich bewailed: 'I am grown so used to him and have so sincere a friendship for him that I am quite depressed at his leaving me.'[93] At home Omai, rich and self-important, all too soon found himself isolated and resented. Did the English spoil him, confuse him so he didn't know who he was? Was he just an amusing pet to them? Yes, probably all that, though there was genuine reciprocal affection and interest too. Omai died in 1780, some two years after Cook dropped him off, so it all ended in tears. His fame in England continued, however; John O'Keefe's play, *Omai: A Voyage 'Round the World*, was performed at the Theatre Royal in Covent Garden in 1785.

Sake Dean Mahomed was another outsider who became an insider in the most unlikely of circumstances. Born in Bihar, Bengal, in 1759, he came from an advantaged Muslim family. At the age of ten Mahomed joined the army and rose through the ranks under the patronage of Captain Baker, an Irishman, who, in 1782, returned home to Cork in Ireland. Mahomed went with him. In 1794, his opus, *The Travels of Dean Mahomet*, was printed, 'the first book to be written and published in English by an Indian'.[94] In 1807 this plucky Indian joined the household of Sir Basil Cochrane in Portman Square, London. Three years later Mahomed set up the first curry house. The business failed (see Chapter 4) and he lost all his money, but not all his English friends.

In the early 1800s he realized railway connections would make Brighton a desirable destination for moneyed Londoners. He moved to the seaside town, opened up a spa. At Mahomed's Bathhouse the well-heeled were pampered with Indian body and head massages called 'shampooing', guaranteed to heal the heart, mind and body. Those were not wholly empty claims. At first people thought he was a cheating 'wog', but he offered sceptics free treatment and they became converts. Mahomed's cures seemed to work when all other remedies had failed. Doctors referred patients to this man, known by then as Dr Brighton. Sufferers of asthma, gout, lumbago, rheumatism apparently got better under his skilled hands. Among his exalted clients were Lord Castlereagh, Lord Canning, Lady Cornwallis, Sir Robert Peel, and the blue-blooded of England and Europe.

Mahomed became a local star, went to horse races, 'gorgeous in Eastern costumes with his pretty Irish wife by his side and a dagger in his girdle'.[95] With the Royal Pavilion orientalizing Brighton, Mahomed's Baths were in the right place at the right time.

Migrants who chose not to court English society but to stay outside and fight the powerful became prominent and respected activists. The state punished them savagely for not knowing their place. William Cuffay, a tailor, was one of the unacknowledged Africans who joined English radicals.[96] Born in 1788 in Kent, he was the descendant of slaves. With fellow tailors he went on strike in 1834, and later became a leader of the Chartist movement. He was found guilty of agitation and deported to Tasmania on a prison ship. Fellow Chartist and friend Thomas Martin Wheeler recalled one of Cuffay's rousing speeches: '[I] gazed with unfeigned admiration upon the high intellectual forehead and animated features of this diminutive Son of Africa's despised and injured race . . . he spoke the English tongue pure and grammatical, and with a degree of ease and facility which would shame many who boast of the purity of their Saxon or Norman descent.'[97]

William Davidson was born in Kingston, Jamaica, in 1786. His father was the attorney general there. At the age of fourteen, young Davidson was sent to Edinburgh to study. After that came a traineeship with a Liverpool lawyer. A few years later he ran off to sea, joined the navy and eventually became an apprentice to a cabinet maker in Lichfield, Staffordshire. When he mastered the craft, married Sarah Lane, a poor widow and mother of four. They settled in London. 'He was a popular figure who invited neighbours to his birthday party and entertained them with wine and radical songs.'[98] By this time Davidson had become a dauntless campaigner. Inspired by Thomas Paine's writings, he joined reading and political societies and passionately defended the rights of poor people to improve them selves, get fair wages and rise against state oppression, using violence if necessary. In 1819, George Edwards, a government spy, introduced Davidson to the Cato Street conspirators – men, mostly shoemakers, who were plotting to assassinate the most hated members of the British Cabinet. Encouraged by Edwards, these plotters, including Davidson, tried to buy arms and prepare for their day of freedom. The police were there, all ready to stop this insurrection, arrest the leaders and re-establish state control.

On the morning of 1 May 1820, William Davidson was hanged with four white comrades. At his trial an unbowed Davidson asked: 'Would you not rather govern a country of spirited men, than cowards?'[99] They strung them up and then beheaded all four. The crowd hissed, wept, shouted, some fainted. Davidson's was the last such public beheading in England. There were many more working-class, black heroes, but most of them took their tales with them to the grave.

By the end of the nineteenth century, Indians and Africans were a fairly common sight in London and many of England's towns and cities. They would have been merchants cutting deals, students at public schools or universities, visitors, servants, street traders and entertainers, liberationists and myriad others. As in previous centuries, some, not all, found the natives hospitable, helpful and easy to charm.

English fondness for foreigners surfaced in the most guarded of bastions. Cornelia Sorabji (1866–1954) was an Indian Parsee whose father had converted to Christianity. From the age of eight, Sorabji knew she was going to be a lawyer, come what may. She achieved top marks at school, Deccan College, Poona,[100] and later at Bombay University. Her results should have entitled her to a scholarship to study law in England, but that offer was only open to men. The determined Sorabji approached eminent Englanders for financial help so she could go to Oxford, return to India and offer legal help to subjugated women, a plea bound to melt their hearts. A group led by a Lord and Lady Hobhouse raised the money. Florence Nightingale donated a sum, met Sorabji and encouraged her reformist passions.[101]

In 1889 she joined Somerville Hall in Oxford. The aspirational young woman met and made a deep impression on Benjamin Jowett, Regius Professor of Greek and Master of Balliol. He became her mentor and lifelong friend. With his staunch backing, Sorabji became, in 1892, the first woman to sit the exam for the degree of Bachelor of Civil Law.[102] Thirty years later she was among the first cohort of women to be called to the Bar.

Sorabji's story proves that 'Not all the British who ruled over India saw themselves as masters of the "natives" and the Indians as the "inferior" race.'[103] The graceful Indian woman was admired and assisted by influential figures such as Alfred Lord Tennyson, H. H. Asquith, A. J. Balfour, Arnold Toynbee, William Gladstone and Eleanor Rathbone. Queen Victoria, King Edward VII, King George V and Queen Mary sent her handwritten notes and invited her to palace functions. She attended, always in gossamer saris or Parsee gowns, bedecked with flowers and jewels.

In India, Sorabji is still regarded as a brown memsahib who liked the English better than Indians – and there is some truth in that. She didn't mix with many Indians apart from her own family. Worse still, though she thought British rule was morally indefensible, she criticized Gandhi for inciting mass fervour and argued against Indian National Congress demands for full independence. Sorabji typified the 'temperate native': individuals who were unthreatening and made the English feel good about themselves.

Like Sorabji, Mahatma Gandhi had the backing of establishment figures, but most of his support came from working-class and poor Englanders. When he sailed to the United Kingdom in 1931 to argue for Indian independence, thousands of Englanders came out to cheer the leader Churchill called a 'half naked fakir'.[104] He was hugely popular even in manufacturing towns where his boycott of English fabrics was leading to a loss of jobs. Poignant photographs show Lancashire women gathered around the skinny man with the loin-cloth, their arms raised in support of his cause. He met the Pearly King and Queen in the East End, and when he was driven to meet Charlie Chaplin – an ally – the car couldn't move because enthusiastic crowds packed the pavements and roads.[105]

The first three MPs of colour in the British parliament were, like Sorabji, Parsees: Dadabhai Naoroji, elected as a Liberal in 1892; Sir M. M. Bhownagree, a Tory; and the fiery communist Shapurji Saklatvala, who won his seat in 1924 by 542 votes. There was no 'ethnic vote' then; they were voted in by Englanders. All three packed halls when they spoke and Saklatvala even managed to fill Trafalgar Square with white working-class citizens who felt he spoke for them.

Royals, too, could be entranced by exotic foreigners. In 1889, tongues started wagging. Queen Victoria was once more being un-Victorian, forgetting her place, forgetting her race. A bearded, turbaned, Muslim servant called Abdul Karim had caught her eye and ear (now that John Brown was dead) and she had elevated him to the post of Munshi, wise teacher, proclaiming proudly that it was the 'first time in the world that any Native has been in such a position'. Professor David Dabydeen explains why the queen was so keen on Karim: '[She was] enchanted and enraptured by the idea of being Empress of India. He told her stories about India, fables about India. India for her was exotic; it was a place of spices, of saris, and a place of peacocks.'[106] She gave Karim land in Agra for his family and cottages near all the royal residences, had his portrait painted, and he became her most trusted confidante. I think, though old, she may have felt tremors of forbidden love too.

The royal household, parliamentarians and men in their fine clubs were apoplectic. They humiliated Karim, harassed his family and passed unpleasant gossip about him to the queen. The lady was not for listening or turning, and accused Karim's foes of racial prejudice and jealousy.[107] The Munshi smoked hookahs in smoking rooms reserved for prime ministers, and starred in Christmas plays at the palace (once playing the King of Egypt sitting on a lion throne). Never before had an outsider been permitted to perform in these plays. With Karim, Victoria, who was such a stickler when it came to protocol, disdained social rules.

He did undoubtedly use his friendship with the queen to get extra cash and high status, but no real evidence has thus far been found of real skulduggery. It was almost as if the two of them found a way of sneaking away, out of the epic drama of Victorian imperialism, to live and play, if not as equals, at least as friends. When Victoria died, Karim was banished to India, their letters were burned, and the old order re-established.

Sex and Love

Meet the Fletchers.[108] I sat near them on a train to Birmingham: Rose, Sam, two kids and gran. Sam had dark-brown skin and green eyes, Rose was blonde, and the kids a beautiful blend of both. We got talking about family histories. Sam's father was half African, half Cornish, and his mum was part Brazilian. They had divorced and Sam was brought up by his West African relatives in Wolver hampton. Rose's mum June recalled her husband's best friend, a Sikh soldier he'd met during the war: Ranjit Singh had died trying to protect two young soldiers from Lancashire. 'Herbie never got over that. I think Herbie loved Ranjit more than he loved anyone, even me.' These folk were little England's immigrant and miscegenation nightmare, and big England's affirmation.

Cross-racial sex and love was and is a by-product of England's cultural promiscuity. Barriers, injunctions and social machinations have been unable to curb or inhibit this unstoppable force of English nature.

As early as 1663, Lancashire-born Job Charnock, the East India Company agent credited with founding Calcutta, famously rescued a beautiful young Rajput widow from a suttee pyre just before they set her alight. She became his common-law wife and bore him four children. Charnock was a dour man, at times brutal to his Indian servants, but with 'Maria' – the name he gave his widowed bride – he was loyal and loving till the end. Every year after she died, he sacrificed a cock over her grave, 'after the pagan fashion', muttered his fellow countrymen.[109] From the seventeenth century onwards, wherever they went, English chaps could not stay away from 'ethnic' beauties and temptresses, and some Englishwomen too were unable or unwilling to keep away from dark-skinned men.

An unusual unfinished painting hangs in the British Library in London. It was painted either by Francesco Renaldi in Calcutta or by Johann Zoffany in Lucknow. In the centre is the English gentleman William Palmer (1740–1816), gazing affectionately at his bibi (Indian common-law wife), Faiz Baksh. She has an oval face, tender eyes and peachy, kissable lips. She is sitting cross-legged on the ground, baby in lap, wearing embroidered Mughal clothes, fine jewels and a headscarf. Two older children and ayahs or relatives look on happily. 'By pictorially reifying their cultural identities . . . the portrait marks the coexistence of two cultures in the same household.'[110]

Palmer was a high-ranking East India Company official; Baksh was descended from Emperor Shah Jahan. They were together for thirty-five years and had six children, all educated in England.[111] Though the children were brought up as Christians, Baksh herself remained a Muslim and was buried near a mosque in Hyderabad.[112]

The scene would not have been untypical at the time, certainly not in India. 'During the eighteenth century, parties, balls and banquets were held in the grand mansions of Calcutta. The British ruling classes mingled with their Indian colleagues as equals and many had Indian wives.'[113] Between 1770 and 1830, there was 'wholesale interracial exploration and surprisingly widespread cultural assimilation and hybridity'.[114]

Contemporary official documents reveal these relationships were normal during this period. Jemdanee, a much-desired concubine, became the bibi of the English diarist William Hickey (1749–1830). In *An Indian Lady*, thought to be a portrait of Jemdanee, she is pensive, erotic, bejewelled, dressed in diaphanous clothes, sitting on a bed, with bells around her ankles.[115] Hickey wrote of her: '[she] was respected and admired by all my friends for her extraordinary sprightliness and good humour'. They sent her perfumes and jewels and were, I imagine, wildly jealous of Hickey. Sadly Jemdanee died giving birth. The grieving Hickey lamented, 'Thus did I lose as gentle and affectionately attached a girl as ever a man was blessed with.'[116]

Hickey's friend Colonel Cooper also had 'a beautiful Hindostanee woman to whom he was greatly attached'. She patiently tried to wean him from 'the destructive and baneful practice of drinking brandy or other spirits profusely even in the mornings'. Some of these men gave up beef or pork and did become teetotallers at the behest of their Indian lovers.[117] To please and keep their men, some bibis took up European habits too.

William Dalrymple has studied the wills of white men living in India in the eighteenth century and found that in the earlier decades many provided for their cherished bibis and their mixed-race children. In 1742, for example, Major Thomas Naylor left his companion Muckmul Patna 40,000 rupees, a bungalow, bullocks, jewels and more.[118] Half the children in baptismal records were of mixed race, 'demonstrating that having a European father and Indian mother was pretty much the accepted norm'.[119] Intermarriage was subtly encouraged so men would be more content and stay put in India.

However, not all eighteenth-century liaisons and relationships were loving and respectful. For some British men, Indian women were theirs to be used, abused and degraded. From 1786 onwards, 'half-caste' children were barred from education and jobs: 'the prohibitions instituted by Cornwallis and later affirmed by Wellesley brought anxieties about interracial relationships into the forefront of colonial policies . . . High-level officials were discouraged from keeping Indian companions and lower-level soldiers and employees of the company were allowed and enabled to turn to prostitutes to satisfy their heterosexual impulses. These kinds of measures contributed to a growing sense that the proximity between Britons and Indians required careful regulation if the British were to retain political authority on the Indian subcontinent.'[120]

Pseudo-scientific human classification gave validity to this political recoiling from miscegenation. And that, in turn, led to sexual and emotional withdrawal from unsuitable unions. Those who couldn't abide by these rules were barred from judgemental colonial circles: 'If in the eighteenth century the sexual scene for British officials was characterized by an active rate of overt sexual intimacy with Indians, by the twentieth century the predominant atmosphere was one of physical aloofness and suppressed eroticism'.[121] Affectionate relationships were replaced by prostitution. The women underwent medical examinations and were rejected if they were found to have caught sexually transmitted diseases.[122]

After the Indian Uprising of 1857, Queen Victoria and her government transferred the rule of India from the East India Company to the Crown. With the arrival of British memsahibs, mistresses had to be dumped and records of the liberal past were erased: 'In the 1780s to the 1800s, there's no embarrassment at all about talking about their posh Mughal wives, their Anglo-Indian children, the fact that they have converted to Islam. The same biographies printed in the 1830s and 1840s have those passages omitted . . . I mean deliberately erased. It's not an accidental thing, it's a deliberate cover up. It's a kind of Stalinist air brushing.'[123]

Many missionaries knew the empire was unjustifiable but, nevertheless, forcefully condemned cross-racial couplings and mixed-race children: 'the presence of missionaries of the ruling race encouraged the British to think they were more moral than Indians and that the preservation of social distance was morally justifiable . . . [the British] often suspected the Indians were, by nature, more lascivious than they were themselves.'[124]

In Burma – where there were few Englishwomen or missionaries – it was common for British officials to have Burmese wives and mistresses, but by the middle of the nineteenth century, bishops and the British authorities were forcing the men to abandon their partners. Promotion was denied to those who refused and they were stigmatized. In 1900, Sir Frederick Fryer, Chief Commissioner of Burma, wrote to Lord Curzon: 'The most troublesome cases are those in which civil servants marry Burmese women. The woman, once married, is under no restraint and I was once obliged to tell an officer I would not give him charge of a district if he allowed his wife to live in the district with him.'[125] Some men, sorrowfully, did forsake their women and their Anglo-Burmese families as a result of these pressures.[126]

As the colonial ambitions of England grew, sexual contact between whites and non-whites had to be delegitimized or downgraded to physical release and no more. Marriage was a symbol of common humanity and so endangered the racial and cultural hierarchy.

The story gets more complicated and interesting. If sex was a marker of colonial separation, it was also, conversely, one of colonialism's main stimuli. Authors Kenneth Ballhatchet and Ronald Hyam maintain that sexual frustration was, arguably, one big reason why British men joined the imperial enterprise. 'Expansion was not only about Christianity and commerce, it was also a matter of copulation and concubinage.'[127] Englanders – some featured in this chapter – went looking for sexual satisfaction or adventures, or needed sex out in the colonies to make the heat and dust, loneliness and cultural isolation more bearable.

One Mr S. Sneade Brown sent candid missives from India: 'I have observed that those who have lived with a native woman for any length of time never marry a European . . . [native women are] so amusingly playful, so anxious to oblige and please that a person after being accustomed to their society shrinks from the idea of encountering the whims or yielding to the fancies of an Englishwoman.'[128] An officer known as GR wrote graphically about sexual acts with males and females and suggested that Indian love-making techniques would liberate and excite white women as much as their men. In his list of the world's best lovers, Japanese prostitutes were at the top, Kashmiris next and then the Chinese.[129]

Homosexual Englishmen went south and east for sex, some of it, again, unpleasantly taken. Erotic memoirs describe sexual acts with tough Pathans, delicate Indian boys and young Middle Eastern men with beautiful skin and supple limbs. Power imparity meant frequent exploitation by whites and compliance by underlings, or mutual accommodation by both.[130] E. M. Forster's first sexual experience (at the age of thirty-nine) was with Mohamed el Adl, a tram conductor in Alexandria. The writer felt freed at last but was constantly anxious about the imbalance and lack of real trust in the relationship.[131]

Sex brought out the best and the worst sides of English behaviour abroad. In India, Ceylon, Burma and the Arab lands, paedophilia and abuse of boys and girls was common. (It still happens.) Rape occurred with alarming frequency, prostitutes were seen as subhuman, and the victims had no recourse or redress: 'English colonials were caught in the push and pull of an irreconcilable conflict between desire and aversion for interracial sexual unions'.[132]

THE HOME FRONT

The English at home were just as conflicted from the sixteenth century onwards. In life and plays one finds 'stock prejudices against blacks in Elizabethan and Jacobean culture, the link between blackness and the devil, the myth of black sexuality'.[133] These intensified during periods of social and political disruption, when the forces of English conservatism were pitted against the daring of English defiance. Black migration, mixed-race sex and love could not be stopped yet could not be accepted.

In 1723, the *Daily Journal*, a London newspaper, panicked: 'T''is said that a great number of blacks come daily into this city, so that t'is thought in a short time if they be not suppressed, the city will swarm with them.'[134] Mrs Hester Piozzi, a friend of Samuel Johnson, a blue stocking and a Christian, remarked on 'a black Lady, covered in finery in the Pit at the Opera, and tawny children playing in the squares with their nurses'.[135] At a dinner attended by William Wilberforce, 'a black man led in a white woman with a party-coloured child, the fruit of their mutual loves'.[136]

In 1792, Olaudah Equiano, the venerated abolitionist discussed above, married Susan Cullen, daughter of James and Anne Cullen from near Ely in Cambridgeshire. They had two daughters, one of whom died aged four. A memorial inscription to her was put up in Chesterton Parish Church in north Cambridgeshire, and congregations remembered the family for many years thereafter.[137] Poor white women unabashedly carried on mixing freely with black men and produced pretty broods of 'tawny' children.

Through the Victorian era, 'black people were tolerated, after a fashion, if they had money, knew their place and kept it. For black to marry white was, in the eyes of many, not just stepping out of place; it was contrary to nature.'[138] Yet stern edicts and social disapprobation were ineffectual before the whirlwinds of desire. Indigent white women took up with charming black sailors, who had such tales to tell. The women would never see the world but wanted to know about it. 'Not only were they accepted by white women as equals, many times they were regarded as white man's superior.'[139] Dickens, the most prolific novelist of that period, saw it all but such relationships never appear in his vast canon. One wonders why.

In the first decades of the twentieth century, the sight of white women with black lovers triggered terrible race riots in London, Liverpool and Cardiff. A few black men were murdered during these mob attacks. The *Liverpool Echo* explained why: 'One of the chief reasons of the anger behind the present disturbances lies in the fact that the negro is nearer to the animal than is the average white man and there are women in Liverpool who have no self respect.'[140]

In the early 1930s, Margaret Simey, a Liverpool councillor, gave voice to the unspoken thoughts of many: 'Black men were thought to be very much more vigorous than white men. People felt that women fell for them for that reason, for sexual indulgence, that sort of thing. People could not accept that any decent Englishwoman could live in those dockside communities. It was beyond their imaginations. They thought only prostitutes could do this.'[141] Her friend Muriel Fletcher produced an official report on this 'danger' and concluded that these couples were doomed, as were their children, because they would 'inherit a certain slackness' and low morals.[142]

One might have thought such prejudices were perfectly acceptable then. Not so. There was such a furore against the report that Miss Fletcher had to flee Liverpool.[143] The egalitarian, cosmopolitan and just side of England kicked in, supported, unknowingly, by the writer J. B. Priestley. He mused about how, in a slum tenement in Liverpool, 'Port Said and Bombay, Zanzibar and Hong Kong had called here. The babies told that tale plainly enough. They were all shades, Asia and Africa came peeping out of their eyes . . . The woolly curls of the negro, the smooth brown skin of the Malay, the diagonal eye of the Chinese, they were all there, crazily combined with features that had arrived in Lancashire by way of half a dozen different European countries from Scandinavia to Italy . . . While violent racism still exists, all the dice are loaded against children of mixed blood. But nature herself, whatever she may do to them in later life, displays no sharp animosity against these half-caste infants but takes care to work most cunningly and beautifully with their physical characteristics.'[144] What a eulogy to such children, to the rainbow nation of England.

During the Second World War, Caribbeans, Africans and Indians joined the British army and, again, were soon were drinking, dancing with and bedding young white women who could not hold back. The relationships often led to marriages, some of which lasted through to death. A whole new generation of biracial children was born, the beginnings of what was to become an entire new census category.

Surveys show that since 2010, Englanders no longer fear or loathe miscegenation. Only around 15 per cent of British citizens – the majority of them white English – object to mixed-race relationships, and among the young the figure is as low as 5 per cent. Crossovers are common in all classes, including the powerful, professional middle classes.[145]

The 2012 Olympics were as much a celebration of mongrel England as of the sporting prowess of team GB. Lord Coe, or Seb Coe, as he is better known, mastermind of the London games, is the son of a white father and an Indian mother; Somali-born Mo Farah, track and field gold-medal winner, has a white wife and mixed-race children; Jessica Ennis, the Olympic heptathlon gold medallist, is herself mixed race. Boris Johnson's wife is half Indian; Vince Cable, Liberal-Democrat MP and Secretary of State for Business, Innovation and Skills, was married to an Asian woman and has mixed-race children. Nobody needs to conceal their heritage; it makes them special. Top pop stars like Leona Lewis, Marvin and Aston from JLS are mixed and proud; the novelist Zadie Smith's mum is Jamaican, her father (now passed away) an Englishman; Hanif Kureshi's father was Pakistani and his mother English. The list of mixed-race celebs is long and growing.

We now have third, even fourth, generations of mixed-race young people who carry their identities with panache. According to the 2011 census, over 1.5 million Britons are biracial. The real figure is bound to be substantially higher, because some such individuals describe themselves as black or identify as white.

Hard-right-wingers of the twenty-first century object vehemently to any racial mixing. Their imagined 'new' England is white Anglo-Saxon unsullied by grubby sex with outsiders. Startlingly, more people of colour in modern Britain oppose these liaisons than do indigenous Britons. Neither camp will be able to halt the flow to heterogeneity.

Miscegenation, the amalgamation of the flesh, now is part of the English DNA, its deep identity. Despite hatred and revulsion, England has gone on and on mixing and merging her blood, joining streams from here, there and everywhere.

Epilogue

As I WAS FINISHING this book and suffering from deep authorial anxieties, my English husband said: 'Don't worry. It's brilliant, like a museum, full of interesting stuff I didn't know and most of us don't.' But itemizing the unknown or unfamiliar was never my entire purpose. Didn't he see that? A big sulk followed, tears too. The facts have to have more than intrinsic value; they must make an argument about the past, present and future of the country in which we both live and will die. He said he did see it, understood the book's pitch and strong political message.

I truly hope other readers do too. So much is at stake. Within ten years, there will be a fully (re)formed, recognizable England, which I hope will be self-assured but not arrogant or defensive, maybe even with its own legislature, which I have supported since 1990. In some ways this is an exhilarating time for the nation. It is in the process of becoming itself, an entity not submerged into Britishness but a distinct and still dominant part of it. Will it be a dream come true or an unending nightmare even for its most ardent patriots? Immigrants, their children and grandchildren will be in that England of the future, some still fighting to belong or not to belong, others integrated into its body and soul.

We non-indigenous inhabitants can't simply opt out of the debate on Englishness. We must be part of the nation's conversations and aspirations. Most of us have nowhere else to go, and wouldn't leave even if we could. England is in us now, as we are in her. Yet, like most native Englanders, migrants have their own simplistic, impressionistic ideas about this nation's relationship with the East and South. That relationship wasn't only about racist domination and colonial exploitation, endless resistance and violence. But the paradigm of perpetual conflict has taken hold. Young Muslims passionately believe that since the crusades, there has been continual, bloody enmity between their people and Europeans. You find these views among the least and most educated, the unemployed as well as rich entrepreneurs and successful professionals. They need to know better and to stop excluding themselves from the drama of 'new' England.

It may seem an odd comparison, but in the early 1960s, the national mood in pre-independence Uganda was not dissimilar to that in England today: high hopes mixed with frustration and fears, idealism mingled with anger and vengefulness, and a national anthem pumping out willed optimism. For five years after independence, we did live in the Promised Land. After that came chaos and bitterness, as in so many ex-colonies, partly because there had not been much debate or thought given to what kind of country politicians and the people would make. Remarkably, post-apartheid South Africa did that. Rights, entitlements, binding values, stories, difficult historical reckoning but without retribution – these were debated, analysed and processed. And though the country has not delivered to the poor and there are inter-ethnic tensions, all citizens were subtly re-educated to think differently about who they are and what their nation is or should be.

I hope that emergent England, with its astonishing talents and pizzazz, will go through similar assessments and examinations, come to understand and embrace its modern self and its rich, cosmopolitan history. The alternative narrative offered in this book is just a small contribution to that undertaking.

Epilogue

To change a nation's self understanding requires commitment from its leaders, big and small, from opinion formers across the media, artists, historians, critics, dramatists and authors, the establishment and those who are semi-detached from power but remain influential. I do not feel we have that commitment yet, except from a few Utopians, visionaries and dissenters.

Dishearteningly, in the second decade of this century, some populist political leaders keenly promote discredited, whitewashed, jingoistic British history. The huge popularity of the nostalgia industry, TV costume dramas in big houses, and the crop of award-winning historical novels shows how England, in particular, is retreating from the present and future. People always scuttle backwards when they are full of angst and inchoate desires. And millions of the English are full of both. Ukip, the party that is strongly against the EU and immigration, gives them hope and comfort.

Here and now, the ever more urgent question is just what kind of England will emerge in the coming years? Will it become soulless, colourless, mean, closed off and small? Or will it choose (for it is a choice) to be open, big, international, roving and curious, easy with diversity because it always has been, ever since the boats first went out and came in? 'Only connect . . . And live in fragments no more,' counsels one of the characters at the end of *Howard's End* by E. M. Forster, one of my favourite English novelists. This quote is an entreaty for unity and harmony between the human heart and head and between cultures. Over the long period of colonization, too many of Forster's own people had lived by rules and lost empathy and sensitivity, natural capacities which the English once possessed.

Some of my interviewees for this book – progressive nationalists such as Billy Bragg, MP John Cruddas, and the sport and culture pundit Mark Perryman – promise me the country will not betray the future by denying the best of itself and its story. They helped me believe this book was worth the hours, days, months and years I spent on it. Perryman gets the last word: 'There is no denying we have an imperial, martial history . . . But there are other components we can extract from our national past to construct an identity of today and tomorrow, a softer, light-hearted but proud patriotism.'[1] Amen to that.

Notes

Introduction

1   Fernandez-Armesto is a British historian of Spanish heritage; quoted in *The Isles*, Norman Davies, Macmillan, 1999, p.1057

2   The best book on the community is *The Ismailis*, Farhad Daftary and Zulfikar Hirji, Thames and Hudson, 2008

3   For examples see *Western Representations of the Orient*, Edward Said, Routledge, 1978; *Orientalism*, Ziauddin Sardar, OUP, 1999; *The Post Colonial Exotic*, Graham Huggan, Routledge, 2001

4   See, for example, the *Middle East Forum*, November 2003, and claims made by *militantmuslimmonitor.org*

5   Letter to Denis Mackail, 22 April 1959

6   In *The Lion and the Unicorn: Socialism and the English Genius*, Secker and Warburg, 1941

7   Letter to J. M. Murray, 3 April 1914

8   See *The Life and Times of Abdullah Quilliam*, Ron Geaves, Kube Publishing, 2010

9   See BBC story on Quilliam and his mosque, www.bbc.co.uk/news/uk-england-merseyside-28018673, 27 June 2014

10 See *Victorian Woking*, J. R. and S. E. Whiteman, Woking, 1970; *A History of Woking*, Alan Crosby, Phillimore and Co, 1982; also the Lightbox museum in Woking, www.thelightbox.org.uk

11 Admired by D. H. Lawrence and E. M. Forster; his translation of the Koran was considered a great literary achievement by the *Times Literary Supplement*

12   See www.wokingmuslim.org for information on these men

13   See Tina Cockett in *Victory News Magazine*, 18 May 2004; archival information has also been unearthed by Richard Christopher; the India Office Surveyor's records 1915–1817 and the National Archives hold original sources

14   Interviewed by David Hytner, Guardian, 11 May 2011

15   Personal interview

16   Personal interview

17   He is also the author of *Ghosts of Empire*, Bloomsbury, 2011

18   Personal interview

19   Nehru went to Harrow public school and Cambridge, while Gandhi was at the Inner Temple, London, and was called to the Bar in 1891

20   Nehru's sister confirmed the affair in *The Hindu*, 14 November 2008

21   Personal interview

22   Quoted in *The Amazing English*, Ranjee Shahani, Adam and Charles Black, 1948, p. 141

23   See 'England's Green and Pleasant Land', www.nationalarchives.gov.uk/utk/england/land.htm

24   See research by Cardiff University on these trends, published 20 April 2014

25   Linda Colley, *Observer*, 13 June 2004

26   *Economist*, 1 October 1998

27   Lecture delivered in April 2009, posted on the archbishop's website.

28   *The Making of English Identity*, CUP, 2003, p. 16

29   Shahani, *The Amazing English*, p. 1

30   Sardar, *Orientalism*, pp. 11, 71

31   Davies, *The Isles*

1 England Stirs

1   'England, Your England', in *Inside the Whale and Other Essays*, Penguin, 1969, p. 65

2   In a rousing speech in Zurich in 1949, Churchill claimed Europe was 'home of the great parent races of the Western world', the centre of most ancient and modern developments in science, philosophy and culture, which, if united, would be glorious and prosperous. This was a post-imperial pep talk as well as post-war idealism.

Notes

3   *Crossing Borders*, Continuum, 2001, p. 19

4   He did not want me to name him or give away any information about his fortune and lands

5   *Guardian*, 19 December 2011

6   *Hansard*, 14 November 1977

7   1 October 1998

8   *Empire*, Jeremy Paxman, Viking, 2011, pp. 19–23

9   Personal interview

10 Personal phone interview

11 Essay in *Wormholes*, Random House, 2010

12 *Journal of Modern History*, 47, 4, p. 622

13 The single was released in 1981

14 Ipsos MORI, November 1999

15 Office of National Statistics survey

16 Devolution and Constitutional Change, Briefing No. 35

17 Ipsos MORI, 16 January 2007

18 *The Dog That Finally Barked: England as an Emerging Political Community*, Institute for Public Policy Research; report on the Future of England Survey by IPPR, Cardiff University and Edinburgh University

19 SurveyMonkey, Englishness survey, July 2011, designed by Graham Johnson, University of Lincoln

20 *The Making of English National Identity*, Krishan Kumar, CUP, 2003, Preface

21 *The Day Britain Died*, Andrew Marr, Profile Books, 2000, p. 61

22 *Notes on the English Character*, 1920

23 Kumar, *English National Identity*, p. 7

24 CEP website, January 2011

25 There are many other theories about where he was from and his exact ethnicity

26 See the debates on www.opendemocracy.net, 7 May–July 2008, after Ken Clarke and others put forward the mood-not-movement hypothesis

27 No official figures for EDL membership are collected by the organization; estimates vary between 40,000 and 60,000. *Inside EDL*, Jamie Bartlett and Mark Littler, Demos, 2011, provides useful insights into what the authors claim is 'the biggest populist movement

in a generation'. In the 2014 EU and council elections, Ukip did exceptionally well in England and got the highest number of MEPs into the European parliament as well as a large number of council seats. The party sees itself as the third party in British politics.

28 It was broadcast on Channel 4 and was entitled *The New Empire within Britain*. The full text is online on many websites. The quote is from Kipling's 'The White Man's Burden'.

29 John Walsh in the *Independent* magazine, 8 October 2011

30 Personal interview

31 That is what he does with precision and panache and to great acclaim at his restaurant at the Mandarin Oriental Hotel in London's Knightsbridge

32 *Richard II*, Act 2, Scene 1

33 The speech uses England to mean Britain, but in my view that was an indicator of the dominance of the big nation which subsumed all others who shared the isles

34 Some academics believe he did go to Italy

35 See the excellent essay 'The Tempest vs. Robinson Crusoe – The Ambivalence of Mastery' by JNellymin, blog for LIT 2120 (Sec 3613), 18 January 2011, http://lit2120cole. wordpress.com/2011/01/18/the-tempest-vs-robinson-crusoe-the-ambivalence-of-mastery/; see also *Derek Walcott*, John Thieme, Manchester University Press, 1999, Chapter 4, which discusses Walcott's understanding of Man Friday

36 Project Gutenberg ebook of *The True-Born Englishman* (1701), 2009, pp 1–3

37 *The English Flag*, 1891

38 *Heretics*, reprinted Serenity Press, 2009, p. 78

39 Methuen, 1927

40 Ibid. p. 1

41 There have been serious diplomatic incidents when modern British leaders and diplomats have behaved arrogantly and with insensitivity. Margaret Thatcher, Tony Blair and Gordon Brown were among those who have claimed the greatness of the Empire. Citizens of those nations have found such behaviour unacceptable.

42 *Spectator*, Issue 69, 1713, quoted in Peter Ackroyd, *London: The Biography*, Vintage, 2001, p. 701

43 *New Statesman*, 30 March 2011

44 Reported in the *Telegraph*, 17 April 2011

45 See the coverage in the press for the week of 13 March 2011

46 Random House, 2010

47 It came out in 2004 and remains one of the most popular British films ever made

48 Marr, *The Day Britain Died*, p. 87

49 *England Calling: 24 Stories for the 21st Century*, ed. Julia Bell and Jackie Gay, Weidenfeld and Nicolson, 2001, p. ix

50 *Guardian*, 16 May 2011

51 *Guardian*, 13 June 2004

52 *The English*, Penguin, 1998, p. 3

53 *Real England*, Portobello, 2008, p. 12

54 Ibid. p. 13

55 *After Identity*, Lawrence and Wishart, 2007, p. 43

56 Baldwin's speech at the annual dinner of St George, 6 May 1924

57 Major's speech to Conservatives in Europe, 22 April 1993; the last line is a quote from George Orwell's *England your England*, 1941

58 Quoted by Safraz Manzoor, *Observer Review*, 5 July 2010

59 *Watching the English*, Hodder and Stoughton, 2004, p. 17

60 Catherine Bennett, *Guardian*, 24 July 2004

61 For example, *Goodness Gracious Me*, BBC, 1998; *The Desmonds*, Channel 4, 1989; the film *Bhaji on the Beach*, written by Gurinder Chadha and Meera Syal. Black pop stars broke out of the ghetto and into mainstream cultural life.

62 'Last Orders', *Guardian*, 5 April 2005

63 In 'This Sceptred Isle', report by British Future, April 2012

64 Personal interview. The IPPR Future of England Survey quoted above found 'tentative evidence of a growth of English identification among ethnic minorities'.

65 When asked for their opinions, a large proportion express strong views against multi-culturalism and multiracialism, yet they live in a mixed society without much actual, day-to-day rancour. Germans, the French and others appear to be much less accommodating.

66 *Guardian*, 20 April 2011

67 *Guardian*, 16 May 2011

68 *Independent*, 28 January 2012

69 'On Race and Englishness', in *The English Question*, ed. Selina Chen and Tony Wright, Fabian Society, 2000, p. 13

70 *Imagined Nation: England after Britain*, Lawrence and Wishart, 2009, p. 29

71 Personal interview

72 Personal interview

73 Personal interview

74 Some of these interviews were carried out by Charles Cotton, PhD student at the University of Lincoln and the rest by me

75 *Telegraph*, 15 March 2011

76 Personal interview

2 England and the Other Abroad

1 Observer, 7 October 2007

2 *The Rise of Oriental Travel: English Visitors to the Ottoman Empire*, Palgrave Macmillan, 2004, p. xiii

3 The Vikings and similar North European pillagers, traders and adventurers were also out and about in earlier centuries

4 Hakluyt amassed written accounts by mariners in this tome. He was a fervent advocate of English expansionism. See *The Cambridge History of English and American Literature*, ed. A. W. Ward, A. R. Waller et al., CUP, 1907–21, Vol. IV

5 'England's Forgotten Worthies', James A. Froude, in *Short Studies on Great Subjects*, Longman 1876, p. 26

6 Personal interview

7 See *Captives: Britain, Empire and the World 1600–1850*, Linda Colley, Pimlico, 2003, p. 48

8 See MacLean, *The Rise of Oriental Travel*, p. xxi

9 Quote from *The Infidels*, Andrew Wheatcroft, Viking, 2003, p. 38 and notes

10 *Othello*, Act V, Scene 2, 350–54

11 *Turks, Moors and Englishmen in the Age of Discovery*, Nabil Matar, Columbia, 1999, p. 20

12   Michael Boyd, personal interview

13   *The World Encompassed*, Francis Drake, 1628, p. 10

14   See Colley, *Captives*, p. 49

15   Ibid. p.62

16   *A True and Faithful Account of the Religion and Manners of Mohammetans*, Joseph Pitts, London, 1704

17   Quoted by William Dalrymple, *Observer*, 31 January 2010

18   William Sherlock, *An Exhortation to Those Redeemed Slaves Who Came in a Solemn Procession to St Pauls Cathedral*, William Rogers, London, 1702, p. 17

19   Colley, *Captives*, p. 105

20   Ibid. p. 107

21   The first is espoused by radical Muslims, the second by Westerners such as the political scientist Samuel Huntington, author of the influential essay 'Clash of Civilizations', *Foreign Affairs Magazine*, 1993

22   Matar, *Turks, Moors and Englishmen*, pp. 65–70

23   *The True Story of Captain John Smith*, Katherine Pearson, 1901, full text online, p. 86

24   An apothecary from Walsingham, for example, arrived in Istanbul to learn about these remedies; in Matar, *Turks, Moors and Englishmen*, p. 69

25   *British Beginnings in Western India*, H. G. Rawlinson, Clarendon Press, 1920, p. 27

26   Quoted by William Dalrymple in 'When Albion's Sons Went Native', *Biblio: A Review of Books*, March–April 2000, Vol. VI, pp. 7–8

27   Quoted in *Islam in Britain: 1558–1685*, Nabil Matar, CUP, 2008, p. 35

28   In *Life in Istanbul, 1588: Scenes from a Traveller's Picture Book*, Bodleian Library, 1977, fig. 8

29   Matar, *Islam in Britain*, p. 53

30   This quote was sent to me by Brian Sewell in a letter, 23 August 2001; it is from Fellow's journals as he travelled around Turkey in the 1840s

31   *Pashas*, James Mather, Yale UP, 2009, p. 21

32   MacLean, *Rise of Oriental Travel*, p. 81

33   Noel Malcolm, 'How Fear Turned to Fascination', *Telegraph*, 2 May 2004

34   In Mather, *Pashas*, p. 8

35 London, 1636, p. 1

36 *The Embassy of Sir Thomas Roe, to the Great Court of the Great Moghul*, Hakluyt Society, 1899, Vol. 1, p. 122

37 Paul Halsall, *Indian History Sourcebook*, Fordham University, New York, June 1998

38 See *The Queen's Slave Trader*, Nick Hazlewood, HarperCollins, New York, 2004

39 *A Short History of Slavery*, James Walvin, Penguin, 2007, p. 43

40 For a full account see *Slavery from the Roman Times to the Early Transatlantic Trade*, W. D. Phillips Jnr, Manchester University Press, 1985

41 See Jackie Kay's article on slavery, *Guardian*, 24 March 2007

42 Paxman, *Empire*, p. 26

43 April 1767, p. 152

44 See *Dissenters and Mavericks*, Margery Sabin, OUP, 2002

45 Speech on the Impeachment of Warren Hastings, printed by W. Richardson, London, 1788

46 Burke's speech on Fox's India Bill, 1 December 1783, printed by J. Dodsley, London, 1784

47 *An Indian Affair*, Archie Baron, Channel 4 Books, 2001, p. 8

48 *Indian Tales of the Raj*, University of California Press, 1987, p. 7

49 Some historians do believe the Empire came about as a result of events and happenings; see Richard Overy, 'Britain's Accidental Empire', *Telegraph*, 1 November 2007, and *The Decline and Fall of the British Empire*, Piers Brendon, Jonathan Cape, 2007

50 See the excellent, nuanced critique 'British Orientalism in India', Anirudh Raghavan, http://www.academia.edu/2565126/British_Orientalism_in_India_Nature_and_Impact_on_Indian_Society_A_Historiographical_Survey_

51 See *The Tigers of Mysore*, Praxy Fernandes, Viking, 1991, for a full account of the way the ruler's reputation was stained

52 Colley, *Captives*, p. 322

53 Mihir Bose told me this story

54 See Robert Irwin's defence of Hastings in *For Lust of Knowing*, Allen Lane, 2006

55 *Battles of the Honourable East India Company: Making of the Raj*, M. S. Narvane, APH Publishing, 2006, p. 19

56 Paxman, *Empire*, p. 81. Hastings had fallen out with one Philip Francis who had joined the company. Francis took his revenge by persuading high-minded parliamentarians that Hastings was dishonourable and had brought Britain into disrepute.

57 Personal interview

58 Quoted by Piers Brendon, *History Today*, Vol. 57, Issue 10

59 *The Expansion of England*, Macmillan, 1914, p. 78

60 'Notes on the English Character', *Abinger Harvest*, Harcourt, 1936

61 *Road to Wigan Pier*, Penguin, 2001, p. 155

62 See *Lord William Bentinck: The Making of a Liberal Imperialist, 1774–1839*, J. Rosselli, Chatto and Windus, 1974

63 In *The Taj Mahal*, Giles Tillotson, Profile Books, 2008, p. 51

64 Norman Davies, personal interview, and *The Isles*, p. 601

65 Picture in the National Army Museum collection; can be seen online

66 *The Lion and the Tiger: The Rise and Fall of the British Raj, 1600–1947*, Denis Judd, OUP, 2004, p. 16

67 A number of intellectuals and journalists hold this view, as I found on my 2012 research trip to India

68 The story also appeared in the *Independent*, 12 June 2012

69 *My African Journey*, Hodder and Stoughton, 1908, pp. 88–151

70 See Mehdi Hassan's incisive column, *Guardian*, 21 April 2011

71 *From Sepoy to Subedar*, ed. James Lunt, Shoe String Press, 1970, pp. 24–32

72 Full account in *Late Victorian Holocausts*, Mike Davis, Verso, 2003

73 Mike Marqusee, *Guardian*, 24 May 2012

74 Shireen Mazari, *New Internationalist*, 6 July 2000; also see *The Corporation That Changed the World*, Nick Robins, Pluto Press, 2011

75 Mazari, ibid.

76 Yasmin Alibhai-Brown, *Independent*, 12 November 1998

77 *The Great Hedge of India*, Robinson, pp. 222–3

78 Paxman, *Empire*, p. 95

79 *From the Ruins of Empire*, Allen Lane, 2012

80 Dennis Masaka, 'Zimbabwe in Land Contestation', *Journal of Sustainable Development*

in Africa, Vol. 13, 2011

81   *Zimbabwe: A Land Divided*, Robin Palmer and Isobel Birch, Oxfam, 1992, p. 8

82   George Monbiot listed some methods: 'men were castrated with pliers. Others were raped, sometimes with knives, broken bottles, rifle barrels, and scorpions. Women had similar instruments forced into their vaginas. [Guards] sliced off ears and fingers, gouged out eyes, mutilated women's breasts with pliers, poured paraffin over people and set them alight', *Guardian*, 9 October 2009

83   See Barnaby Rogerson, *Independent*, 16 September 2011

84   *Acts of Union and Disunion*, Linda Colley, Profile Books, 2014, p. 120

85   Jackie Kay, *Guardian*, 24 March 2007

86   See Andrew O. Lindsay's paper on the subject in *International Journal of Scottish Literature*, Issue 4, 2008

87   Kumar, *English National Identity*, p. 171

88   *Britons: Forging the Nation*, Pimlico, 1994, p. 130

89   See 'The Opium Wars: How Scottish Traders Fed the Habit', *Scotsman*, 6 September 2005

90   *A History of the Asians in East Africa*, J. S. Mangat, Clarendon Press, 1969, p. 23

91   *Mixed Feelings*, Yasmin Alibhai-Brown, Women's Press, 2001, p. 19

92   Personal interview

93   See press coverage, 15 January 2005

94   Tory MP Rory Stewart's words, during a personal interview

95   Orwell Lecture, January 2009

96   Personal interview

97   Tharoor's blog, September 2010

98   See Anna Lillios on Durrell in *Magill's Survey of World Literature*, Salem Press, Vol. 17, pp. 23–4

99   *Imperial Fictions*, Rana Kabbani, Pandora, 1986, p. 31

100 Quoted in *Life of William Beckford*, J. W. Oliver, London, 1932, p. 66

101 Letter to Mr Hamilton, 4 January 1783

102 Blunt's papers are in the Fitzwilliam Museum, Cambridge; his biography can be found on the museum website

103 When I was in Jordan, I learnt about Glubb Pasha from old men and women who still remember him

104 Personal interview

105 *New Statesman*, 13 February 2006

106 *Orientalism*, Edward Said, Penguin, 1995, p. 2

107 Baron, *An Indian Affair*, p. 105

108 *The Asiatic Society of Bengal and the Discovery of India's Past*, OUP, 1988

109 *Grammar of the Persian Languages*, William Jones, 1785, Preface

110 Irwin, *For Lust of Knowing*, p. 3; when not fuming, Irwin convincingly defends benign Orientalists

111 Quoted in an Arabic newspaper interview; el-Ghitani translated it for me

112 *Staging Islam in England*, Matthew Birchwood, D. S. Brewer, 2007, pp. 9–11

113 Brian Sewell, personal interview

114 *Guardian*, 7 April 2011

115 *Daily Mail*, 10 February 2010

116 See Laurie Penny in the *New Statesman*, 10 June 2010, and Johann Hari, *Independent*, 31 July 2009; Roberts's full analysis of this massacre is in *The History of the English Speaking People Since 1900*, Weidenfeld and Nicolson, 2006, Chapter 4

117 *Guardian*, 28 June 2006

118 Personal interview

119 Interview with Stephen Moss, *Guardian*, 3 May 2012

120 He did not want me to name him

121 Letter to Emile de la Rue, 23 October 1857 in *The Letters of Charles Dickens*, Clarendon Press, 1974, pp. 337–8

122 *Guardian*, 6 August 1997

123 See press reports on 8 March 2011

124 They did not want to be named

125 Paxman, *Empire*, p. 101

3 England and the Other at Home

1 In *The Battle of Britishness*, Tony Kushner, Manchester University Press, 2012, title page

2   *Observer magazine*, 30 October 2011

3   *Guardian*, 6 February 2012

4   Shahani, *The Amazing English*, p. 137

5   Simon Jenkins, *Guardian*, 3 July 2012

6   *Independent*, 23 February 2006

7   Published in 1850, VII, lines 215 onwards

8   Ackroyd, *London*, p. 701

9   Personal interview

10 Personal interview

11 Personal interview

12 Kushner, *The Battle of Britishness*, p. 5

13 Personal interview

14 Personal interview

15 *Guardian*, 3 November 1999

16 See the news coverage of 25 January 2011

17 *Staying Power: The History of Black People in Britain*, Peter Fryer, Pluto Press, 1984,
    p. 1

18 Personal interview, April 2011

19 See Andrew Curry, 'Raiders or Traders?', *Smithsonian Magazine*, July 2008

20 *Guardian*, 10 November 2009

21 Read Anthony Julius's *Trials of the Diaspora: A History of Anti-Semitism in England*,
    OUP, 2010

22 See *Immigrants and Industries of London 1500–1700*, Lien Bich Luu, Ashgate, 2005; it
    contains a vast amount of information on these migrants and native attitudes

23 *The Three Ladies of London*, 1590

24 *Bloody Foreigners*, Robert Winder, Little, Brown, 2004, p. 66

25 Nabil Matar, 'Renaissance England and the Turban', in *Images of the Other: Europe
    and the Muslim World Before 1700*, ed. David Blanks, Cairo American University Press,
    1996

26 Matar, *Turks, Moors and Englishmen*, p. 20; this groundbreaking historian has upturned
    many assumptions about the relationship between England and the East

27 Ibid. p. 5

28 The painting can be seen in the Wikipedia entry on the envoy; it is owned by the University of Birmingham

29 Matar, *Turks, Moors and Englishmen*, p. 34. See also *Britain and the Islamic World, 1558–1713*, Gerald MacLean and Nabil Matar, OUP, 2011

30 Matar, *Turks, Moors and Englishmen*, pp. 35–6; Robert Blake published an account of this visit in 1637, available online, Cornell University archives

31 Matar, *Turks, Moors and Englishmen*, p. 41

32 See *Muslims in Britain: An Introduction*, Sophie Gilliat-Ray, CUP, 2010, pp. 13–14

33 There are many examples in Colley, *Captives*

34 A print of the panel appeared in the *Burlington Magazine*, LXXVI, 1940

35 *Londinum Triumphans*, John Tatham, London, 1663, p. 5

36 Fryer, *Staying Power*, p. 30

37 *The London Spy*, August 1699, Part X, p. 13

38 Quoted in Fryer, *Staying Power*, p. 10

39 *Diary*, 5 April 1669

40 See Ackroyd, *London*, p. 73

41 See the British Library and National Archives websites: www.bl.uk/; www.nationalarchives.gov.uk/

42 *Asians in Britain: 400 Years of History*, Rozina Visram, Pluto Press, 2002, p. 24

43 Ibid.

44 *Principal Navigations*, Vol. 2, 1599, quoted in Susan Benson's *Ambiguous Ethnicity*, CUP, 1981, p. 4

45 Published in 1778; see my book, *Mixed Feelings*, p. 30

46 *Candid Reflections*, London, 1772, pp. 48–9, quoted in Fryer, *Staying Power* pp. 157–8

47 Cobbett's weekly *Political Register*, 16 June 1804

48 Fryer, *Staying Power*, has a whole chapter on this subject

49 *Public Advertiser*, quoted in ibid. p. 61

50 *Poems*, J. Johnson, 1800, p. 404

51 *Hogarth's Blacks: Images of Blacks in Eighteenth Century English Art*, David Dabydeen, Manchester University Press, 1987, p. 39

52   Fryer, *Staying Power*, pp. 94–5

53   Ibid.

54   *The Interesting Narrative of the Life of Olaudah Equiano, Or Gustavus Vassa, the African. Written by Himself*, 1789, reprinted Modern Library, New York, 2004

55   Fryer, *Staying Power*, p. 106

56   *Life of Olaudah Equiano*

57   *General Magazine and Impartial Review*, III, 1789, p. 315

58   *Gentleman's Magazine*, XXXIV, 1764, p. 493

59   *Boswell's Life of Johnson*, Clarendon Press, pp. III, 200; this provocative toast took place some time in the early 1770s

60   *Anecdotes of the Late Samuel Johnson*, Hester Lynch Piozzi, 1786

61   *Black Personalities in the Era of the Slave Trade*, James Walvin, Allen and Unwin, 1973, p. 21

62   See *The Limits of the Human: Fictions of Anomaly, Race and Gender in the Long Eighteenth Century*, Felicity Nussbaum, CUP, 2003 and Fryer, *Staying Power*, pp. 72–3

63   *Oxford Dictionary of National Biography*, www.oxforddnb.com

64   A wonderful book on the subject is *London in the Eighteenth Century: A Great and Monstrous Thing*, Jerry White, Vintage, 2013

65   See *Black Presence: Asian and Black History in Britain*, National Archives, www.nationalarchives.gov.uk/pathways/blackhistory

66   In Fryer, *Staying Power*, p. 81

67   *Harris's List of Covent Garden Ladies . . . for the year 1788*, p. 84

68   *Vagabondiana; Or Anecdotes of Mendicant Wanderers through the Streets of London*, 1814, p. 33

69   See *The Black Figure in 18th-Century Art*, David Dabydeen, BBC History website

70   See *The Idea of Race in Science 1900–1960*, Nancy Stepan, Macmillan, 1982, and *Colour, Class and the Victorians*, Douglas Lorimer, Leicester University, 1978

71   Profiled by Kate Kellaway, *Observer*, 2 October 2005

72   See www.100greatblackbritons.com

73   See *Black Victorians; Black Victoriana*, ed. Gretchen Holbrook Gerzina, Rutger's

University Press, 2003

74 A wonderful, detailed essay on Fanque is available on the *Smithsonian* website posted by Mike Dash, 8 September 2011

75 *Sir Arthur Sullivan: His Life, Letters and Diaries*, Herbert Sullivan and Newman Flower, Cassell and Co., 1950

76 Winder, *Bloody Foreigners*, pp. 193–4

77 *Truth Magazine*, Vol. 34, 2 November 1883

78 *London Labour and the London Poor*, Griffin, Bohn and Co, 1861, Vol. III, p. 185

79 Fryer, *Staying Power*, pp. 85–6

80 Visram, *Asians in Britain*, p. 99

81 This and the quote from the *Daily Mail* is in 'Siege of Sidney Street', *The Cable*, Commemorative Issue 14, p. 6

82 18 December 1910

83 11 June 1919

84 *English Journey*, Tauchnitz, 1935, p. 31

85 Ibid. p. 167

86 Ibid. p. 181

87 *Life and Labour of the People of London*, 1889, Vol. I, p. 583

88 2 March 1934, quoted by Anne Karpf in the *Guardian* magazine, 7 June 2002

89 20 August 1938

90 www.liverpoolmuseums.org.uk

91 See *Sunday Times*, 29 September 2013, and *Asian Britain: A Photographic History*, Susheila Nasta, Westbourne Press, 2013

92 Collected and printed by Bernard Gardin and Dominique Zanardi; reprinted in the *Independent* magazine, May 2009

93 'The Indian sepoy in the First World War', Santandu Das, www.bl.uk/world-war-one/articles/the-indian-sepoy-in-the-first-world-war

94 All examples in *Indian Voices of the Great War: Soldiers' Letters 1914–1918*, David Omissi, Macmillan, 1999

95 Personal interview in July 2010

96 *The Colour of Love*, Yasmin Alibhai-Brown and Anne Montague, Virago, 1992, p. 71

97 *Observer*, 7 July 1996

98 Headline Review, 2004

99 See Trevor and Mike Phillips, *Windrush: The Irresistible Rise of Multiracial Britain*, HarperCollins, 1999

100 *Because They Know Not*, Phoenix, 1959, p. 29

101 Comprehensive accounts can be found in Zig Layton-Henry's *The Politics of Immigration*, Blackwell, 1992, and *The Politics of Race in Britain*, Allen and Unwin, 1984

102 See the column by Mehdi Hassan on Churchill's racism, *Guardian*, 21 April 2011

103 In a letter he wrote to the *Times*, quoted by Winder, *Bloody Foreigners*, p. 198

104 Speech in 1969, quoted in Layton-Henry, *The Politics of Race*, p. 77

105 James wrote: 'The blacks will know as friends only those whites who are fighting in the ranks beside them. And whites will be there,' quoted by Chris Brazier in *New Internationalist*, Issue 145, March 1985

106 Images reproduced in *Between Empire and Equality*, Commission for Racial Equality, 2000

107 Personal interview

108 I interviewed Heath for radio three times, twice in 1992, and once in 1997

109 Personal interview

110 Winder, *Bloody Foreigners*, p. 4

111 *Guardian*, 7 April 2004

112 Winder, *Bloody Foreigners*, p. 3

113 *Guardian*, 13 October 2010

114 *Sunday Times* magazine, 8 August 2010

115 Professor Tariq Modood and his colleagues at Bristol University have carried out substantial research on Islamaphobia

116 See article in the *Independent*, 3 January 2012

117 'Becoming England', in *Imagined Nation: England after Britain*, Lawrence and Wishart, 2008, p. 30

118 Personal interview

119 Personal interview

120 See the *Economist*, 27 September 2013

121   See the *Independent*, 20 August 2010

122   See press reports, 6 December 2009

123   Personal interview

124   The survey was carried out by the recruitment website www.totaljobs.com and was reported in the *Evening Standard*, 21 December 2011

125   Personal interview, autumn 2011

4 *Trade, Things and Appetites*

1   *Evening Standard*, 26 October 2011

2   In *British Beginnings in Western India*, H. G. Rawlinson, OUP, 1920, p. 21

3   See *The Vikings*, R. Chartrand, K. Durham, et al., Osprey Press, 2005

4   See *The Oxford Illustrated History of the Crusades*, ed. Jonathan Riley-Smith, OUP, 2001

5   *London: The Illustrated History*, Museum of London, Cathy Ross and John Clark, Penguin Books, 2011, p. 79

6   See *Dutch Ships in Tropical Waters: The Development of the Dutch East India Company (VOC) Shipping Network in Asia 1595–1660*, Robert Parthesius, Amsterdam University Press, 2010

7   *Consuming Splendor: Society and Culture in Seventeenth-Century England*, CUP, New York, 2005, pp. 2–3

8   See the website of the Fitzwilliam Museum

9   The first is owned by the Fitzwilliam Museum and the second by the British Museum

10   Mather, *Pashas*, p. 35; his erudite tome has been an invaluable resource for this book

11   Ibid.

12   *From the Rising of the Sun: English Images of the Ottoman Empire to 1715*, B. H. Beck, Peter Lang, 1987, p. 20

13   V. J. Parry, in *A History of the Ottoman Empire to 1730*, ed. M. A. Cook, CUP, 1976, p. 123

14   See *William Harborne and the Trade with Turkey, 1578–1582*, S. A. Skilliter, British Academy, OUP, 1977; also *The Cambridge History of Turkey*, Vol. 3, ed. Suraiya N. Faroqhi, CUP, 2006

15   *A History of the Levant Company*, A. C. Wood, OUP, 1935, p. 74

16   Beck, *Rising of the Sun*, p. 16

17   *Studies in English Commerce and Exploration in the Reign of Elizabeth*, Albert Lindsay Rowland, Burt Franklin, Philadelphia, 1924, pp. 81–4

18   Act I, Scene 3

19   He later became a consultant to the East India Company. See the online journal, *Norton Anthology of English Literature*.

20   In *Early English Travellers in India*, Ram Chandra Prasad, Motilal Banarsidass, Delhi, 1980, pp. 23, 29

21   Mather, *Pashas*, p. 3

22   *Principal Navigations*, Vol. 2, p. 245

23   Part of a letter quoted in *The Embassy of Sir Thomas Roe to the Court of the Great Mogul*, ed. Sir William Foster, Humphrey Milford, 1926, p. 310

24   'England, India, and the East Indies, 1617 CE', *Internet History Sourcebooks*, ed. Paul Halsall, Fordham University, New York, 2011, www.fordham.edu/halsall/india/1617englandindies.asp

25   *England's Quest of Eastern Trade*, Sir William Foster, A. C. Black, 1933, p. 70

26   Bloomsbury, 2008

27   Full story in MacLean, *Rise of Oriental Travel*

28   *The Sultan's Organ: The Diary of Thomas Dallam 1599*, ed. John Mole, Fortune Books, 2011

29   *The Opium Wars: The Addiction of One Empire and the Corruption of Another*, W. Travis Hanes III and Frank Sanello, Sourcebooks, Illinois, 2002, p. 13

30   *Illustrated London News*, 17 July 1852. A photograph taken of her in 1852, just after her christening, shows her dressed like a doll in a frilly Victorian dress, hands crossed, dark eyes burning into the camera. See 'Princess Victoria Gouramma of Coorg (1841–64)', The Royal Collection, www.royalcollection.org.uk/eGallery/object.asp?category=296&object=2906573&row=98

31   Colley, *Captives*, p. 246

32   Ibid.

33   Robins, *The Corporation*, p. x

34   Baron, *An Indian Affair*, p. 12

35   Ibid. p. 32

36   In ibid. p. 86

37   *Monsoon Traders: The Maritime World of the East India Company*, Huw Bowen et al., Scala Publishers, 2011, p. 13. Hastings could be unethical and greedy too. He did not reform the tax regime and supported the Opium War.

38   In *Indian Ocean Strategy*, Sandeep Singh, www.indianoceanstrategy.com/face.pdf, p. 8

39   In Baron, *An Indian Affair*, p. 79

40   Ibid. p. 80

41   Davis, *Late Victorian Holocausts*, is full of examples

42   *Telegraph*, 8 December 2008, and www.mkgandhi.org

43   For a good summary check out Professor Peter Marshall, *British India and the 'Great Rebellion'*, BBC History, 2011, www.bbc.co.uk/history/british/victorians/indian_rebellion_01.shtml

44   *Plain Tales from the Raj*, ed. Charles Allen, BBC Books, 1975, p. 91

45   Quoted by Nick Robbin in *Resurgence and Ecologist* magazine, Issue 240, January 2007

46   MacGregor, *A History of the World in a 100 Objects*, BBC/Allen Lane, 2010, p. 601

47   See the UK Tea Council website, www.tea.co.uk

48   See Niu Chen, *Notes on an Exhibition of Bone China*, www.beijingtoday.com.cn, and essays by R. C. P. Cubbon for *Tableware International*, 1981, 1982

49   See *Porcelain: Its Nature, Art and Manufacture*, William Burton, B. T. Batsford, 1906, and *Porcelain in History: Pots of Fame*, www.economist.com/node/15814776

50   Garden Visit, www.gardenvisit.com/book/london_parks_and_gardens_1907/ chapter _13_private_gardens/buckingham_palace_gardens

51   Mather, *Pashas*, pp. 56–7

52   Rosemary Crill, 'The Golden Age of the Indian Textile Trade', in *British Asian Style*, ed. Christopher Breward et al., V&A, 2010, p. 15

53   *Clothing: A Global History*, Robert Ross, Polity Press, 2008, p. 30

54   J. B. Priestley comments on this in his travelogue

55   Ross, *Clothing*, p. 7

56   See Sonia Ashmore, 'Hippies, Bohemians & Chintz', in Breward, *British Asian Style*, pp. 106–21

57 Monsoon website

58 See *Hussein Chalayan*, ed. Robert Violette, Rizzoli, 2011

59 Personal communication

60 Ross, *Clothing*, pp. 38–40

61 *Re-Orienting Fashion: The Globalization of Asian Dress*, ed. Sandra Niessen et al., Berg, 2003, p. 2

62 www.masterchef.com/masterchef-champion-2012

63 Xanthe Clay, 16 April 2012

64 www.menumagazine.co.uk/book/curryhistory.html

65 *The Indian Empire: Its People, History, and Products*, W. W. Hunter, Trübner, London, 1886, p. 561

66 *Curry: A Tale of Cooks and Conquerors*, Lizzie Collingham, OUP, 2006, p. 149

67 See *Tipu's Tigers*, Susan Stronge, V&A, 2009

68 Madhur Jaffrey, *Ultimate Curry Bible*, Ebury Press, 2003, p. 30

69 *Zanzibar: City, Island and Coast*, Tinsley Brothers, London, 1872, Vol. 1, pp. 228–30

70 Jaffrey, *Ultimate Curry Bible*, p. 15

71 *The Kenya Settlers' Cookery Book*, St Andrews Guild, 1952

72 *The Settler's Cookbook: A Memoir of Love, Migration and Food*, Portobello Books, 2008

73 See Roman Food in Britain, www.resourcesforhistory.com/Roman_Food_in_Britain.htm; the Museum of London website is a good resource too

74 Press reports, 14, 15 April 2011

75 *Taste: The Story of Britain Through its Cooking*, Kate Colquhoun, Bloomsbury, 2007, p. 54

76 *The Englishman's Food: A History of Five Centuries of English Diet*, J. C. Drummond and Ann Wilbraham, Jonathan Cape, 1964, pp. 37–8

77 See *Spice Crops*, E. A. Weiss, CABI, 2002; see also 'Middle Ages Food', www.middle-ages.org.uk/middle-ages-food.htm

78 Colquhoun, *Taste*, pp. 54–5

79 Ibid. p. 99

80 Ibid. p. 103

81 Drummond, *The Englishman's Food*, pp. 25, 36–7

82 From *The New English Kitchen: Changing the Way You Shop, Cook and Eat*, Rose Prince, Fourth Estate, 2005, quoted in the *Independent*, 27 August 2009

83 An anonymous tract, *Women's Petition Against Coffee*, 1674

84 Baron, *An Indian Affair*, p. 138

85 *Diary*, 16 January 1665

86 *The Art of Cookery*, London, 1747, p. 52

87 Baron, *An Indian Affair*, p. 138

88 Colley, *Captives*, pp. 253–4

89 Jaffrey, *Ultimate Curry Bible*, p. 30

90 *Star of India: The Spicy Adventures of Curry*, Jo Monroe, John Wiley, 2005, p. 63

91 See Visram, *Asians in Britain*, for sketches of these sellers; the originals are in the British Library

92 Collingham, *Curry*, pp. 134–6

93 Ibid. p. 136

94 Ibid. p. 149

95 In Jaffrey, *Ultimate Curry Bible*, p. 29

96 Collingham, *Curry*, 138–9

97 Ibid. p. 145

98 Jaffrey, *Ultimate Curry Bible*, p. 31

99 *A Spicy 200-year Affair: Curry and Why we Love it*, Alun Palmer, 25 June 2010

100 John Day, New York, 1946; all this information is from www.resthof.co.uk/orientalhistory.htm. See screenshot at http://archive.today/Jb5H

101 Ibid.

102 Obituary, *New York Times*, 14 August 1995

103 See www.theoldfoodie.com/2007/04/arabian-delights.html

104 She told me this when she came to dinner around 1999

105 See my food memoir, *The Settler's Cookbook*

106 *Guardian*, 4 February 2011

107 *Sunday Times*, 2 May 2010

108 *BBC News*, 27 April 2007

109 I interviewed Santichatsak for BBC Radio 4 in 2008

110 www.macleans.ca/culture/books/in-conversation-with-jamie-oliver-why-britain-really-is-great

111 *Observer*, 31 October 1999

112 Nick Squires, *Telegraph*, 14 October 2011

113 Marr, *Observer*, 31 October 1999

114 Ibid.

115 Ibid.

5 Buildings, Spaces and Design

1 *Travels in India*, London, 1793, quoted in *Indian Renaissance: British Romantic Art and the Prospect of India*, Hermoine De Almeida and George Gilpin, Ashgate Publishing, 2005 p. 122

2 I heard this story from a British Muslim architect and in the Middle East; it also appears in Birchwood, *Staging Islam*, p. 45

3 Christopher Wren Jr, *Parentalia: Or, Memoirs of the Family of the Wrens*, 1750, p. 307

4 *An Account of Architects and Architecture*, John Evelyn, London, 1733, pp. 9–10

5 *The Diary of John Evelyn*, ed. E. S. de Beer, Clarendon Press, 1955, pp. 267–8

6 Jalal Uddin Khan, 'The Sublime and the Beautiful: William Jones on Ancient Arabian Poetry', *IUP Journal of English Studies*, 5, 2010, pp. 54–65

7 See *Oriental Architecture in the West*, Patrick Conner, Thames and Hudson, 1979, p. 113

8 Ibid. p. 115

9 Ibid. p. 116

10 See *The Bungalow: The Production of a Global Culture*, Anthony King, Routledge, 1984

11 Baron, *An Indian Affair*, p. 133

12 Conner, *Oriental Architecture*, p. 120

13 Baron, *An Indian Affair*, p. 133

14 See www.sezincote.co.uk

15 Brendon, *Decline and Fall*, p. 2

16   Paul Norton, 'Daylesford: S. P. Cockerell's Residence for Warren Hastings', *Journal of the Society of Architectural Historians*, Vol. 22, Issue 3, 1963, p. 128

17   Baron, *An Indian Affair*, p. 133

18   Conner, *Oriental Architecture*, p. 119

19   *The Life and Letters of William Beckford of Fonthill*, Heinemann, 1910, pp. 62–3, letter dated 4 December 1778

20   Ibid. p. 164, letter dated Tuesday 18 October 1782

21   *Gothic Histories*, Clive Bloom, Continuum International Publishing, 2010, p. 38

22   *The Oriental Obsession: Islamic Inspiration in British and American Art and Architecture 1500–1920*, John Sweetman, p. 84. Academic Dr Amy Frost is convinced the summerhouse was not built by Beckford because it is out of sync with his other homes. See also Michael Forsyth's substantive writings on Bath and his view of Beckford's house.

23   See *Elizabeth Barrett Browning: The Hope End Year*, Barbara Dennis, Poetry Wales Press, 1996. Patrick Conner thinks that it was 'so extraordinary in its stockade-like solidity that Edward Moulton-Barrett may well have designed it himself', *Oriental Architecture*, p. 125

24   In Conner, *Oriental Architecture*, pp. 125–6

25   Dennis, *Elizabeth Barrett Browning*, p. 23

26   In Nebahat Avcioglu and Finbarr Barry Flood, 'Globalizing Cultures: Art and Mobility in the Eighteenth Century', *Ars Orientalis*, Vol. 39, March 2011

27   *Poetical Works of Thomas Moore*, Longmans, 1841, p. 136

28   Open University notes on the pavilion

29   *Queen Victoria's Maharajah: Duleep Singh, 1838–93*, Michael Alexander and Sushila Anand, Weidenfeld and Nicolson, 1980, p. 110

30   Ibid. pp. 46–9

31   www.sikhiwiki.org/index.php/Maharajah_Duleep_Singh and http://virtualvictorian.blogspot.co.uk/2013/11/the-maharajah-duleep-singh-sovereign.html

32   Alexander, *Queen Victoria's Maharajah*, p. 111

33   Ibid.

34   Visram, *Asians in Britain*, p. 101

35   Sweetman, *The Oriental Obsession*, p. 195–6

36   See www.literarynorfolk.co.uk

37   Ibid.

38   'Elephant Tea House (1877)' www.world-guides.com/europe/england/tyne-and-wear/
      sunderland

39   *The Past, Present, and Future of British Architecture: Presidential Address at the Opening
      Meeting of the Winter Session 13 November 1901*, Northern Architectural Association, 1901

40   Not his real name

41   Personal interview; see Keenan's *Diplomatic Baggage*, John Murray, 2005

42   Quoted on the Christie's website under the Doris Duke Collection, www.christies.com
      /special_sites/duke_jun04/article.asp?article=2

43   He illustrated many of Rudyard's stories

44   An excellent account of Lockwood Kipling can be found in Mahrukh Tarapor, 'John
      Lockwood Kipling and British Art Education in India', *Victorian Studies*, 24, 1980

45   For a detailed account, see William J. Glover's excellent *Making Lahore Modern*,
      University of Minnesota Press, 2007

46   Sweetman, *The Oriental Obsession*, p. 168

47   Essay by Sunand Prasad, in *India House*, Indian High Commission, 2009

48   *Observer*, 23 February 1930

49   Quoted by Peter Kandela, 'Turkish Baths', *Lancet*, 13 February 1999

50   See www.yorkshire.com/discover/what-to-do/SpecialOccasions/Spas/Harrogate

51   From the *Pillars of Hercules*, quoted by Kandela, *Lancet*, 13 February 1999

52   8 June 1861

53   Quoted from www.virtualvictorian.blogspot.co.uk

54   In *Who's a Pretty Boy Then?: One Hundred and Fifty Years of Gay Life in Pictures*, James
      Gardiner, Serpent's Tail, 1998, p. 8

55   Ibid. pp. 8, 123

56   *Vauxhall Gardens: A History*, David Coke and Alan Borg, Yale University Press, 2011; see
      review, *Guardian*, 22 July 2011

57   *Edinburgh Encyclopaedia*, 1830

58   See *Japanese Gardens in Britain*, Amanda Herries, Shire Books, 2001

59   *The History of the Royal Botanic Gardens*, Ray Desmond, Harvill Press, 1995,

pp. 23–4

60   Ibid.

61   Hazelle Jackson, 'East Meets West: The Japanese Garden in England', *Timetravel-Britain*, www.timetravel-britain.com/articles/gardens/japan.shtml

62   Ibid.

63   Ibid.

64   Sweetman, *The Oriental Obsession*, pp. 107–9

65   Jonathan Jones, *Guardian*, 25 September 2003

66   *Guardian*, 17 May 2008

67   Ibid.

68   See 'Thomas Hope and the Regency Style', V&A website, www.vam.ac.uk/content/articles/t/thomas-hope/

69   See www.arthurlloyd.co.uk, dedicated to music halls and theatre history

70   See www.antiquaprintgallery.com/hyde-park-turkish-expo-museum-corner-dinner-party-1854-108703-p.asp

71   Reproduced in *Empire Building: Orientalism and Victorian Architecture*, Mark Crinson, Routledge, 1996, p. 66

72   10 August 1854

73   20 August 1854

74   'Leicester Square, East Side: Leicester Estate: Nos 17–30', *Survey of London*, Vols 33 and 34: St Anne Soho, 1966, pp. 488–503, www.british-history.ac.uk/report.aspx?compid=41125

75   *Illustrated London News*, 31 January 1852; *The Builder*, 18 March 1854

76   See *Survey of London*, www.british-history.ac.uk

77   Quoted by Lara Kriegel in her perceptive essay in *The Great Exhibition of 1851: New Interdisciplinary Essays*, ed. Louise Purbrick, Manchester University Press, 2001, pp. 146–7

78   Ibid. p. 157

79   *BBC News*, 26 July 2006

80   In *Palace and Mosque: Islamic Art from the Middle East*, Tim Stanley, V&A, 2004, pp. 74–5

81 'The History of Pattern-Designing: A Lecture Delivered in Support of the Society for the Protection of Ancient Buildings, 1882', in *The Collected Works of William Morris: With an Introduction by his Daughter May Morris*, Vol. XXII, *Hopes and Fears for Art: Lectures on Art and Industry*, Longmans Green, 1914, p. 216

82 A programme note for an exhibition of Aitchison's work at Leighton House Museum in 1911

83 *Leighton House Museum*, Daniel Robins and Reena Suleman, Royal Borough of Kensington and Chelsea Museums and Arts Service, 2005, p. 22

84 Ibid.

85 See www.rbkc.gov.uk/subsites/museums/leightonhousemuseum1.aspx

86 Quoted by Sweetman, *The Oriental Obsession*, pp. 191–2

87 *Architect's Journal*, 19 April 2012

88 See *India in Britain*, Kusoom Vadgama, Robert Boyce and BLA Publishing, 1984

89 Memorandum to Churchill's War Cabinet, 'Proposal that His Majesty's Government should Provide a Site for a Mosque in London', *National Archives*, W.P. (G.) (40) 268, 18 October 1940

90 See a transcript of the Granada interview at www.margaretthatcher.org/document /103485

91 *Guardian*, 30 October 2006

92 One big anxiety about this complex is that it is being set up and paid for by Tablighi Jamaat, an ultra-conservative subgroup; I share that anxiety

93 Personal interview

94 See www.suratfirst.blogspot.co.uk for images and www.gluedideas.com; also *Picturesque India: A Handbook for European Travellers*, W. S. Caine, London, 1891

95 *The Idea of India*, Hamish Hamilton, 1997, p. 121

96 Ed. Peter Scriver and Vikramaditya Prakash, Routledge, 2007, p. 3; this well-written collection provides a coherent Orientalist position on the British buildings in South Asia

97 *Essays on Indian Art and Architecture*, Discovery Publishing House, Delhi, 2003, pp. 17–19

98 David Cannadine, *Ornamentalism*, Allen Lane, 2001, p. 48

99 *Asia Before Europe*, K. N. Chaudhuri, 1990, p. 154

100 See www.archinomy.com; also www.oldindianphotos.in/

101 On my trips to Jaipur I have met artists, poets and teachers who still rave about Sir Jacob

102 Crinson, *Empire Building*, p. 11

103 *The Builder*, 5 September 1846; quoted in ibid. p. 112

104 Ibid. pp. 118–19

105 *Alexandria: City of Memory*, Michael Haag, Yale University Press, 2004, p. 11

106 A drawing is reprinted in Crinson, *Empire Building*, p. 177

107 *Financial Times* online, 9 March 2012

6 Ways of Seeing, Thinking, Feeling

1   Act IV, Scene 1

2   It was clearly not possible to cover all the areas of cross-influence, such as music, dance, and later film and technology; some of the individuals in this chapter appear elsewhere in the book

3   See *A Universal History of Numbers*, George Ifrah, Wiley, 2000

4   Irwin, *For Lust of Knowing*, pp. 28–9

5   In his *Book of Optics*, quoted in *Arabick Roots*, a booklet accompanying a Royal Society exhibition, 2011, p. 7

6   *Internet Encyclopaedia of Philosophy*, www.iep.utm.edu/avicenna/

7   Ibid.

8   *Arabick Roots* exhibition, Royal Society, 2011, p. 42

9   Personal interview with Rim Turkmani, Royal Society fellow and curator

10 *Arabick Roots*, p. 11

11 Irwin, *For Lust of Knowing*, p. 90

12 Personal interview

13 Irwin, *For Lust of Knowing*, p. 93

14 The title in Arabic is *Hayy ibn Yaqzan*

15 Irwin, *For Lust of Knowing*, p. 97

16 *William Bedwell the Arabist 1563–1632*, Alastair Hamilton, E. J. Brill and Leiden University Press, 1985, p. 125

17   *Distorted Imagination: Lessons from the Rushdie Affair*, Ziauddin Sardar and Merryl Wyn Davies, Grey Seal Books, 1990, pp. 41–2

18   Self-published, around 1674

19   See *A Seventeenth-Century Defender of Islam: Henry Stubbe*, P. M. Holt, Dr William's Trust, 1972

20   *Arabick Roots*, Foreword

21   Ibid. p. 8; 'proxility' means tediously prolonged or wordy

22   Ibid. pp. 6–11

23   Ibid. p. 14

24   More stories about this extraordinary woman appear in Chapter 7

25   See Lady Mary's letter (no. 36) to Mrs S. C. from Adrianople, *The Turkish Embassy Letters*, Virago Press, 1994

26   See Sanjay Saraf, 'Rhinoplasty in 600 BC', *Internet Scientific Publications*, ISSN 1528 82 93

27   Ibid.

28   Personal interview

29   *The Story of English*, Robert McCrum et al., Viking, 1986, p. 47

30   *Sunday Times*, 10 November 2013

31   *Evolving English*, British Library, 2002, p. 138

32   'The African Writer and the English Language', reprinted in a 1997 anniversary copy of *Transition*, Issue 75–6, pp. 342–9

33   H. L. Mencken, in McCrum, *The Story of English*

34   In *Sunday Times* magazine, 15 April 2012

35   Susie Dent, *The Language Report: English on the Move*, OUP, 2000–7, quoted by Richard Nordquist, www.grammar.about.com/od/fh/g/Hinglish.htm

36   De Almeida and Gilpin, *Indian Renaissance*, pp. 67

37   Sewell, letter, 23 August 2001

38   *Select Views of India, 1758–8*, J. Edwards, 1783

39   Sweetman, *The Oriental Obsession*, p. 101

40   See *White Mughals*, William Dalrymple, Penguin, 2004

41   Some dispute the pictures were by Zoffany

42 Foreword to the exhibition *Martin Yeoman: The Artist as Traveller*, Indar Pasricha Gallery, 2004; see Yeoman's website, www.martinyeoman.com/india2004.asp

43 *Encounters*, Anna Jackson, V&A, 2004, pp. 184–96

44 Ibid. Chapter 15

45 Ibid. p. 165

46 Ibid. p. 282

47 In *Culture and Customs of India*, Carol Henderson, Greenwood Publishing, 1954, p. 65

48 It is in the Museu Nacional de Arte Antiga, Lisbon

49 Jackson, *Encounters*, pp. 202–3

50 Ibid. p. 210

51 *Mrs and Miss Revell in a Chinese Interior*, c. 1780, Peabody Essex Museum, Salem, Massachusetts

52 Jackson, *Encounters*, p. 323

53 Anna Wu, 'The Silent Traveller: Chiang Yee in Britain 1933–55', *V&A Online Journal*, 4, 2012, www.vam.ac.uk/content/journals/research-journal/issue-no.-4–summer–2012/the-silent-traveller-chiang-yee-in-britain–1933–55

54 *Passport to Peking*, OUP, 2010, p. 225

55 Ibid.

56 Ibid; Mrs Atlee, wife of Clement, was one of them

57 See ibid. for photographs of the three friends, including one of their wedding

58 *Modern English Painters*, John Rothenstein, Grey Arrow, 1962, Vol. 2, p. 148

59 In *The Lure of the East: British Orientalist Painting*, Rana Kabbani et al., Yale University Press, 2008, p. 35

60 Ibid. pp. 33–6

61 Ibid. p. 35

62 Ibid. p. 23

63 Personal interview

64 Personal interview

65 See www.saleem-arif-quadri.co.uk to see the range and uniqueness of Quadri's work

66 From programme notes I wrote for an exhibition at Leighton House in 2011

67 *The Art of Integration*, Peter Sanders, Awakening Publications, 2008, p. 6

68 Ibid. images on pp 45, 52,77, 28–9, 72 respectively

69 For example, Lucy Prebble, who wrote *Enron*, and Jezz Butterworth, whose play *Jerusalem* about English angst is considered a modern classic.

70 The great names of the time, Oscar Wilde, Bernard Shaw, J. M. Synge, were mostly Irish

71 The text seems to have been around since the eighth century, or even earlier; there is no agreed recorded date of a first performance

72 See www.theatredatabase.com and *Oxford Handbook of Tudor Drama*, ed. Thomas Betteridge and Greg Walker, OUP, 2012

73 One of the most erudite books on this subject is *Images of Englishmen and Foreigners in the Drama of Shakespeare and His Contemporaries*, A. J. Hoenselaars, Associated University Press, 1992

74 See *English Professional Theatre, 1530–1660*, ed. Glynne Wickham et al., CUP, 2000

75 Personal interview

76 There are many examples of such plays which were a commentary on England; among the best known were John Denham's *The Sophy* (1641), Robert Baron's *Mirza* (1648), Elkanah Settle's *Ibrahim the Illustrious Bassa* (1676). The Eastern rulers are often wise and compassionate and seem to be a subtle contrast to some capricious and unstable English rulers.

77 Birchwood, *Staging Islam*, pp. 8, 64

78 Personal interview

79 Pompa Banerjee, 'The Turkish Influence on English Drama', *Texts of Imagination and Empire*, Folger Institute, 2000, www.folger.edu/html/folger_institute/jamestown/c_bannerjee.htm

80 *Children of Conflict*, E. P. Dutton, 1975, p. 18. Henriques is referring to plays such as Marlowe's *Lust's Domain* and Webster's *The White Devil*; he thought Shakespeare did not succumb to simple binaries or plain stereotypes of non-Europeans, not even in his early plays.

81 'Making More of the Moor', *Shakespeare Quarterly*, Vol. 4, 1990, pp. 433–54

82 Ibid. These unexpected twists and depictions are found in the plays of John Marston (1576–1634), George Peele (1556–96) and Thomas Dekker (1572–1632)

83 Hoenselaars, *Images of Englishmen and Foreigners*, pp. 74–5

Notes

84 Birchwood, *Staging Islam*, pp. 9–14

85 Jennifer Brady, 'Wish Fulfilment in Dryden's *Aurang-Zebe*', *Philological Quarterly*, 83, 2006, pp. 41–60

86 Greg Doran, personal interview. The picture was, curiously, entitled *The Indian Emperor or the Conquest of Mexico*; see *Hogarth*, Ronald Paulson, New Brunswick, 1992

87 *Remarks on the Arabian Nights' Entertainments*, printed for T. Cadell Jr. and W. Davies, London, 1797, pp. 8–12

88 Act IV, Scene 2

89 In *Ira Aldridge: The Negro Tragedian*, Herbert Marshall and Mildred Stock, Rockcliff, 1958

90 Germany, Sweden and Russia were some of the places they settled

91 In *Intersections in Theatrics and Politics*, Lindsey R. Swindall, University of Massachusetts, 2007, p. 107

92 From *Robeson: A Biography*, Martin Bauml Duberman, quoted in Ashcroft's obituary in the *New York Times*, 15 June 1991

93 *Othello*, Act V, Scene 2

94 A. C. Bradley, *Shakespearean Tragedy*, Macmillan, 1904

95 Alan A. Stone, 'Othello' [film review], *Boston Review*, April/May 1996 Vol. XXI No. 2

96 Kabbani, *Imperial Fictions*, pp. 20–21

97 This is how Roderigo describes Othello to Desdemona's father in Act 1, Scene 1

98 *Guardian*, 22 September 2005

99 Ibid.

100 *Richard III, an Arab Tragedy*

101 Al-Bassam, *Guardian*, 22 September 2005

102 See the *Independent*, 13 April 2012, for an article by Arifa Akbar on the global reach of Shakespeare

103 Quoted in the *Guardian*, 1 August 2012

104 *Birmingham Post*, 23 September 2009

105 Programme notes by Richard Dowden

106 Marina Warner, *Guardian*, 9 January 2010

107 Interview August 2011

7 *People*

1 Published in 1922, Project Gutenberg ebook, May 2011, Chapter 1, p. 1

2 Personal interview

3 Jeremy Paxman, personal interview

4 See Boyd Tonkin on Marsden's *The Levelling Sea*, *Independent*, 1 July 2011

5 Ibid.; tragically none of Emidy's manuscripts have survived

6 Countless others died without leaving any trace of their adventurous lives

7 Beck, *Rising of the Sun*, pp. 2–3

8 See Emrys Jones in the *Cambridge Shakespeare Library*, ed. Catherine Alexander, CUP, 2003

9 *Rambler*, May 1751

10 Francis Drake's voyages began in 1570 and Walter Raleigh started his explorations around 1585

11 *Sir Anthony Sherley: His Relations of his Travel to Persia*, London, 1614, p. 64

12 One of the finest is by Anthony Van Dyke; all images can be seen on the Sherley Family Association website, www.shirleyassociation.com/NewShirleySite/NonMembers/England/wistonbrothers.html

13 See entries by Richard Raiswell in *ODNB*

14 *A Voyage into the Levant*, London, 1634

15 Quoted by MacLean, *Rise of Oriental Travel*, p. 166

16 Montagu, *Turkish Embassy Letters*, letter dated 1 April 1717 to an unknown correspondent

17 Ibid.

18 Anita Desai, Introduction to Montagu, *Turkish Embassy Letters*, p. xxxi

19 Fielding, a character in *A Passage to India*, is described by E. M. Forster as someone who did not have a 'herd instinct' and who believed the world is 'a globe of men who are trying to reach one another and can best do so by the help of goodwill, plus culture and intelligence'; many of the women in his novels try to reach out in the same way

20 Kirsten Ellis, *Putting Lady Hester on the Screen*, Writer's Guild website, 25 January 2012, www.writersguild.org.uk/news-a-features/books/260–putting-lady-hester-on-the-screen

21   *Decline to Glory: A Reassessment of the Life and Times of Lady Hester Stanhope*, Roger Day, Salzburg University, 1997, p. 125

22   Ellis, *Lady Hester*

23   Day, *Decline to Glory*, p. 98

24   Ibid. pp. 154–5

25   Ibid. p. 155

26   Quoted by Manoj Mishra, *India Fascinates*, Muse India Archives, www.museindia.com/viewarticle.asp?myr=2009&issid=24&id=1440

27   *'Up the Country': Letters Written to Her Sister from the Upper Provinces of India*, Virago, 1983, Vol. 1, p. 99

28   All these examples are in Mishra, *India Fascinates*

29   See *Victorian and Edwardian Women Travellers: A Bibliography of Books Published in English*, John Theakstone, Martino Publishing, 2007, and Jane Robinson's books, *Wayward Women: A Guide to Women Travellers*, OUP, 1990, and *Unsuitable for Ladies: An Anthology of Women Travellers*, OUP, 1994

30   Mishra, *India Fascinates*

31   *The Wilder Shores of Love*, Lesley Blanch, John Murray, 1956, p. 173

32   Ibid. pp. 176–7

33   See *A Scandalous Life: The Biography of Jane Digby*, Mary S. Lovell, Fourth Estate, 2003

34   Blanch, *The Wilder Shores*, p. 184

35   The only biographical information we have is that she was a youngish woman who left her marriage and travelled around Asia between 1851 and 1852 and published her journals in 1853

36   In *Travels in Kashmir*, Brigid Keenan, Permanent Black, 1989, p. 145

37   Ibid. p. 146

38   Ibid. pp. 145–55

39   Post-colonialists such as Rana Kabbani (*Imperial Fictions*), Professor Ziauddin Sardar and Merryl Wyn Davies (*Distorted Imagination*), writers I admire but don't wholly agree with

40   Quoted in Jason Thompson, 'The Indefatigable Mr Lane', *Saudi Aramco World*, Vol. 59,

No. 2, 2008

41 *An Account of the Manners and Customs of the Modern Egyptians*, London, 1836, p. 98

42 Ibid. p. 279

43 *Edward W. Lane: A Study*, Leila Ahmed, Prentice Hall Press, 1978, in Thompson, *The Indefatigable Mr Lane*, www.saudiaramcoworld.com/issue/200802/the.indefatigable. mr.lane.htm

44 Robinson, *Wayward Women*, quoted in Sahar Abdel-Hakim, 'Sophia Poole: Writing the Self, Scribing Egyptian Women', *Alif*, 22, 2002, pp. 107–26

45 In *Harriet Martineau: Victorian Imperialism, and the Civilizing Mission*, Deborah A. Logan, Ashgate, 2010, pp. 185–6

46 Harriet Martineau's *Eastern Life: Present and Past*, 1848, Vol. 2, pp. 6, 243–4

47 Ibid. Vol. 2, p. 66

48 *A Winter on the Nile*, Anthony Sattin, Windmill, 2011, p. 8

49 New Year's Eve, 1849, in *Letters from Egypt: A Journey on the Nile 1849–1850*, ed. Anthony Sattin, Barrie and Jenkins, 1987

50 Sattin, *A Winter on the Nile*, p. 12

51 November 1849, in Nightingale, *Letters from Egypt*, p. 89

52 Quoted in Michael Mewshaw, 'Barbaric Splendor Suited Him', a review of Thesiger's *The Life of My Choice*, *New York Times*, 20 March 1988

53 *Independent*, 7 May 2010

54 *Wilfred Thesiger in Africa*, Alexander Maitland et al., HarperPress, 2010

55 They include Americans, Scots, Irish, Welsh, other Europeans and those of Eastern heritage – Pico Iyer, for example

56 Keenan, *Diplomatic Baggage*, p. 243

57 Edward Said and other post-colonialists either explicitly or implicitly linked such writing to imperialism; for a full discussion, see *Postcolonial Travel Writing: Critical Exploration*, ed. Justin Edwards and Rune Graulund, Palgrave Macmillan, 2011

58 William Dalrymple, *Guardian*, 19 September 2009

59 In *A Compendium of Eastern Elements in Byron's Oriental Tales*, Naji B. Oueijan, Peter Lang, 1999, pp. 46–7

60 Ibid. p. 21; Rycault wrote histories of the Ottoman Empire in the mid-seventeenth

century

61 Massimiliano Demata, 'Byron, Turkey and the Orient', in *Reception of Byron in Europe*, ed. Richard Cardwell, Continuum International Publishing, 2005, Vol. 1, pp. 446–7

62 His wife destroyed the most prurient jottings; see Blanch, *The Wilder Shores*, pp. 130–33

63 Facts discussed at a seminar on Richard Burton in Mumbai in January 2012

64 *A Personal Narrative of a Pilgrimage to Al-Madinah and Meccah*, Dover Publications, 1964, Vol. 2, pp. 160–62; first published 1855

65 See the preface to the third edition of Burton's *Pilgrimage*, ed. Isabel Burton, G. Bell, 1913, Vol. 1, pp. xxii–xxiii

66 Ibid. p. xxiv

67 Blanch, *The Wilder Shores*

68 Ibid. pp. 18–19

69 Ibid. p. 68

70 Ibid. p. 89

71 Preface, 1895, in Blunt's *A Secret History of the English Occupation of Egypt: Being a Personal Narrative of Events*, Alfred A. Knoff, 1922, p. vii

72 Ibid. p. 44

73 T. E. Lawrence was one of them, Burton too, possibly

74 Christopher Hitchins in *Atlantic Magazine*, June 2007, www.theatlantic.com/magazine/archive/2007/06/the-woman.../305893/

75 Liora Lukitz's biography of Bell, *ODNB*, 2008

76 Letter dated 30 January 1922, *Letters of Gertrude Bell*, Vol. 2, Boni and Liveright, 1927, p. 632

77 Lukitz, *ODNB*

78 Janet Wallach, *Desert Queen: The Extraordinary Life of Gertrude Bell*, Anchor, 2005; Wallach spoke about Bell on BBC Radio 4's *Great Lives*

79 Jack St John Philby in Likutz, *ODNB*

80 In Hitchens, *Atlantic Magazine*

81 *Guardian*, 12 March 2003

82 Ibid.

83   Aka Jack

84   In *Philby of Arabia*, Elizabeth Monroe, Faber, 1970, p. 146

85   Ibid. p. 170

86   The reason for this expulsion was Philby's open criticism of the new ruler and his cronies, whom he thought were corrupt and extravagant; see James Craig's excellent profile in *ODNB*

87   Tom Carver, 'Philby in Beirut', *London Review of Books*, 11 October 2012

88   *Some Memoirs of the Life of Job, the Son of Solomon, High Priest of Boonda in Africa*, London, 1734

89   See the image in the *Independent*, 8 July 2010

90   www.captcook-ne.co.uk/ccne/themes/omai.htm

91   Adam Nicolson, *Telegraph*, 7 January 2003

92   See A. W. R. Chapman, 'Omai Goodness: A Noble Savage', www.hatmandu.net/writing/omai-goodness-a-noble-savage, 2002

93   Chapman, 'Omai Goodness'

94   Visram, *Asians in Britain*, p. 39; see too her earlier *Ayahs, Lascars and Princes: Indians in Britain 1700–1947*, Pluto Press, 1986

95   Visram, *Asians in Britain*, p. 43

96   Fryer, *Staying Power*, p. 237

97   Ibid. pp. 245–6

98   Ibid. p. 216

99   Ibid. p. 219

100 She was the first ever female admitted to Deccan College and the first to get a prestigious scholarship for getting exceptionally high grades

101 See *An Indian Portia: Selected Writings of Cornelia Sorabji 1866–1954*, ed. Kusoom Vadgama, Pardoe Blacker, 2011

102 Foreword by Lady Hale of Richmond, ibid. p. 7

103 Vadgama, *An Indian Portia*, p. 22

104 See Nasta, *Asian Britain*

105 Pictures in Kusoom Vadgama, *India in Britain*, Robert Royce, 1984

106 In *Queen Victoria's Last Love*, Channel 4, 2012

Notes

107 See *Victoria and Abdul*, Shrabani Basu, History Press, 2010

108 Not their real names

109 In *A New Account of the East Indies*, Alexander Hamilton, 1930, Vol. I, pp. 8–9

110 *Sex and the Family in Colonial India*, Durba Ghosh, CUP, 2006, pp. 80–81

111 P. J. Marshall on Palmer, *ODNB*, 2004

112 Baron, *An Indian Affair*, p. 115

113 Ibid.

114 Quoted by Pankaj Mishra in his review of Dalrymple, *White Mughals*, *Guardian*, 5 October 2002

115 The image can be seen in Baron, *An Indian Affair*, p. 30

116 In Dalrymple, *White Mughals*, pp. 40–41; William Hickey's *Memoirs*, ed. A. Spencer, Hurst and Blackett, London, 1913–25, are revelatory

117 Dalrymple, *White Mughals*, pp. 34–7

118 Ibid. pp. 35–6

119 Baron, *An Indian Affair*, pp. 30–31

120 Ghosh, *Sex and the Family*, pp. 8–9

121 *Empire and Sexuality*, Ronald Hyam, Manchester University Press, 1990, p. 120

122 Ibid. p. 122; see also *Race, Sex and Class under the Raj*, Kenneth Ballhatchet, Weidenfeld and Nicolson, 1980

123 Dalrymple, quoted in Baron, *An Indian Affair*, p. 109

124 Ballhatchet, *Race, Sex and Class*, p. 5

125 Ibid. p. 151

126 Ibid. pp. 148–52

127 Hyam, *Empire and Sexuality*, p. 2

128 *Home Letters from India 1828–1841*, reprinted by CUP, p. 17

129 Hyam, *Empire and Sexuality*, p. 133

130 See both Hyam, *Empire and Sexuality*, and Ballhatchet, *Race, Sex and Class*

131 *Sultry Climates: Travel and Sex Since the Grand Tour*, Ian Littlewood, John Murray, 2001, pp. 89–91

132 Hyam, *Empire and Sexuality*, p. 205

133 Karen Newman, *Essaying Shakespeare*, University of Minnesota, 2009, pp. 43–5

134   5 April 1723

135   *The Intimate Letters of Hester Piozzi and Penelope Pennington*, ed. Oswald Knapp, John
      Lane, 1914, p. 243

136   In Fryer, *Staying Power*, p. 235

137   Ibid. pp. 108–109, 162

138   Ibid. p. 234

139   Pat O'Mara, *The Autobiography of a Liverpool Irish Slummy*, 1834, quoted in Winder,
      Bloody Foreigners, p. 169

140   10 June 1919

141   Alibhai-Brown, *Mixed Feelings*, pp. 55–6

142   *Report on an Investigation into the Colour Problem in Liverpool and Other Ports*, Muriel
      E. Fletcher, Liverpool Association for the Welfare of Half-Caste Children, 1930

143   Alibhai-Brown, *Mixed Feelings*, pp. 55–6

144   Priestley, *English Journey*, pp. 247–50

145   See Shyama Perera in the *Independent*, 13 December 2012

Epilogue

1   In his pamphlet *Ingerland Expects*, IPPR, 2002

Index

Abd el-Ouahed ben Messaoud, 99
Abdul Aziz, Rozy, 267
Abgali, Mohammed Ben Ali, 209
Abrahams, Peter, 213
Abu Jaber, Kamel, 86
Achebe, Chinua, 213
Ackroyd, Peter, 93
Acton, Eliza, 158
Acts of Union, 51, 73
Adams, Douglas, 83
Addison, Joseph, 35
Adele, 83
Aga Khan, the, 194
Ahmed, Lalita, 161
Ahmed, Leila, 255
Ahmet I, Emperor, 137
Aitchison, George, 190
Akbar, Emperor, 135
Al Masalha, Mohammad, 86
Al Attar, Suad, 224
Al-Bassam, Sulayman, 239–40
Albert, Prince, 110, 180
'Albion', 2
Alders, Mary, 125
Aldridge, Ira, 234, 240
Alexandra, Queen, 147
Alexandria, St Mark's Church, 202
Alfred the Great, King, 132
Alhambra, the, 185, 195, 202
Al-Hassani, Salim, 209–10
Ali, Mohammed, 225
Alkaid Jaurar bin Abdella, 99

al-Khalili, Jim, 210–11
Al-Kindi, 206
Allahabad, All Saints Cathedral, 199
Allan, William, 223
Allanson-Winn, Rowland George, 7
Allen, Keith, 165
al-Shaykh, Hanan, 243
al-Timimi, Saadi, 122–3
al-Zahawie, Wissam, 87
Ambrose, John, 57
Amin, B. K., 67
Amin, Idi, 118
Amis, Martin, 83
Amritsar massacre, 79
Anderson, John, 57
Andrews, Charles Freer, 9
Angelic Upstarts, 26
Anglo-Saxon Chronicle, 96, 132
Anne of Denmark, Queen, 100
anti-Semitism, 114, 266
anti-white attitudes, rise in, 121
Aquinas, Thomas, 206
Arabian Nights, 232, 243, 254
Arabs
    attitudes to British, 85–9
    and science, 205–11
    and slave trade, 59–60
Archer, Jeffrey, 83
Archers, The, 36
Ardabil Carpet, 189
Ashcroft, Peggy, 234
Ashley, Laura, 146

Gainsborough, Thomas, 104
Gajjer, Manish, 90
Gandhi, Mahatma, 9, 67, 148, 212, 242, 273–4
Garrick, David, 105, 107
Gentleman's Magazine, 63, 210
George III, King, 173, 269
George IV, King, 174
George V, King, 180, 273
Georgiana, Duchess of Devonshire, 104
Gérôme, Jean-Léon, 223
Gibberd, Sir Frederick, 194
Gibbon, Edward, 65
Gill, A. A., 162
Gill, Margaret, 234
Gimson, Andrew, 42
Gladstone, William Ewart, 273
Glancey, Jonathan, 195
Glasse, Hannah, 155
globalization, 21–2, 45, 122
Glubb Pasha, 75–6
Goffe, Thomas, 229
Goldring, William, 201
Goldsmith, Jemima, 91
Goodness Gracious Me, 76
Gopal, Priyamvada, 79
Gordon-Cumming, Constance, 252
Gouramma, Princess, 138
Grant, Bernie, 148
Great Exhibition (1851), 188–9, 202
Greene, Graham, 67
Greig, Geordie, 126
Grimshaw, Ronald, 176
Guildhall, redesign of, 167–8
Gujarat, famine in, 69
Guo, Xiaolu, 215
gurdwaras, 195–6
Gurnah, Abdulrazak, 214
Guru Nanak Gurdwara, 195

Hadrian's Wall, 96
Hafez, 263

Haile Selassie, Emperor, 90
Hakluyt, Richard, 52, 135–6
Halal slaughter, 100
Halley, Edmond, 209
Hamilton, Captain, 55
Hammam Bouquet, 182
Hanley, Lynsey, 45
Harborne, William, 57, 134, 136
Hardy, Thomas, 40, 85
Hare, David, 231, 244
Harris, Robert, 83
Harrison, George, 184
Harrogate, Turkish baths, 181–2
Harvey, John, 137
Hassan bin Talal, Prince, 94
Hastings, Warren, 64–5, 140, 155, 170–2, 185
Hawkins, John, 59–60
Hawkins, William, 56
Heath, Edward, 12, 19, 118
Henriques, E. C., 193
Henriques, Fernando, 229
Henry VIII, King, 134, 175, 227
Hervey, Mrs, 254
Hevelius, Johannes, 209
Heywood, Thomas, 229
Hickey, William, 277
Hickman, Katie, 124, 137
Hindostanee Coffee House, 156
Hirst, Damien, 83
Hitchens, Christopher, 263
HMS *Bonetta*, 109
Hoare, William, 267
Hobhouse, Lord and Lady, 272
Hodges, William, 5, 167, 216
Hogarth, William, 108, 155, 165, 219, 232
Hole, Richard, 232
Holman Hunt, William, 223
Hom, Ken, 161
Hope, Thomas, 186
Hope End, 173
Hornby, Nick, 83